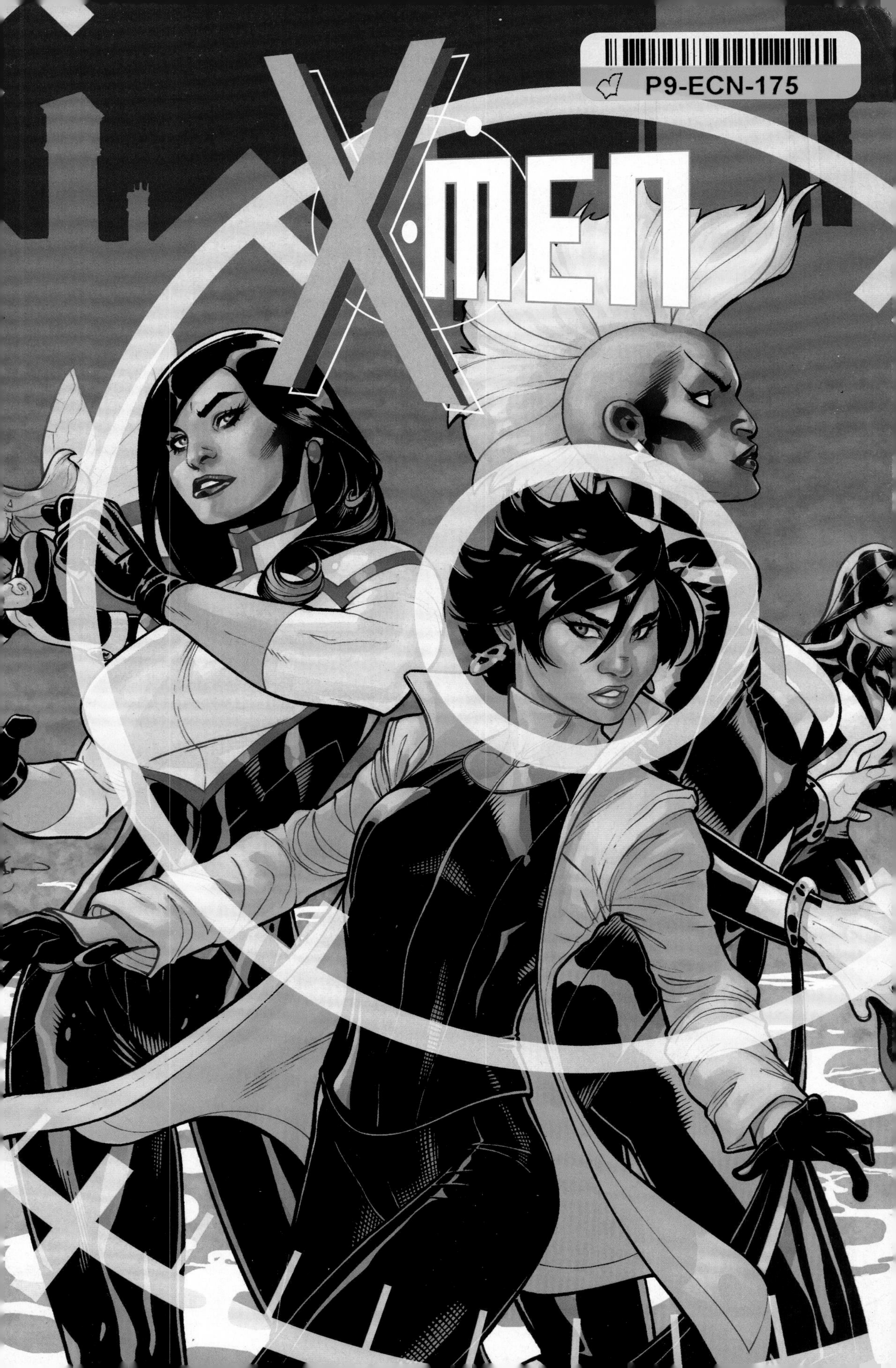
X-MEN

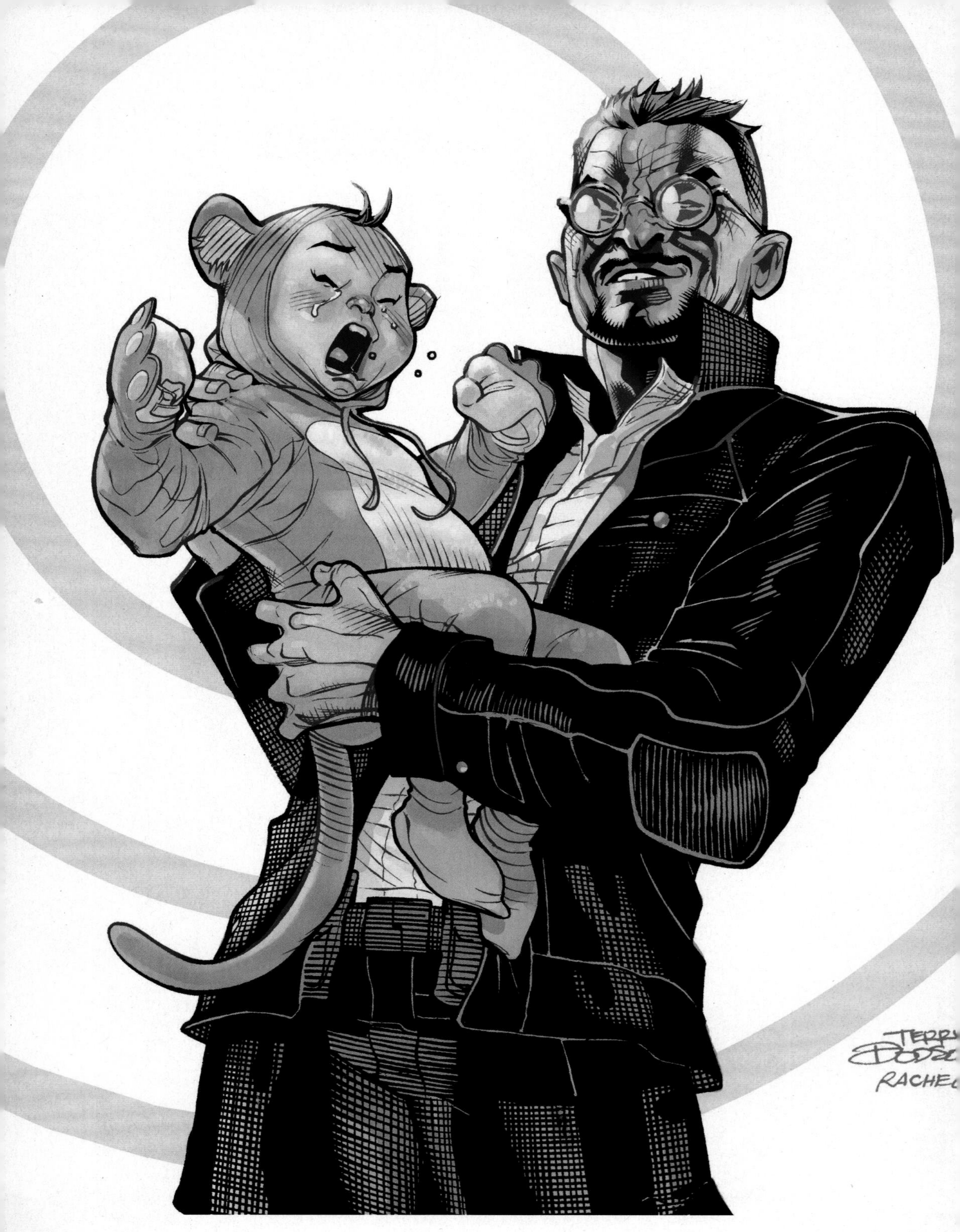
TERRY
DODSON
RACHEL

BLOODLINE

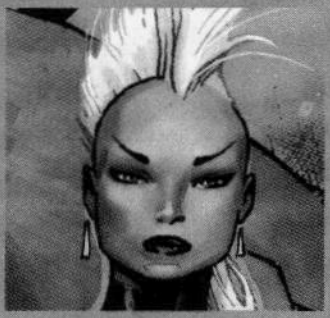
STORM

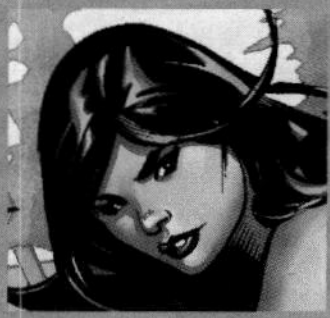
MONET

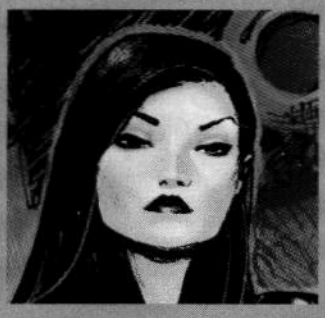
PSYLOCKE

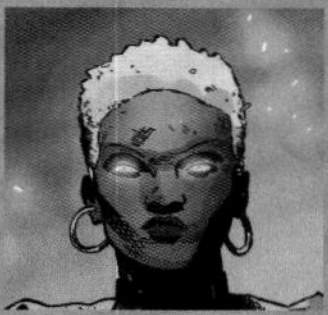
KYMERA

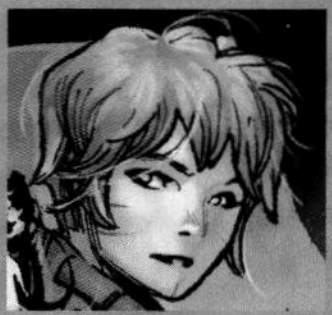
RACHEL GREY

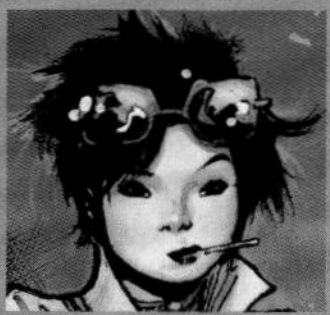
JUBILEE

BRIAN WOOD
WRITER

X-MEN #13-14

CLAY **MANN** — **PENCILER**

CLAY **MANN** & SETH **MANN** — **INKERS**

PAUL **MOUNTS** — **COLORIST**

X-MEN #15-16

MATTEO **BUFFAGNI** WITH GERARDO SANDOVAL (#16) — **ARTISTS**

PAUL **MOUNTS** — **COLORIST**

BROMO-SUPERIOR

PHIL **BRIONES** — **ARTIST**

MATT **MILLA** — **COLORIST**

X-MEN #17

PACO **DIAZ** & PHIL **BRIONES** — **ARTISTS**

PAUL **MOUNTS** — **COLORIST**

LETTERERS: VC'S JOE CARAMAGNA WITH CHRIS ELIOPOULOS (#16)
COVER ART: TERRY DODSON & RACHEL DODSON
ASSISTANT EDITOR: FRANKIE JOHNSON
EDITORS: DANIEL KETCHUM & TOM BRENNAN
X-MEN GROUP EDITOR: NICK LOWE

COLLECTION EDITOR: **JENNIFER GRÜNWALD** ASSISTANT EDITOR: **SARAH BRUNSTAD**
ASSOCIATE MANAGING EDITOR: **ALEX STARBUCK** EDITOR, SPECIAL PROJECTS: **MARK D. BEAZLEY**
SENIOR EDITOR, SPECIAL PROJECTS: **JEFF YOUNGQUIST** SVP PRINT, SALES & MARKETING: **DAVID GABRIEL**

EDITOR IN CHIEF: **AXEL ALONSO** CHIEF CREATIVE OFFICER: **JOE QUESADA**
PUBLISHER: **DAN BUCKLEY** EXECUTIVE PRODUCER: **ALAN FINE**

X-MEN VOL. 3: BLOODLINE. Contains material originally published in magazine form as X-MEN #13-17. First printing 2014. ISBN# 978-0-7851-8972-5. Published by MARVEL WORLDWIDE, INC., a subsidiary of MARVEL ENTERTAINMENT, LLC. OFFICE OF PUBLICATION: 135 West 50th Street, New York, NY 10020. Copyright © 2014 Marvel Characters, Inc. All rights reserved. All characters featured in this issue and the distinctive names and likenesses thereof, and all related indicia are trademarks of Marvel Characters, Inc. No similarity between any of the names, characters, persons, and/or institutions in this magazine with those of any living or dead person or institution is intended, and any such similarity which may exist is purely coincidental. **Printed in Canada.** ALAN FINE, EVP - Office of the President, Marvel Worldwide, Inc. and EVP & CMO Marvel Characters B.V.; DAN BUCKLEY, Publisher & President - Print, Animation & Digital Divisions; JOE QUESADA, Chief Creative Officer; TOM BREVOORT, SVP of Publishing; DAVID BOGART, SVP of Operations & Procurement, Publishing; C.B. CEBULSKI, SVP of Creator & Content Development; DAVID GABRIEL, SVP Print, Sales & Marketing; JIM O'KEEFE, VP of Operations & Logistics; DAN CARR, Executive Director of Publishing Technology; SUSAN CRESPI, Editorial Operations Manager; ALEX MORALES, Publishing Operations Manager; STAN LEE, Chairman Emeritus. For information regarding advertising in Marvel Comics or on Marvel.com, please contact Niza Disla, Director of Marvel Partnerships, at ndisla@marvel.com. For Marvel subscription inquiries, please call 800-217-9158. **Manufactured between 8/15/2014**

They are the faculty and students of the Jean Grey School for Gifted Youngsters, a school meant to protect and train mutants, the next step in human evolution. They are the X-Men!

After finding an infant boy alone in the wreckage of a destroyed building, Jubilee — an orphan herself — took the child, named him Shogo, and decided to raise him with the X-Men as part of their extended family.

Not long after Shogo and Jubilee arrived at the Jean Grey institute, trouble followed in the form of Arkea, a malevolent and infectious alien being capable of destroying the world. After briefly inhabiting Shogo, Arkea fought the X-Men and formed a new evil sisterhood. Storm, Rachel Grey, Psylocke, Monet, Jubilee, and Karima Shapandar then teamed up to take down the sisterhood, destroying Arkea permanently in the process.

The fight left lasting impressions on the team, shaking some of them to the core and causing others to doubt Storm's leadership. Throughout this, there has been one bright spot — Jubilee has officially started the process for adopting Shogo.

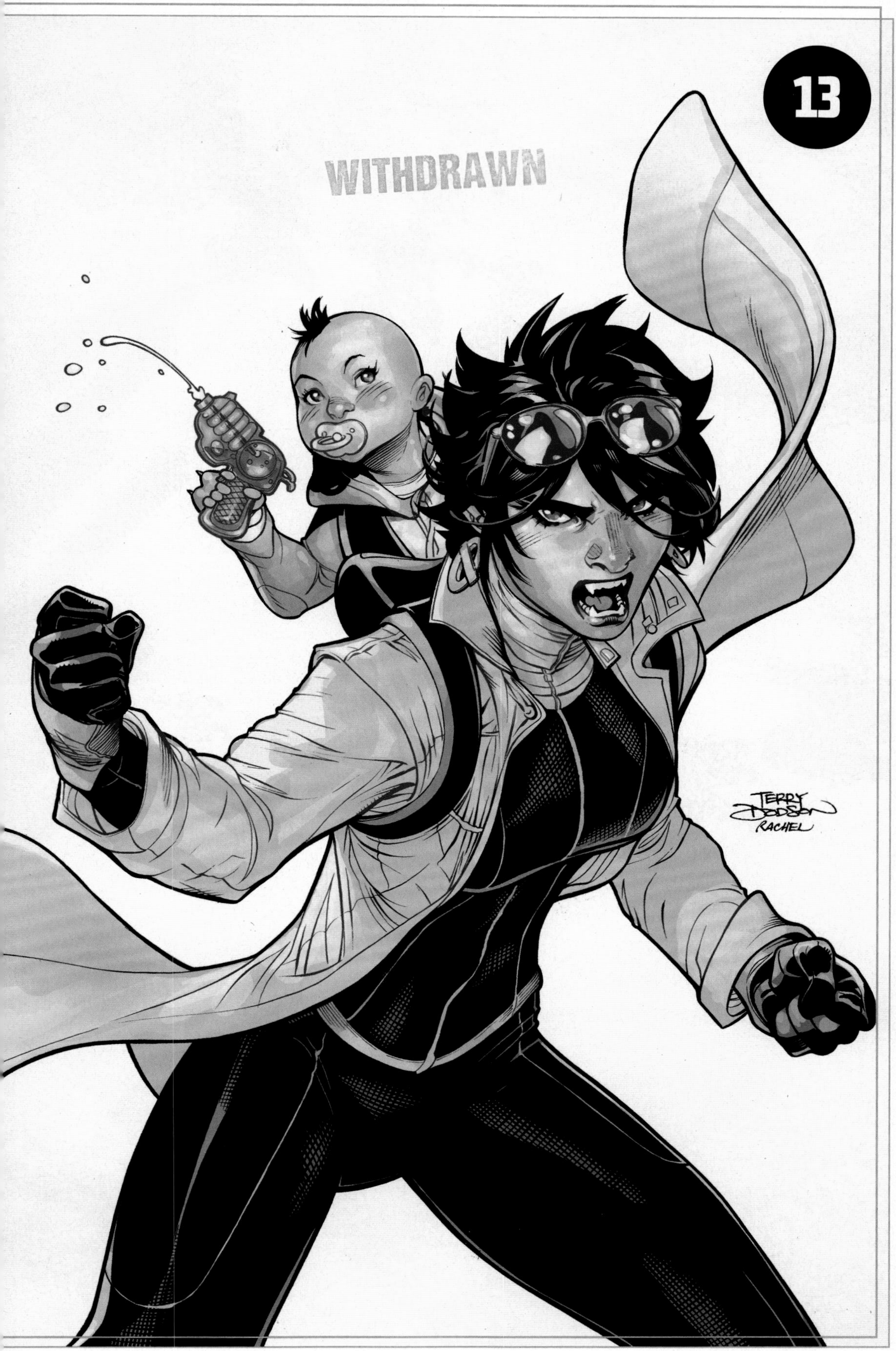
13
TERRY DODSON
RACHEL

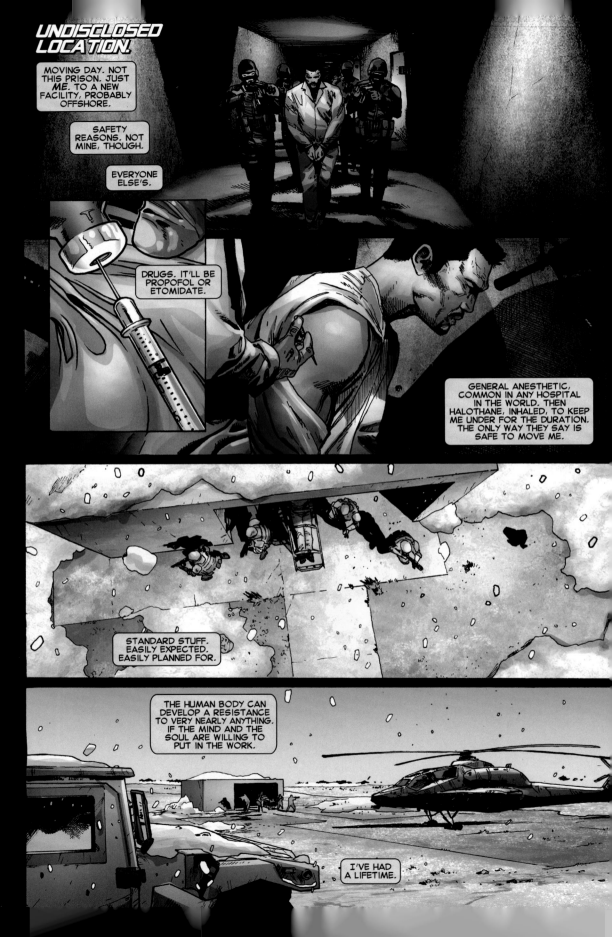

MOVING DAY. NOT THIS PRISON. JUST *ME*. TO A NEW FACILITY, PROBABLY OFFSHORE.

SAFETY REASONS. NOT MINE, THOUGH.

EVERYONE ELSE'S.

DRUGS. IT'LL BE PROPOFOL OR ETOMIDATE.

GENERAL ANESTHETIC, COMMON IN ANY HOSPITAL IN THE WORLD. THEN HALOTHANE, INHALED, TO KEEP ME UNDER FOR THE DURATION. THE ONLY WAY THEY SAY IS SAFE TO MOVE ME.

STANDARD STUFF. EASILY EXPECTED. EASILY PLANNED FOR.

THE HUMAN BODY CAN DEVELOP A RESISTANCE TO VERY NEARLY ANYTHING. IF THE MIND AND THE SOUL ARE WILLING TO PUT IN THE WORK.

I'VE HAD A LIFETIME.

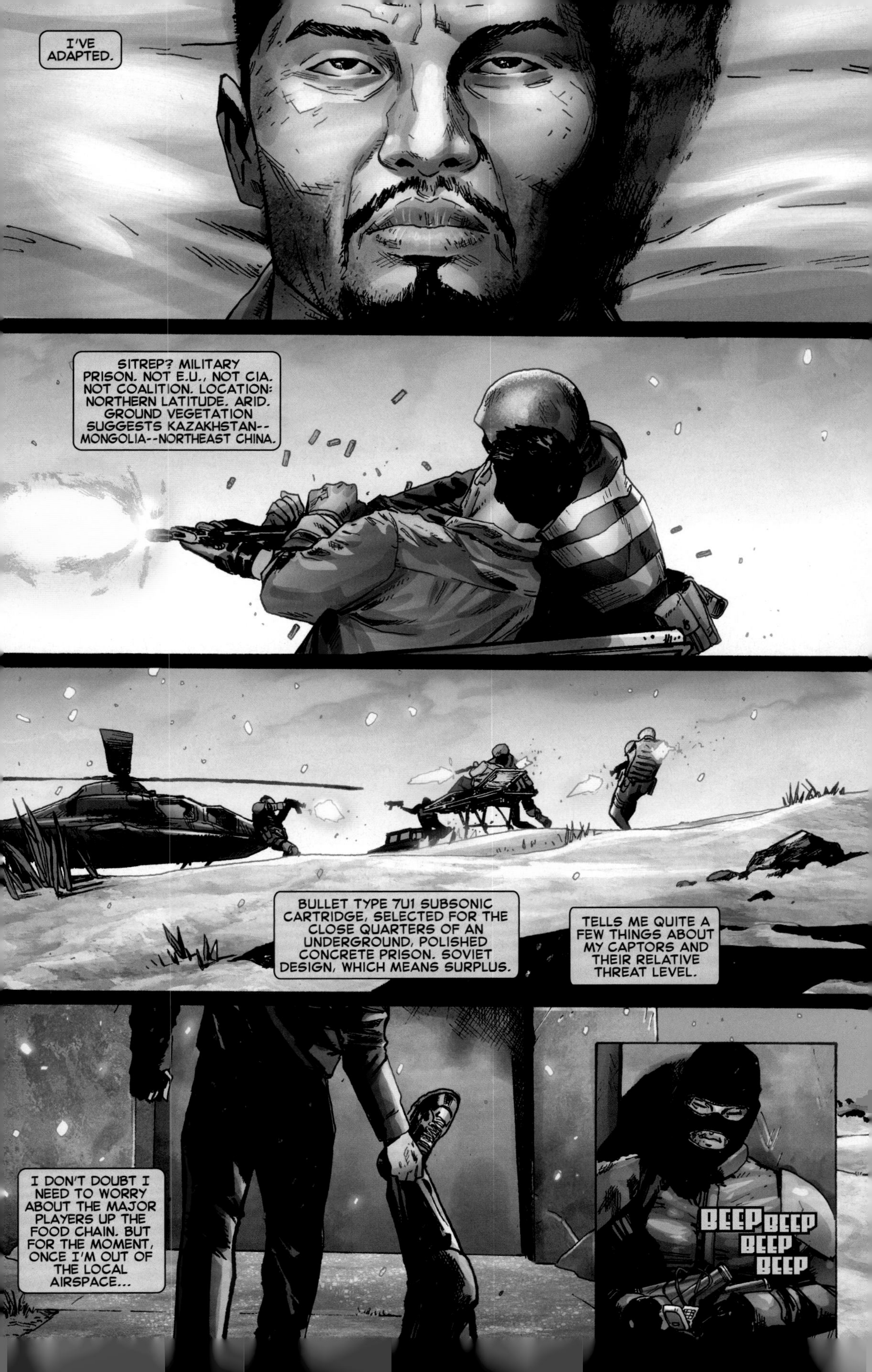
I'VE ADAPTED.
SITREP? MILITARY PRISON. NOT E.U., NOT CIA. NOT COALITION. LOCATION: NORTHERN LATITUDE. ARID. GROUND VEGETATION SUGGESTS KAZAKHSTAN--MONGOLIA--NORTHEAST CHINA.
BULLET TYPE 7U1 SUBSONIC CARTRIDGE, SELECTED FOR THE CLOSE QUARTERS OF AN UNDERGROUND, POLISHED CONCRETE PRISON. SOVIET DESIGN, WHICH MEANS SURPLUS.
TELLS ME QUITE A FEW THINGS ABOUT MY CAPTORS AND THEIR RELATIVE THREAT LEVEL.
I DON'T DOUBT I NEED TO WORRY ABOUT THE MAJOR PLAYERS UP THE FOOD CHAIN. BUT FOR THE MOMENT, ONCE I'M OUT OF THE LOCAL AIRSPACE...
BEEP BEEP
BEEP
BEEP

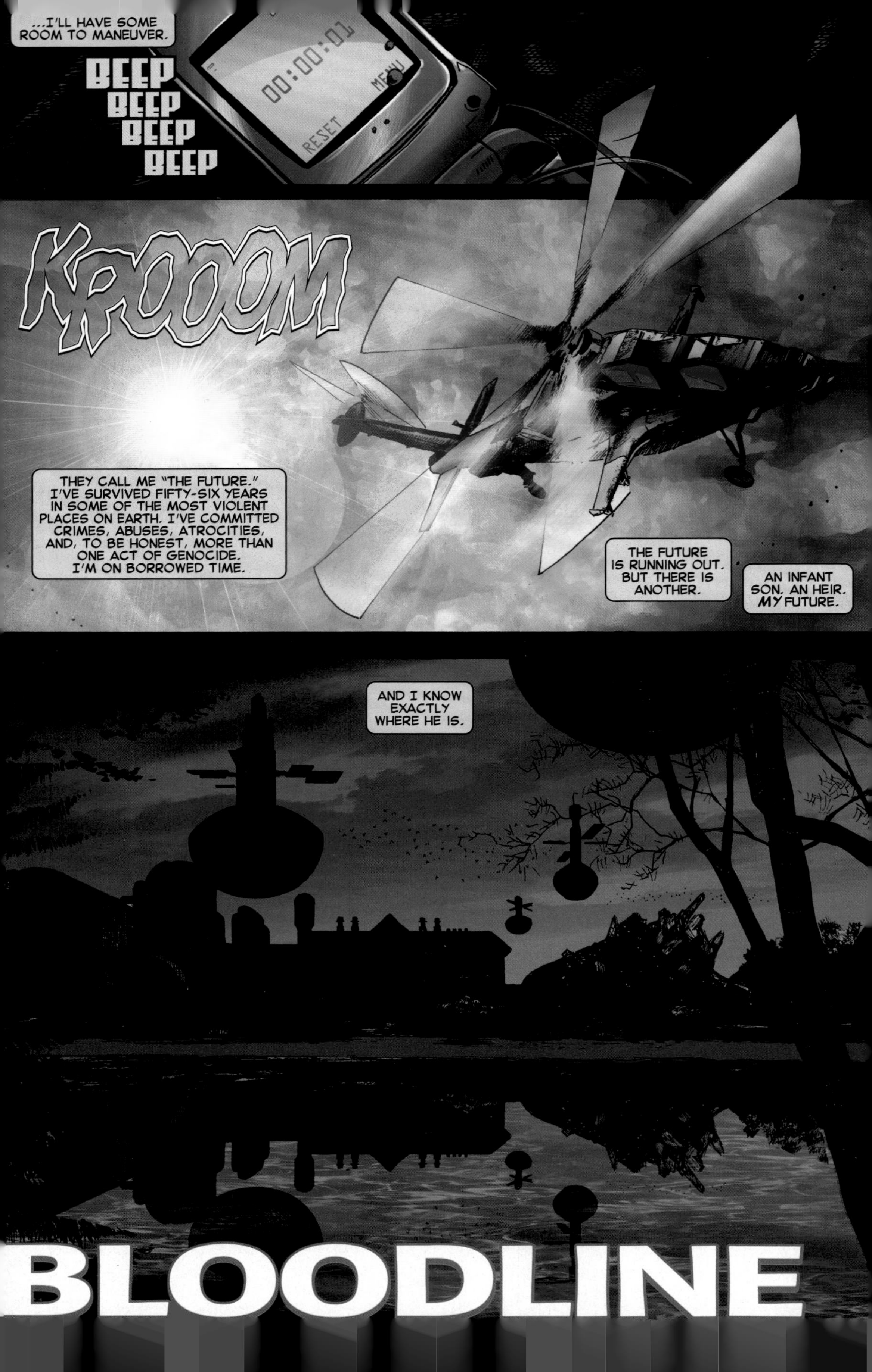
...I'LL HAVE SOME ROOM TO MANEUVER.
00:00:01
RESET
MENU
BEEP BEEP BEEP BEEP
KROOOM
THEY CALL ME "THE FUTURE." I'VE SURVIVED FIFTY-SIX YEARS IN SOME OF THE MOST VIOLENT PLACES ON EARTH. I'VE COMMITTED CRIMES, ABUSES, ATROCITIES, AND, TO BE HONEST, MORE THAN ONE ACT OF GENOCIDE. I'M ON BORROWED TIME.
THE FUTURE IS RUNNING OUT. BUT THERE IS ANOTHER.
AN INFANT SON. AN HEIR. MY FUTURE.
AND I KNOW EXACTLY WHERE HE IS.
BLOODLINE

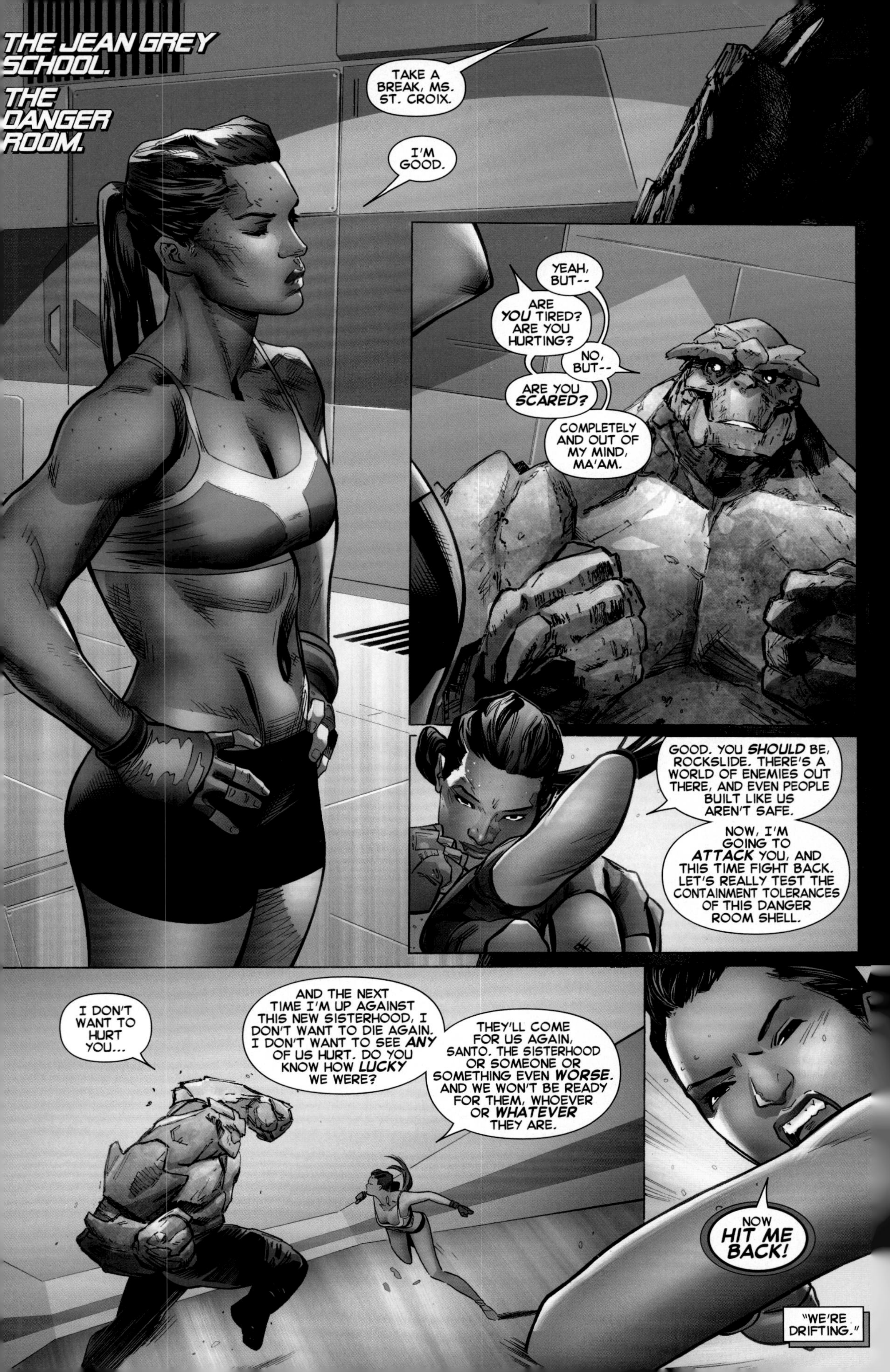
THE JEAN GREY SCHOOL.
THE DANGER ROOM.
TAKE A BREAK, MS. ST. CROIX.
I'M GOOD.
YEAH, BUT--
ARE YOU TIRED? ARE YOU HURTING?
NO, BUT--
ARE YOU SCARED?
COMPLETELY AND OUT OF MY MIND, MA'AM.
GOOD. YOU SHOULD BE, ROCKSLIDE. THERE'S A WORLD OF ENEMIES OUT THERE, AND EVEN PEOPLE BUILT LIKE US AREN'T SAFE.
NOW, I'M GOING TO ATTACK YOU, AND THIS TIME FIGHT BACK. LET'S REALLY TEST THE CONTAINMENT TOLERANCES OF THIS DANGER ROOM SHELL.
I DON'T WANT TO HURT YOU...
AND THE NEXT TIME I'M UP AGAINST THIS NEW SISTERHOOD, I DON'T WANT TO DIE AGAIN. I DON'T WANT TO SEE ANY OF US HURT. DO YOU KNOW HOW LUCKY WE WERE?
THEY'LL COME FOR US AGAIN, SANTO. THE SISTERHOOD OR SOMEONE OR SOMETHING EVEN WORSE. AND WE WON'T BE READY FOR THEM, WHOEVER OR WHATEVER THEY ARE.
NOW HIT ME BACK!
"WE'RE DRIFTING."

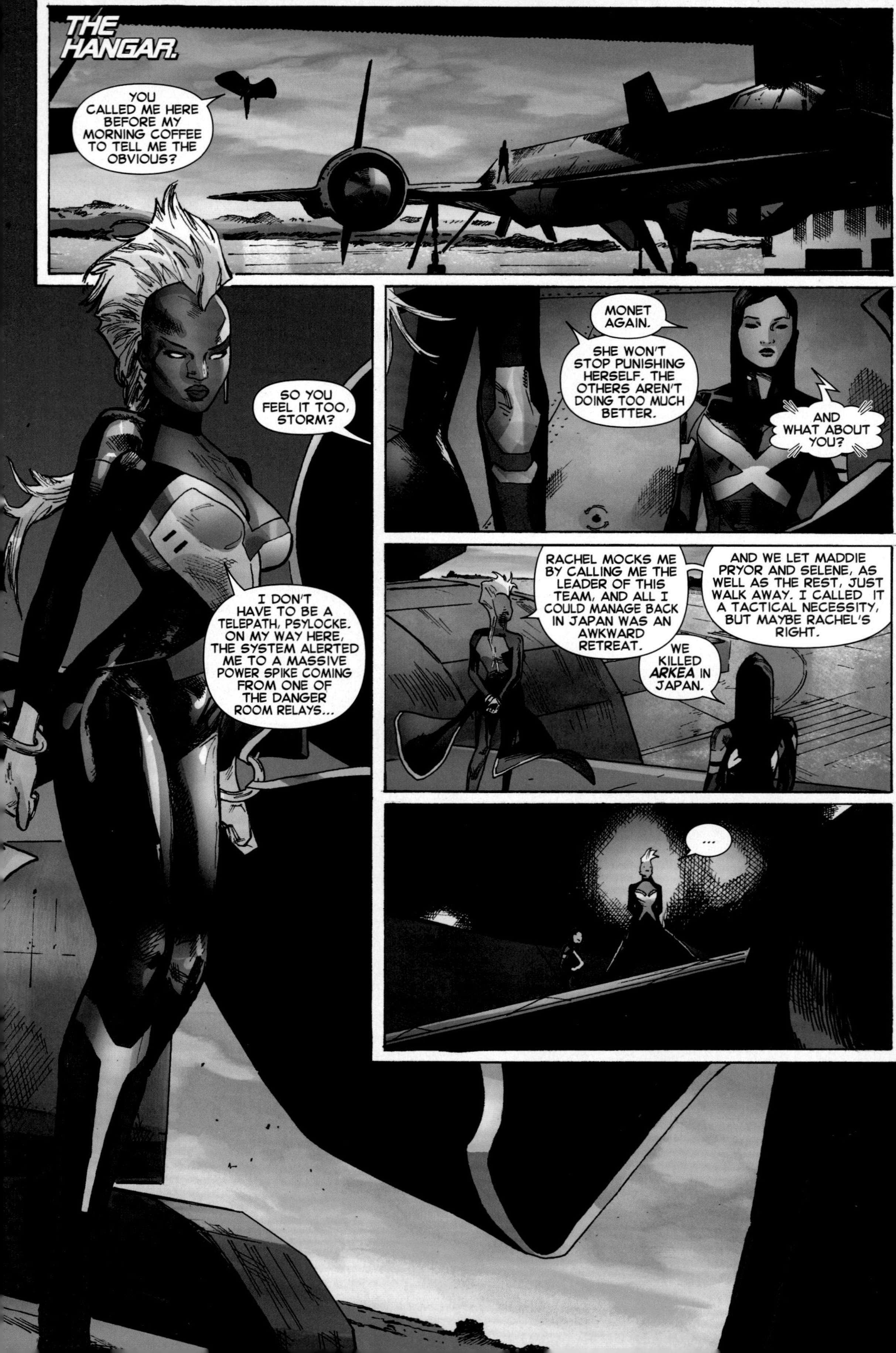
THE HANGAR.
YOU CALLED ME HERE BEFORE MY MORNING COFFEE TO TELL ME THE OBVIOUS?
SO YOU FEEL IT TOO, STORM?
I DON'T HAVE TO BE A TELEPATH, PSYLOCKE. ON MY WAY HERE, THE SYSTEM ALERTED ME TO A MASSIVE POWER SPIKE COMING FROM ONE OF THE DANGER ROOM RELAYS...
MONET AGAIN.
SHE WON'T STOP PUNISHING HERSELF. THE OTHERS AREN'T DOING TOO MUCH BETTER.
AND WHAT ABOUT YOU?
RACHEL MOCKS ME BY CALLING ME THE LEADER OF THIS TEAM, AND ALL I COULD MANAGE BACK IN JAPAN WAS AN AWKWARD RETREAT.
WE KILLED ARKEA IN JAPAN.
AND WE LET MADDIE PRYOR AND SELENE, AS WELL AS THE REST, JUST WALK AWAY. I CALLED IT A TACTICAL NECESSITY, BUT MAYBE RACHEL'S RIGHT.
...

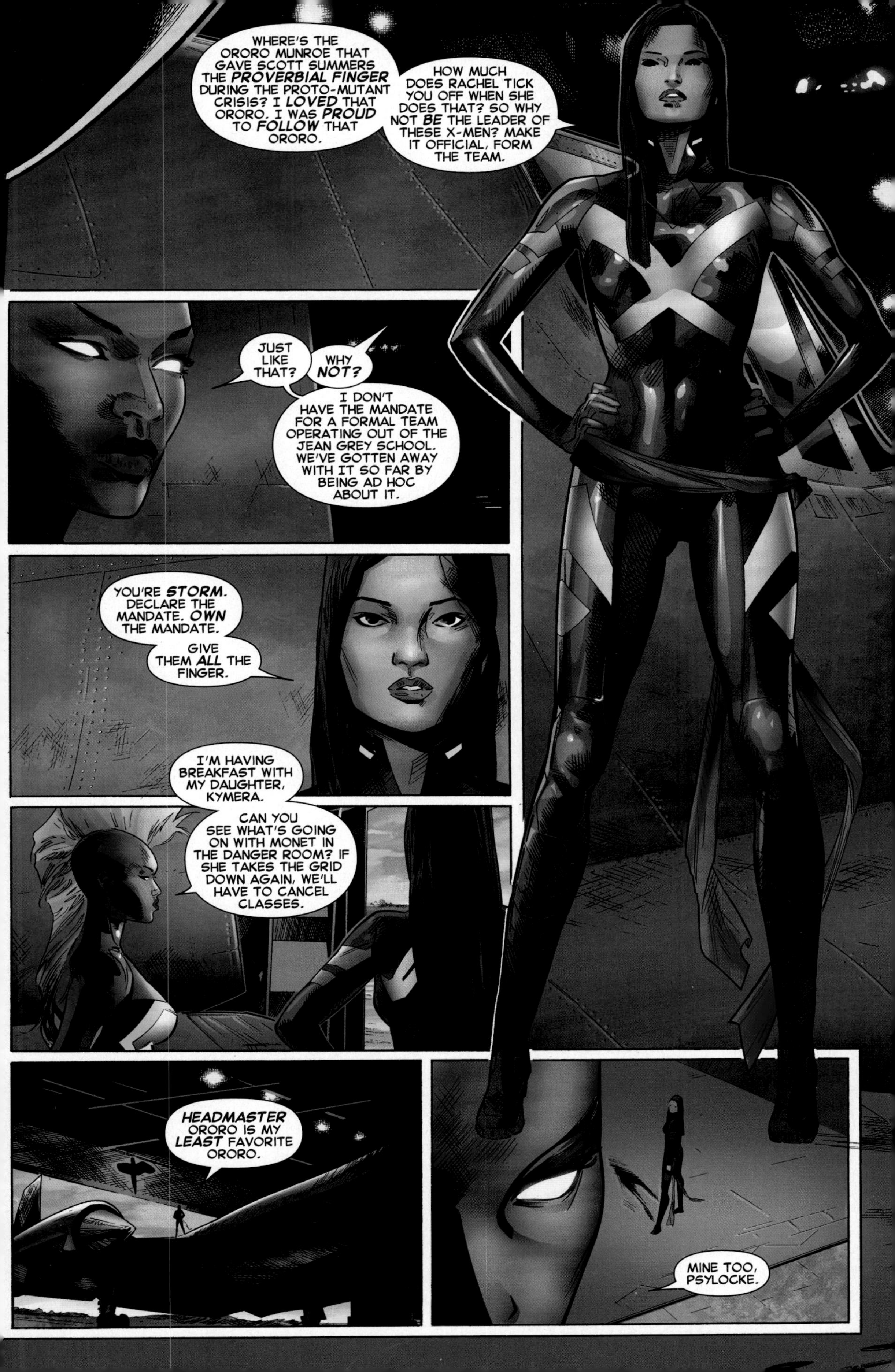
WHERE'S THE ORORO MUNROE THAT GAVE SCOTT SUMMERS THE *PROVERBIAL FINGER* DURING THE PROTO-MUTANT CRISIS? I *LOVED* THAT ORORO. I WAS *PROUD* TO *FOLLOW* THAT ORORO.
HOW MUCH DOES RACHEL TICK YOU OFF WHEN SHE DOES THAT? SO WHY NOT *BE* THE LEADER OF THESE X-MEN? MAKE IT OFFICIAL, FORM THE TEAM.
JUST LIKE THAT?
WHY *NOT?*
I DON'T HAVE THE MANDATE FOR A FORMAL TEAM OPERATING OUT OF THE JEAN GREY SCHOOL. WE'VE GOTTEN AWAY WITH IT SO FAR BY BEING AD HOC ABOUT IT.
YOU'RE *STORM*. DECLARE THE MANDATE. *OWN* THE MANDATE.
GIVE THEM *ALL* THE FINGER.
I'M HAVING BREAKFAST WITH MY DAUGHTER, KYMERA.
CAN YOU SEE WHAT'S GOING ON WITH MONET IN THE DANGER ROOM? IF SHE TAKES THE GRID DOWN AGAIN, WE'LL HAVE TO CANCEL CLASSES.
HEADMASTER ORORO IS MY *LEAST* FAVORITE ORORO.
MINE TOO, PSYLOCKE.

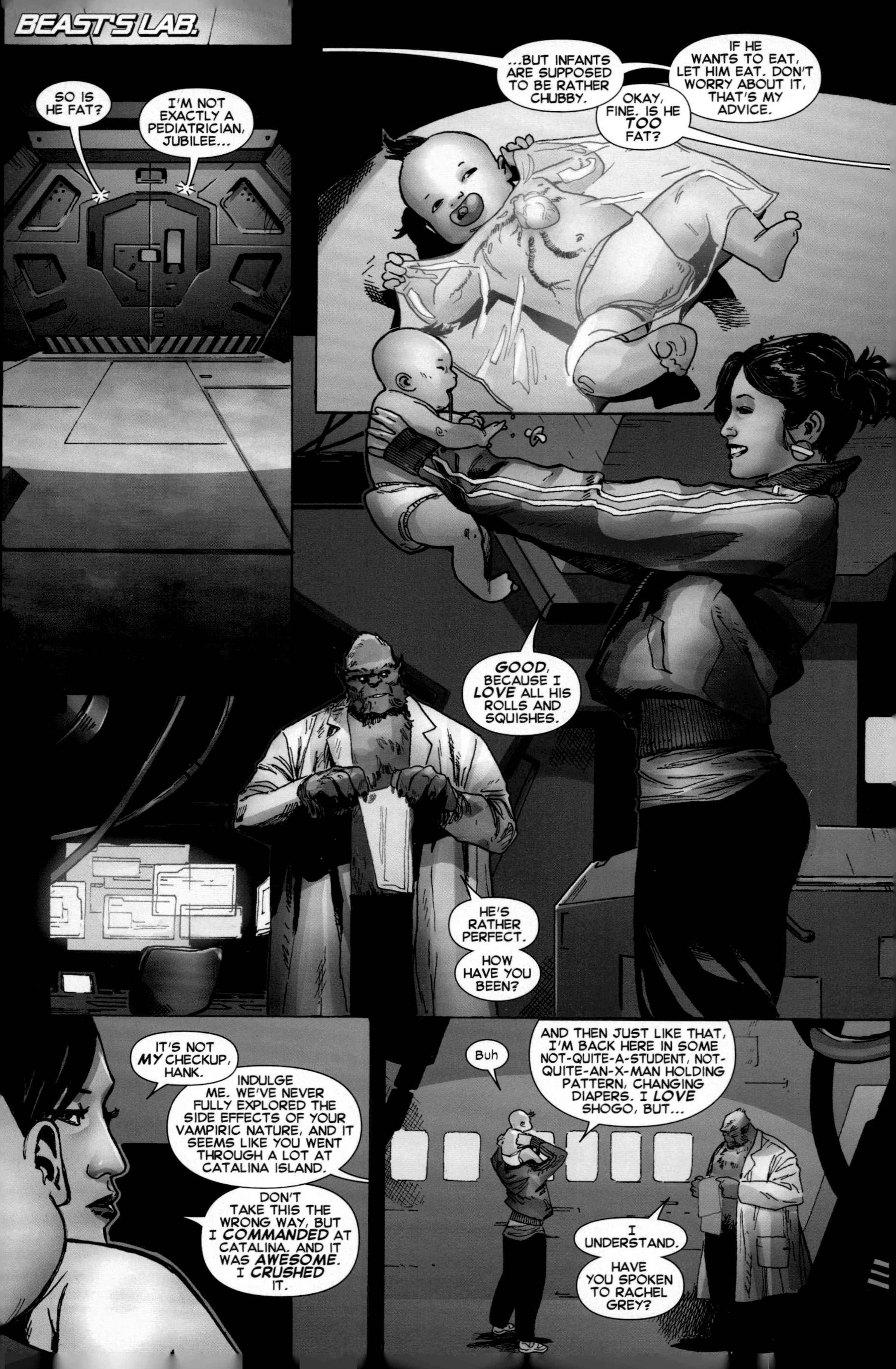
BEAST'S LAB.
SO IS HE FAT?
I'M NOT EXACTLY A PEDIATRICIAN, JUBILEE...
...BUT INFANTS ARE SUPPOSED TO BE RATHER CHUBBY.
IF HE WANTS TO EAT, LET HIM EAT. DON'T WORRY ABOUT IT, THAT'S MY ADVICE.
OKAY, FINE. IS HE TOO FAT?
GOOD, BECAUSE I LOVE ALL HIS ROLLS AND SQUISHES.
HE'S RATHER PERFECT.
HOW HAVE YOU BEEN?
IT'S NOT MY CHECKUP, HANK.
INDULGE ME. WE'VE NEVER FULLY EXPLORED THE SIDE EFFECTS OF YOUR VAMPIRIC NATURE, AND IT SEEMS LIKE YOU WENT THROUGH A LOT AT CATALINA ISLAND.
DON'T TAKE THIS THE WRONG WAY, BUT I COMMANDED AT CATALINA. AND IT WAS AWESOME. I CRUSHED IT.
Buh
AND THEN JUST LIKE THAT, I'M BACK HERE IN SOME NOT-QUITE-A-STUDENT, NOT-QUITE-AN-X-MAN HOLDING PATTERN, CHANGING DIAPERS. I LOVE SHOGO, BUT...
I UNDERSTAND.
HAVE YOU SPOKEN TO RACHEL GREY?

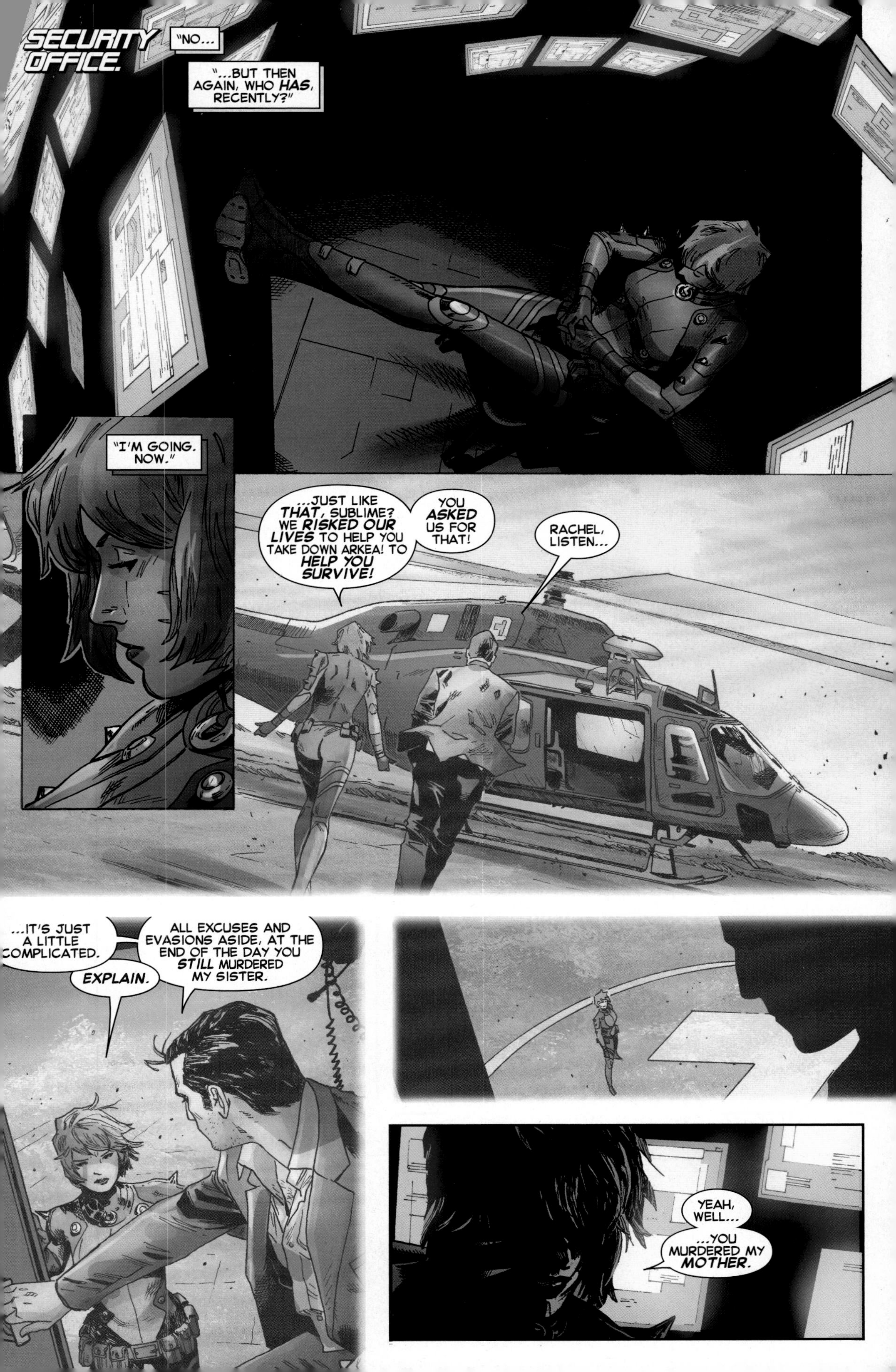
SECURITY OFFICE.
"NO...
"...BUT THEN AGAIN, WHO HAS, RECENTLY?"
"I'M GOING. NOW."
...JUST LIKE THAT, SUBLIME? WE RISKED OUR LIVES TO HELP YOU TAKE DOWN ARKEA! TO HELP YOU SURVIVE!
YOU ASKED US FOR THAT!
RACHEL, LISTEN...
...IT'S JUST A LITTLE COMPLICATED.
EXPLAIN.
ALL EXCUSES AND EVASIONS ASIDE, AT THE END OF THE DAY YOU STILL MURDERED MY SISTER.
YEAH, WELL...
...YOU MURDERED MY MOTHER.

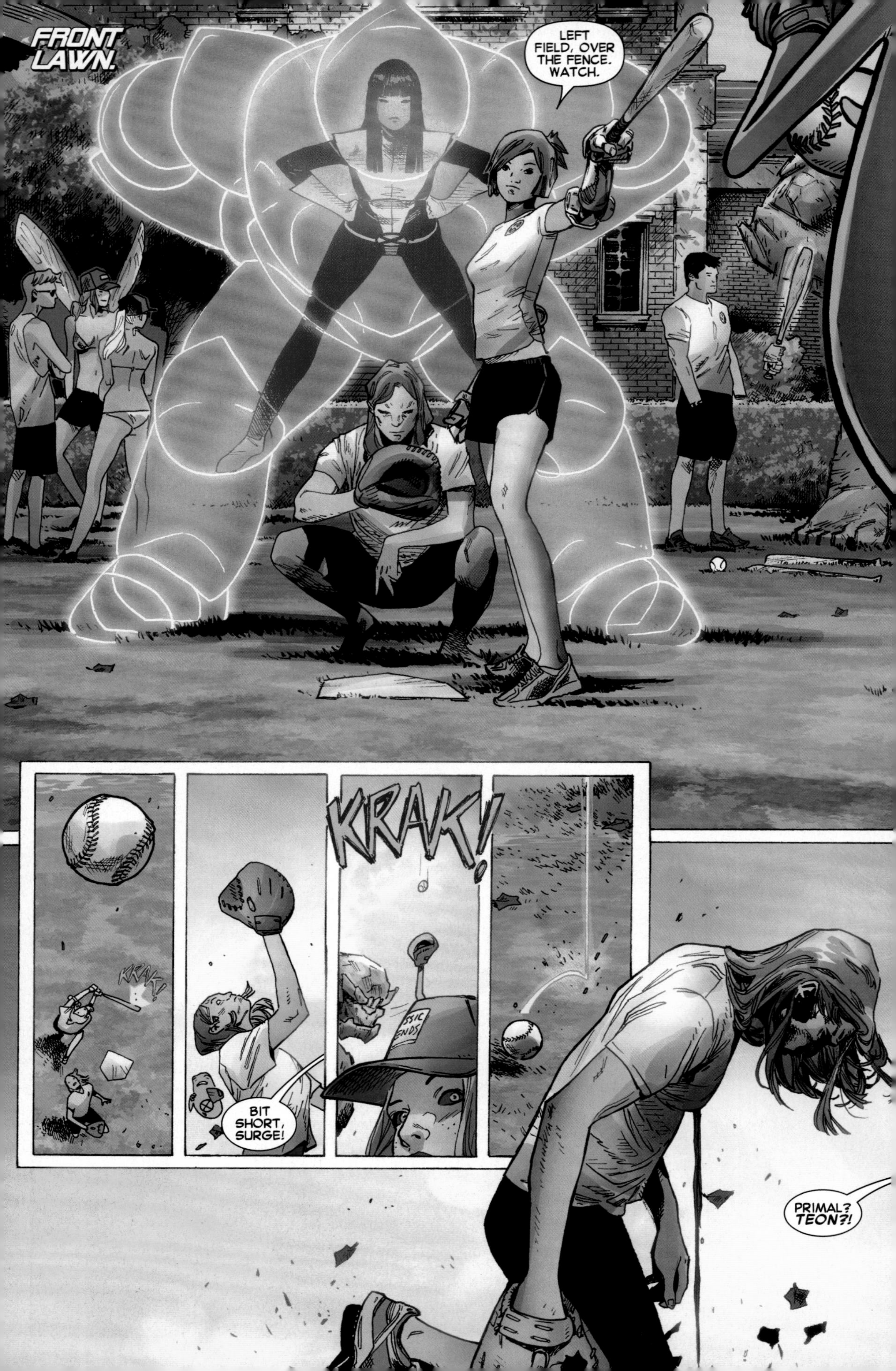
FRONT LAWN.
LEFT FIELD, OVER THE FENCE. WATCH.
KRAK!
KRAK!
BIT SHORT, SURGE!
PRIMAL? TEON?!

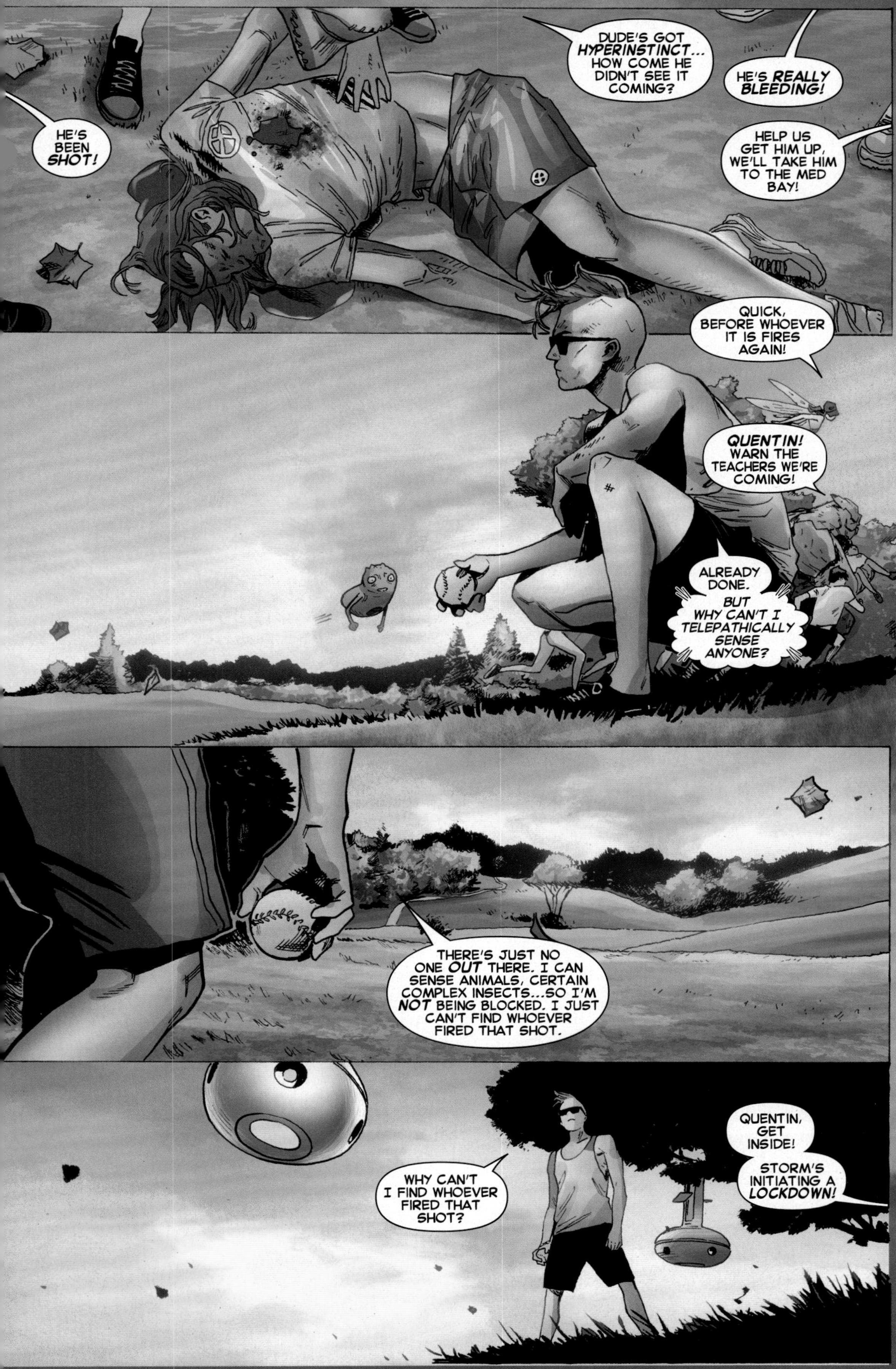
HE'S BEEN SHOT!
DUDE'S GOT HYPERINSTINCT... HOW COME HE DIDN'T SEE IT COMING?
HE'S REALLY BLEEDING!
HELP US GET HIM UP, WE'LL TAKE HIM TO THE MED BAY!
QUICK, BEFORE WHOEVER IT IS FIRES AGAIN!
QUENTIN! WARN THE TEACHERS WE'RE COMING!
ALREADY DONE.
BUT WHY CAN'T I TELEPATHICALLY SENSE ANYONE?
THERE'S JUST NO ONE OUT THERE. I CAN SENSE ANIMALS, CERTAIN COMPLEX INSECTS...SO I'M NOT BEING BLOCKED. I JUST CAN'T FIND WHOEVER FIRED THAT SHOT.
WHY CAN'T I FIND WHOEVER FIRED THAT SHOT?
QUENTIN, GET INSIDE!
STORM'S INITIATING A LOCKDOWN!

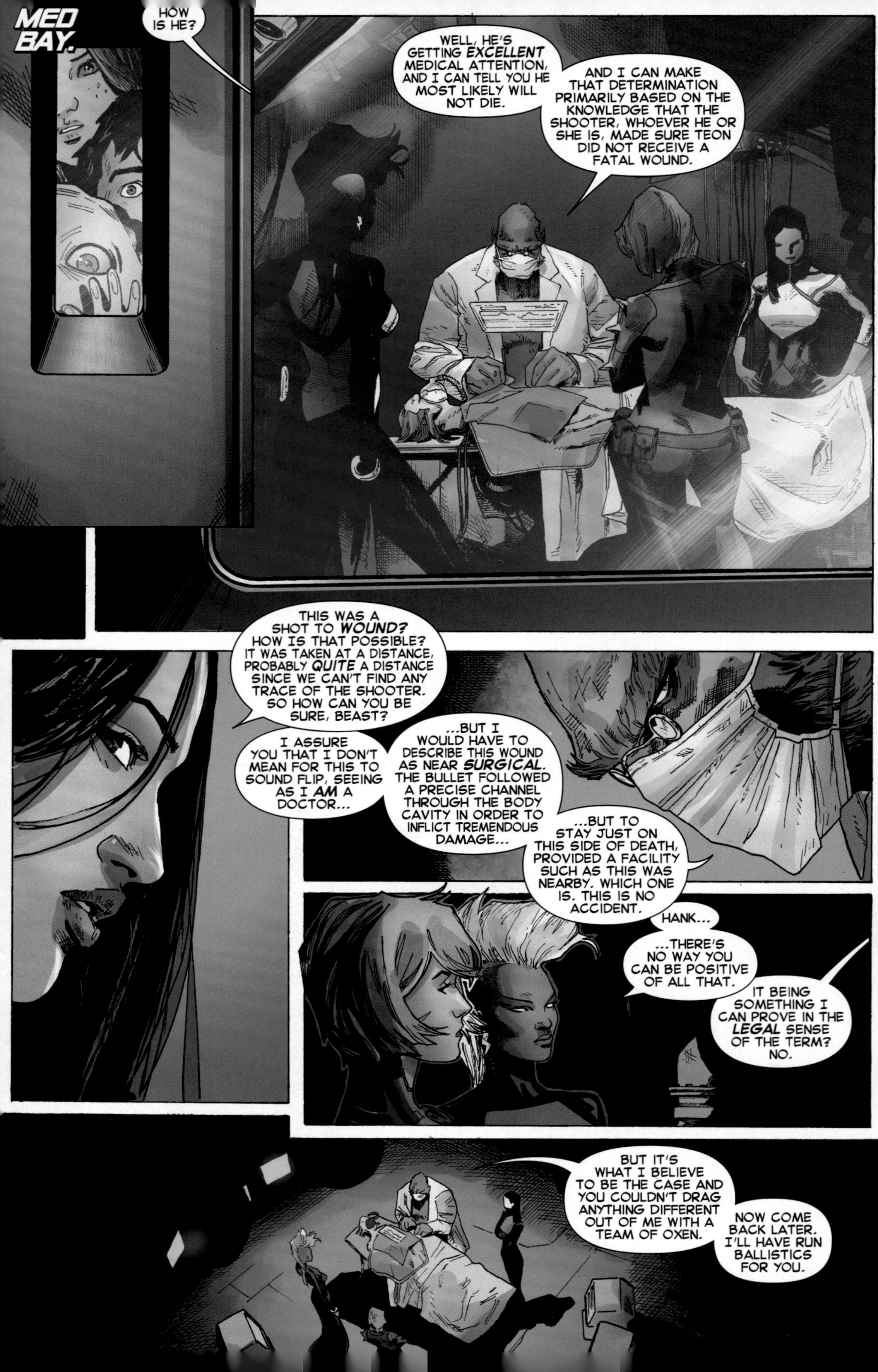
MED BAY.
HOW IS HE?
WELL, HE'S GETTING EXCELLENT MEDICAL ATTENTION, AND I CAN TELL YOU HE MOST LIKELY WILL NOT DIE.
AND I CAN MAKE THAT DETERMINATION PRIMARILY BASED ON THE KNOWLEDGE THAT THE SHOOTER, WHOEVER HE OR SHE IS, MADE SURE TEON DID NOT RECEIVE A FATAL WOUND.
THIS WAS A SHOT TO WOUND? HOW IS THAT POSSIBLE? IT WAS TAKEN AT A DISTANCE, PROBABLY QUITE A DISTANCE SINCE WE CAN'T FIND ANY TRACE OF THE SHOOTER. SO HOW CAN YOU BE SURE, BEAST?
I ASSURE YOU THAT I DON'T MEAN FOR THIS TO SOUND FLIP, SEEING AS I AM A DOCTOR...
...BUT I WOULD HAVE TO DESCRIBE THIS WOUND AS NEAR SURGICAL. THE BULLET FOLLOWED A PRECISE CHANNEL THROUGH THE BODY CAVITY IN ORDER TO INFLICT TREMENDOUS DAMAGE...
...BUT TO STAY JUST ON THIS SIDE OF DEATH, PROVIDED A FACILITY SUCH AS THIS WAS NEARBY. WHICH ONE IS. THIS IS NO ACCIDENT.
HANK...
...THERE'S NO WAY YOU CAN BE POSITIVE OF ALL THAT.
IT BEING SOMETHING I CAN PROVE IN THE LEGAL SENSE OF THE TERM? NO.
BUT IT'S WHAT I BELIEVE TO BE THE CASE AND YOU COULDN'T DRAG ANYTHING DIFFERENT OUT OF ME WITH A TEAM OF OXEN.
NOW COME BACK LATER. I'LL HAVE RUN BALLISTICS FOR YOU.

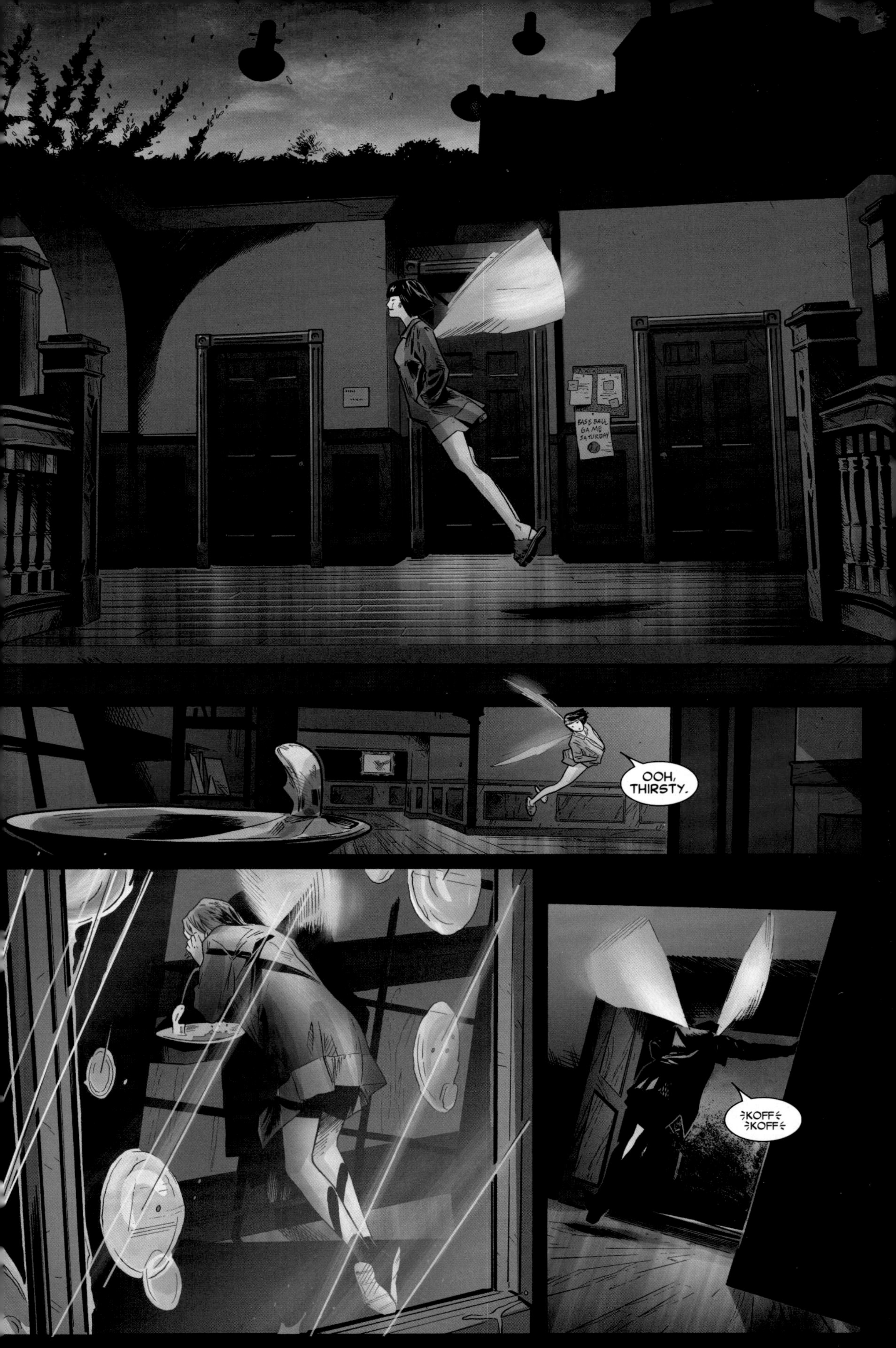
BASEBALL GAME SATURDAY
OOH, THIRSTY.
KOFF KOFF

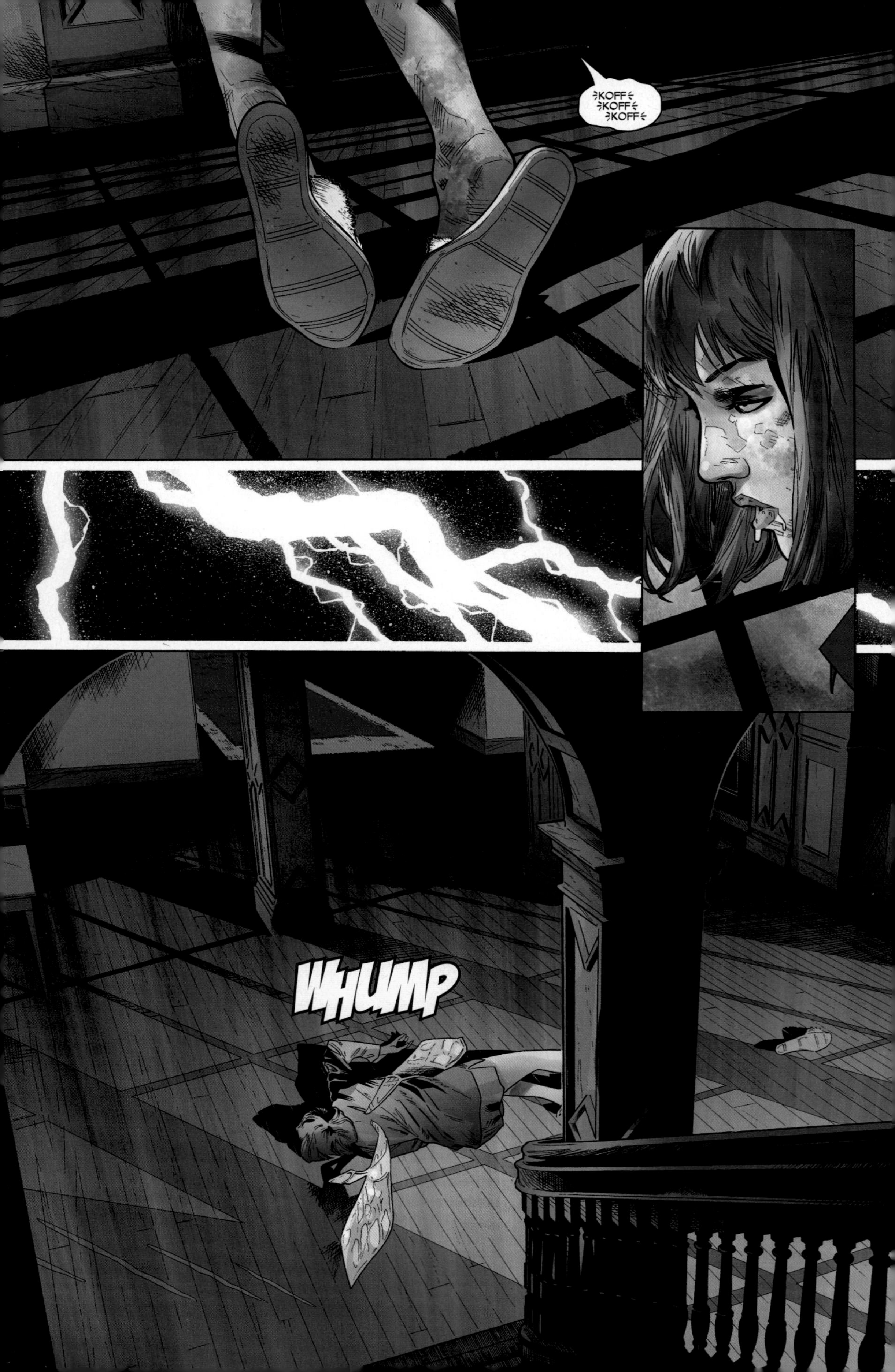
KOFF KOFF KOFF
WHUMP

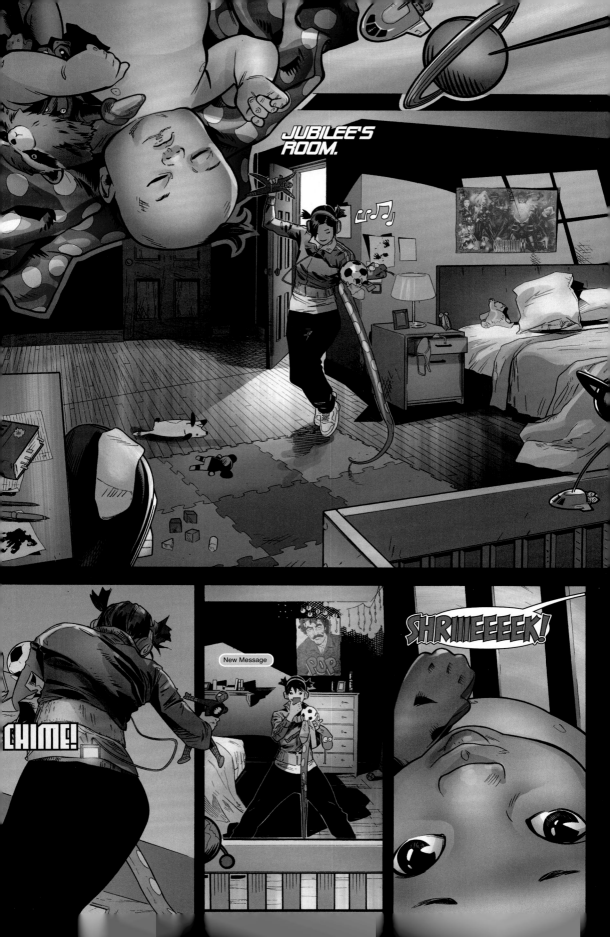

JUBILEE'S ROOM.

New Message

SHRIIIEEEEK!

CHIME!

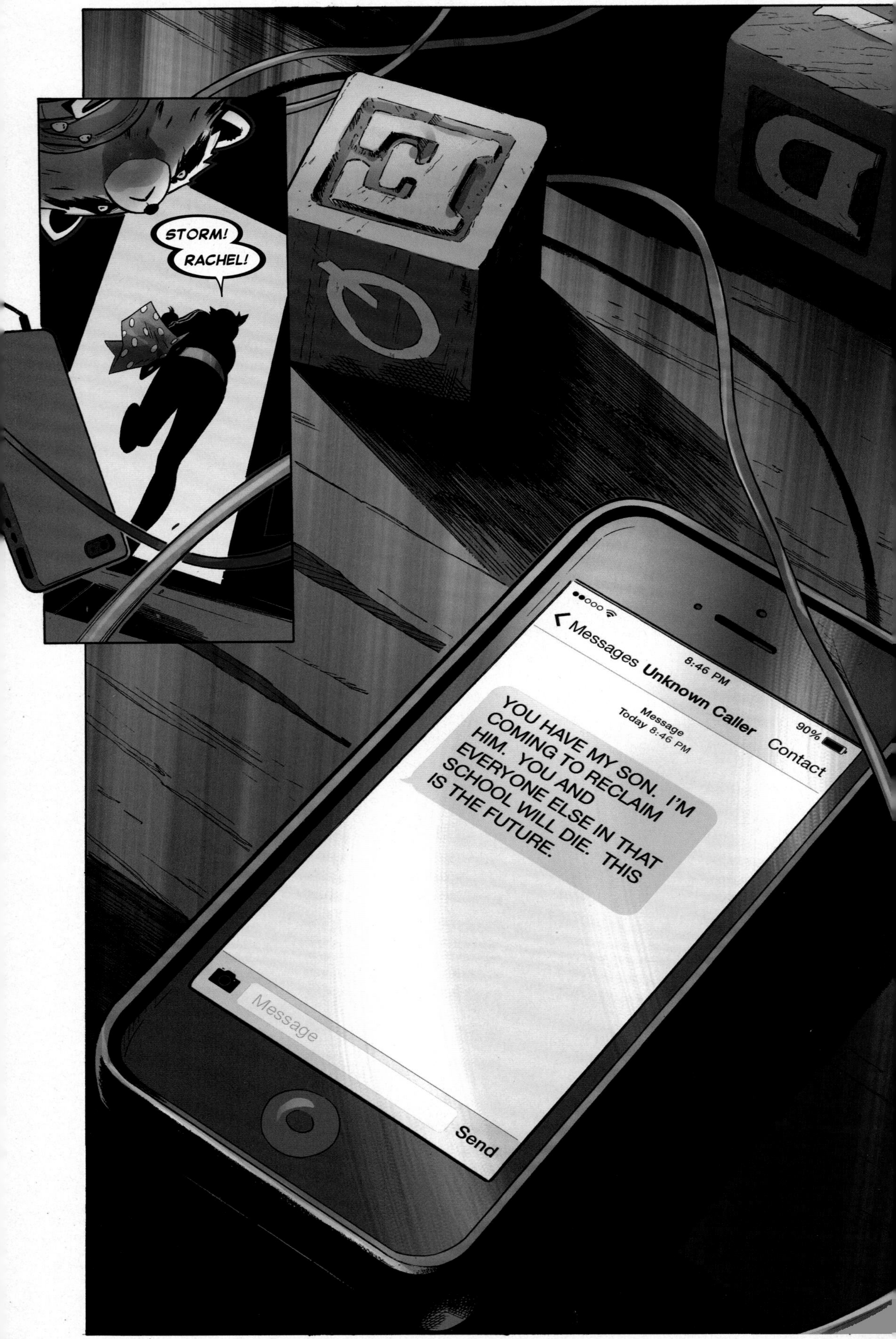
STORM! RACHEL!
Messages
Unknown Caller
8:46 PM
90%
Contact
Message
Today 8:46 PM
YOU HAVE MY SON. I'M COMING TO RECLAIM HIM. YOU AND EVERYONE ELSE IN THAT SCHOOL WILL DIE. THIS IS THE FUTURE.
Message
Send

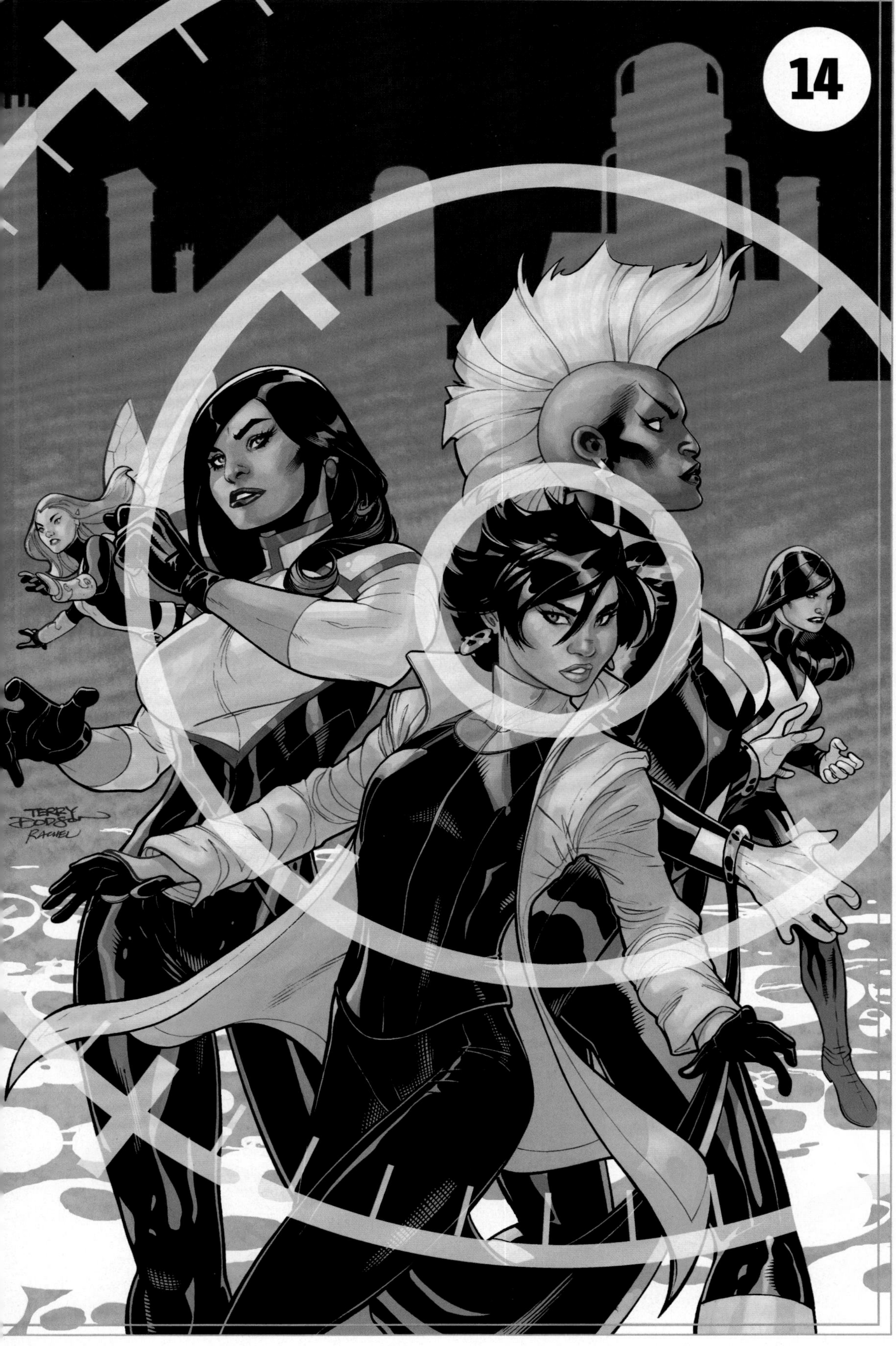
14
TERRY DODSON RACHEL

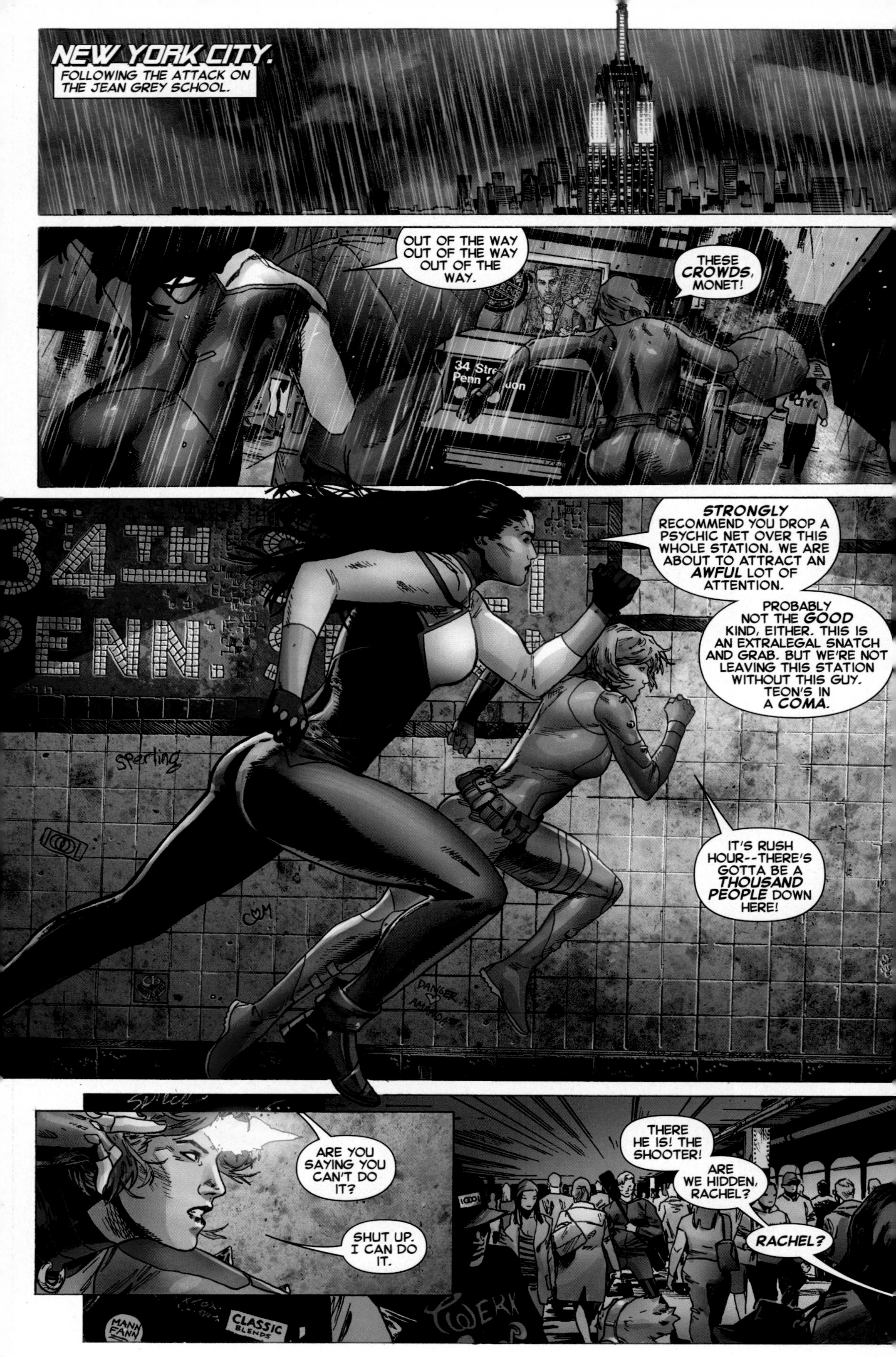

NEW YORK CITY.
FOLLOWING THE ATTACK ON THE JEAN GREY SCHOOL.
OUT OF THE WAY OUT OF THE WAY OUT OF THE WAY.
THESE CROWDS, MONET!
34 Stre
Penn S uon
STRONGLY RECOMMEND YOU DROP A PSYCHIC NET OVER THIS WHOLE STATION. WE ARE ABOUT TO ATTRACT AN AWFUL LOT OF ATTENTION.
PROBABLY NOT THE GOOD KIND, EITHER. THIS IS AN EXTRALEGAL SNATCH AND GRAB. BUT WE'RE NOT LEAVING THIS STATION WITHOUT THIS GUY. TEON'S IN A COMA.
IT'S RUSH HOUR--THERE'S GOTTA BE A THOUSAND PEOPLE DOWN HERE!
34TH
PENN.
ARE YOU SAYING YOU CAN'T DO IT?
SHUT UP. I CAN DO IT.
THERE HE IS! THE SHOOTER!
ARE WE HIDDEN, RACHEL?
RACHEL?
CLASSIC BLENDS

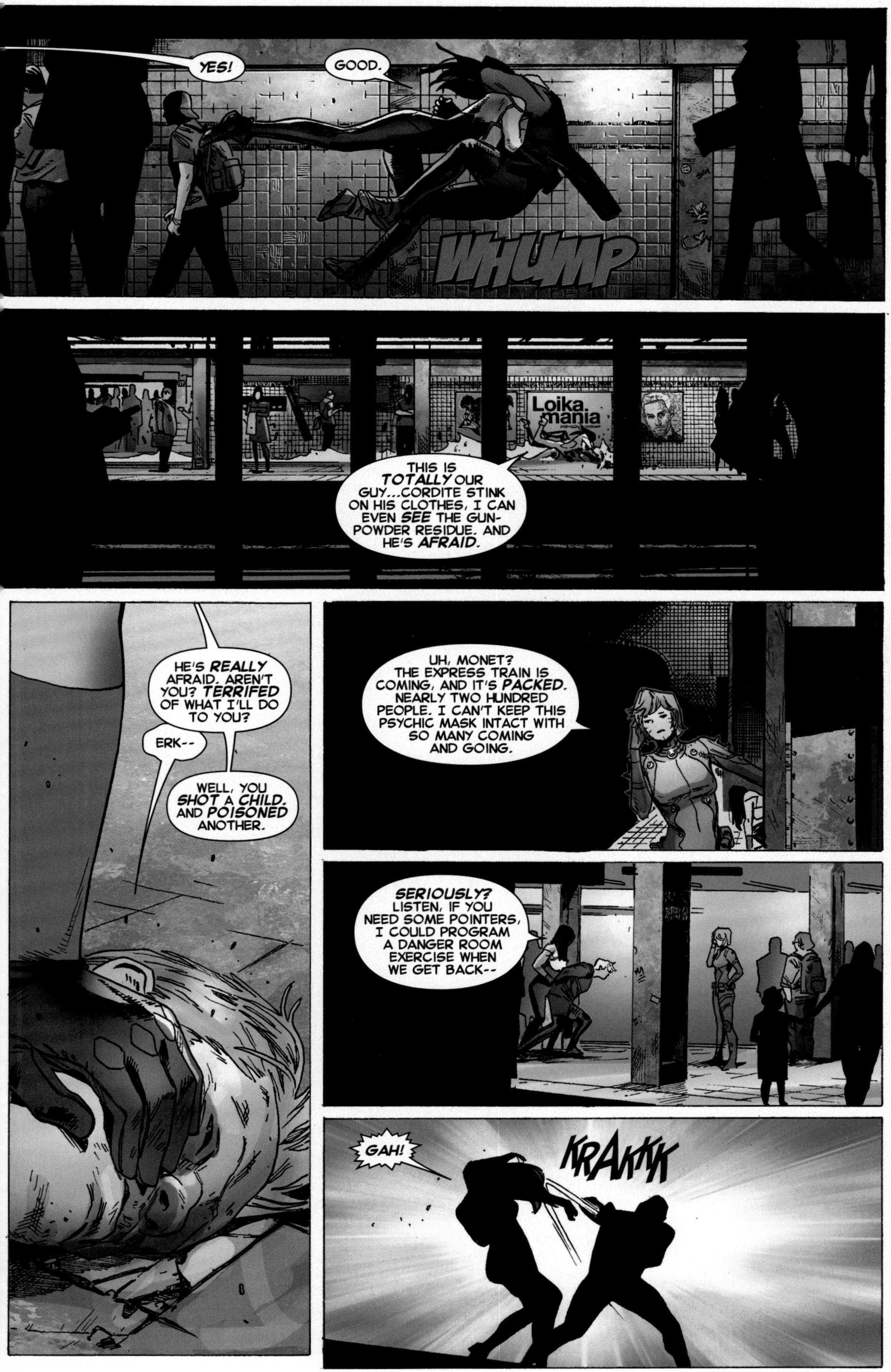
YES!
GOOD.
WHUMP
Loika.mania
THIS IS TOTALLY OUR GUY...CORDITE STINK ON HIS CLOTHES, I CAN EVEN SEE THE GUN-POWDER RESIDUE. AND HE'S AFRAID.
HE'S REALLY AFRAID. AREN'T YOU? TERRIFED OF WHAT I'LL DO TO YOU?
ERK--
WELL, YOU SHOT A CHILD. AND POISONED ANOTHER.
UH, MONET? THE EXPRESS TRAIN IS COMING, AND IT'S PACKED. NEARLY TWO HUNDRED PEOPLE. I CAN'T KEEP THIS PSYCHIC MASK INTACT WITH SO MANY COMING AND GOING.
SERIOUSLY? LISTEN, IF YOU NEED SOME POINTERS, I COULD PROGRAM A DANGER ROOM EXERCISE WHEN WE GET BACK--
GAH!
KRAKKK

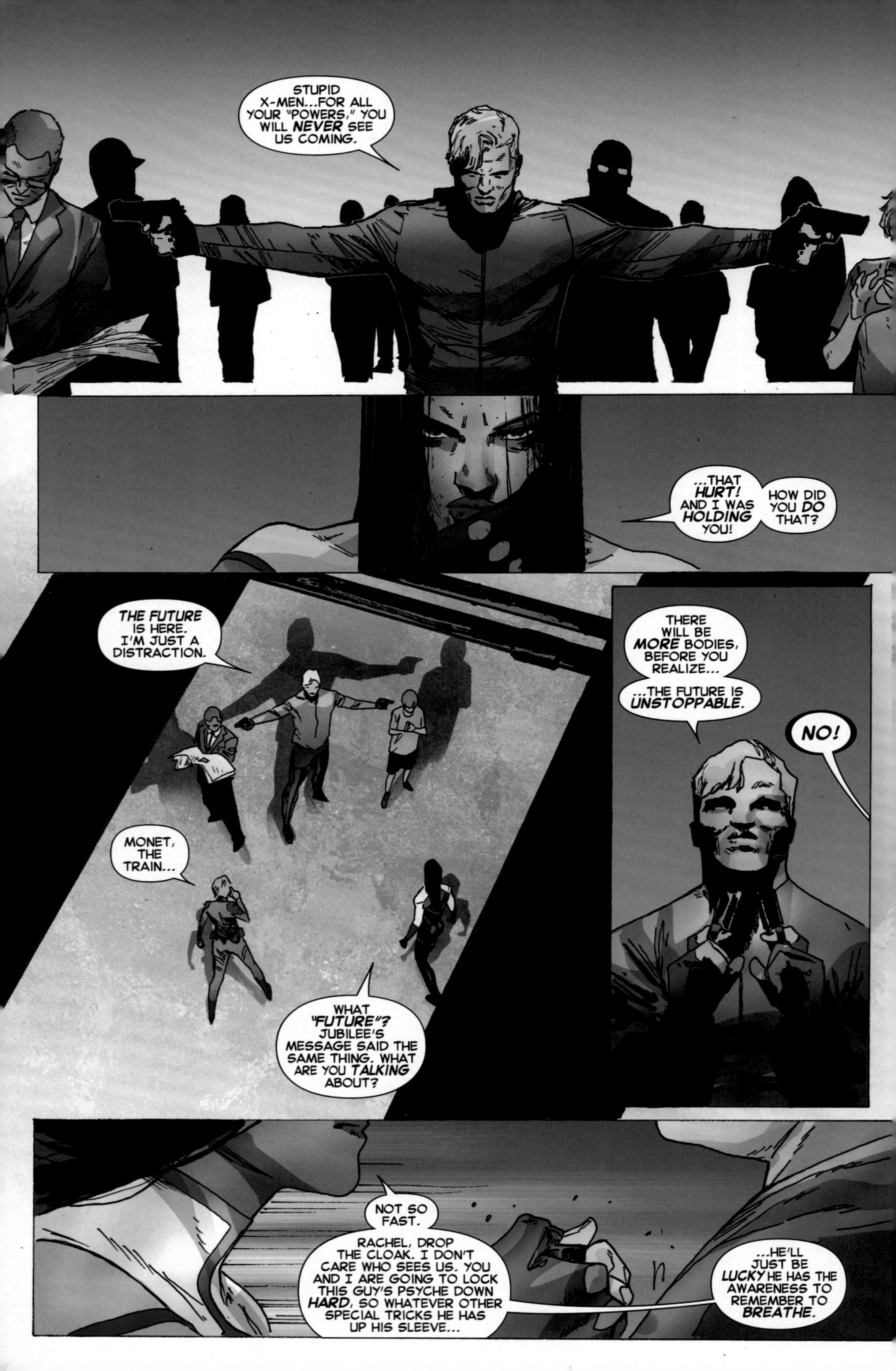
STUPID X-MEN...FOR ALL YOUR "POWERS," YOU WILL NEVER SEE US COMING.
...THAT HURT! AND I WAS HOLDING YOU!
HOW DID YOU DO THAT?
THE FUTURE IS HERE. I'M JUST A DISTRACTION.
MONET, THE TRAIN...
WHAT "FUTURE"? JUBILEE'S MESSAGE SAID THE SAME THING. WHAT ARE YOU TALKING ABOUT?
THERE WILL BE MORE BODIES, BEFORE YOU REALIZE...
...THE FUTURE IS UNSTOPPABLE.
NO!
NOT SO FAST.
RACHEL, DROP THE CLOAK. I DON'T CARE WHO SEES US. YOU AND I ARE GOING TO LOCK THIS GUY'S PSYCHE DOWN HARD, SO WHATEVER OTHER SPECIAL TRICKS HE HAS UP HIS SLEEVE...
...HE'LL JUST BE LUCKY HE HAS THE AWARENESS TO REMEMBER TO BREATHE.

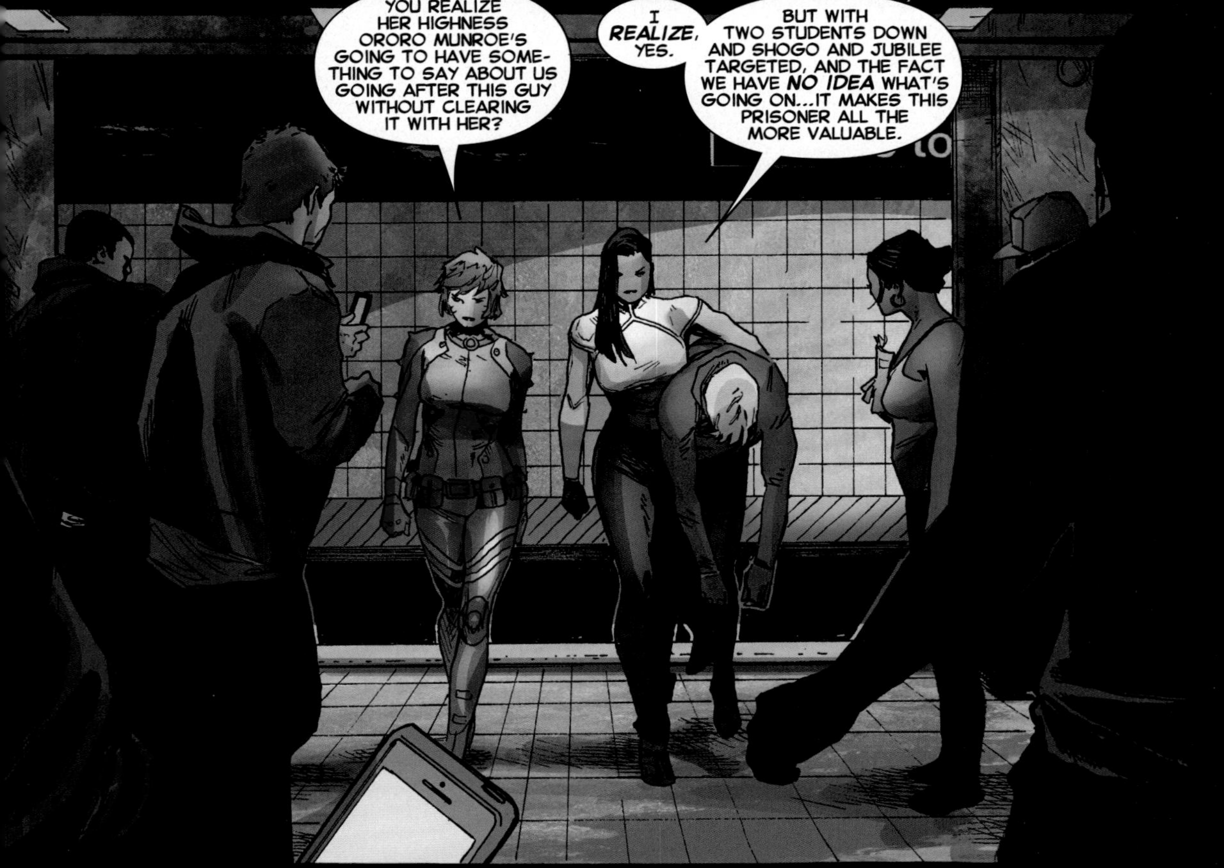
YOU REALIZE HER HIGHNESS ORORO MUNROE'S GOING TO HAVE SOME-THING TO SAY ABOUT US GOING AFTER THIS GUY WITHOUT CLEARING IT WITH HER?
I REALIZE, YES.
BUT WITH TWO STUDENTS DOWN AND SHOGO AND JUBILEE TARGETED, AND THE FACT WE HAVE NO IDEA WHAT'S GOING ON...IT MAKES THIS PRISONER ALL THE MORE VALUABLE.

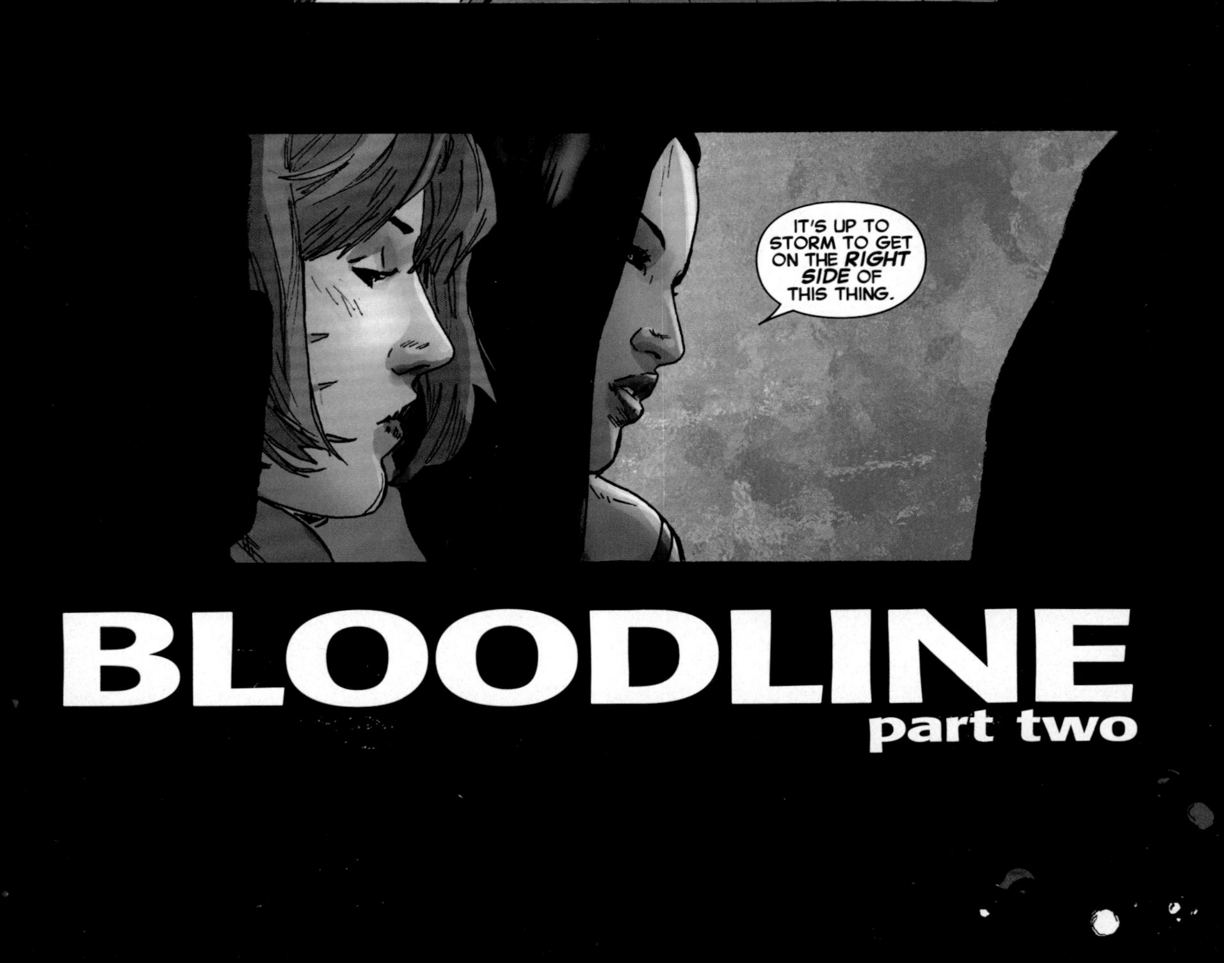
IT'S UP TO STORM TO GET ON THE RIGHT SIDE OF THIS THING.

BLOODLINE
part two

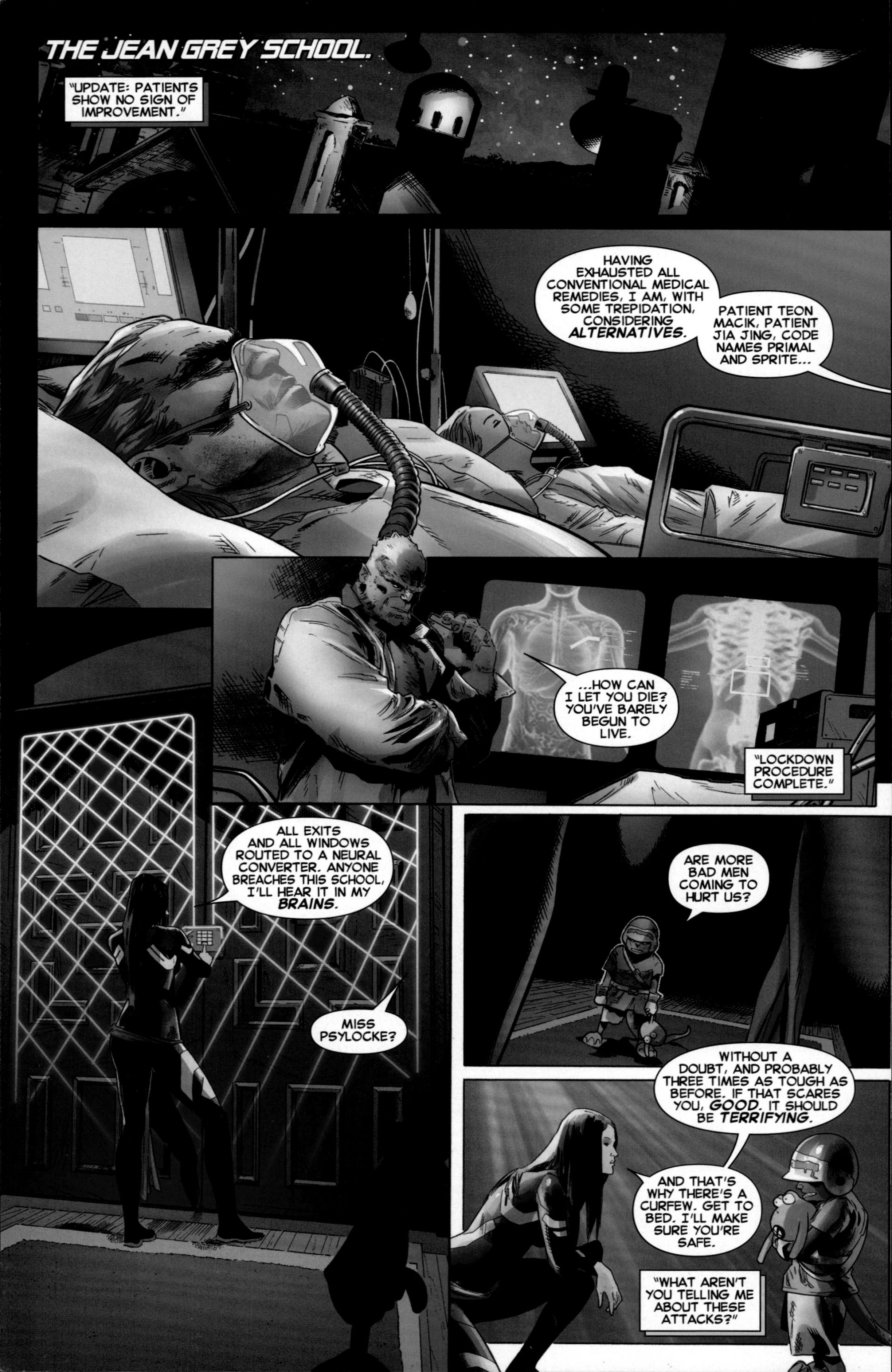
THE JEAN GREY SCHOOL.
"UPDATE: PATIENTS SHOW NO SIGN OF IMPROVEMENT."
HAVING EXHAUSTED ALL CONVENTIONAL MEDICAL REMEDIES, I AM, WITH SOME TREPIDATION, CONSIDERING ALTERNATIVES.
PATIENT TEON MACIK, PATIENT JIA JING, CODE NAMES PRIMAL AND SPRITE...
...HOW CAN I LET YOU DIE? YOU'VE BARELY BEGUN TO LIVE.
"LOCKDOWN PROCEDURE COMPLETE."
ALL EXITS AND ALL WINDOWS ROUTED TO A NEURAL CONVERTER. ANYONE BREACHES THIS SCHOOL, I'LL HEAR IT IN MY BRAINS.
MISS PSYLOCKE?
ARE MORE BAD MEN COMING TO HURT US?
WITHOUT A DOUBT, AND PROBABLY THREE TIMES AS TOUGH AS BEFORE. IF THAT SCARES YOU, GOOD. IT SHOULD BE TERRIFYING.
AND THAT'S WHY THERE'S A CURFEW. GET TO BED. I'LL MAKE SURE YOU'RE SAFE.
"WHAT AREN'T YOU TELLING ME ABOUT THESE ATTACKS?"

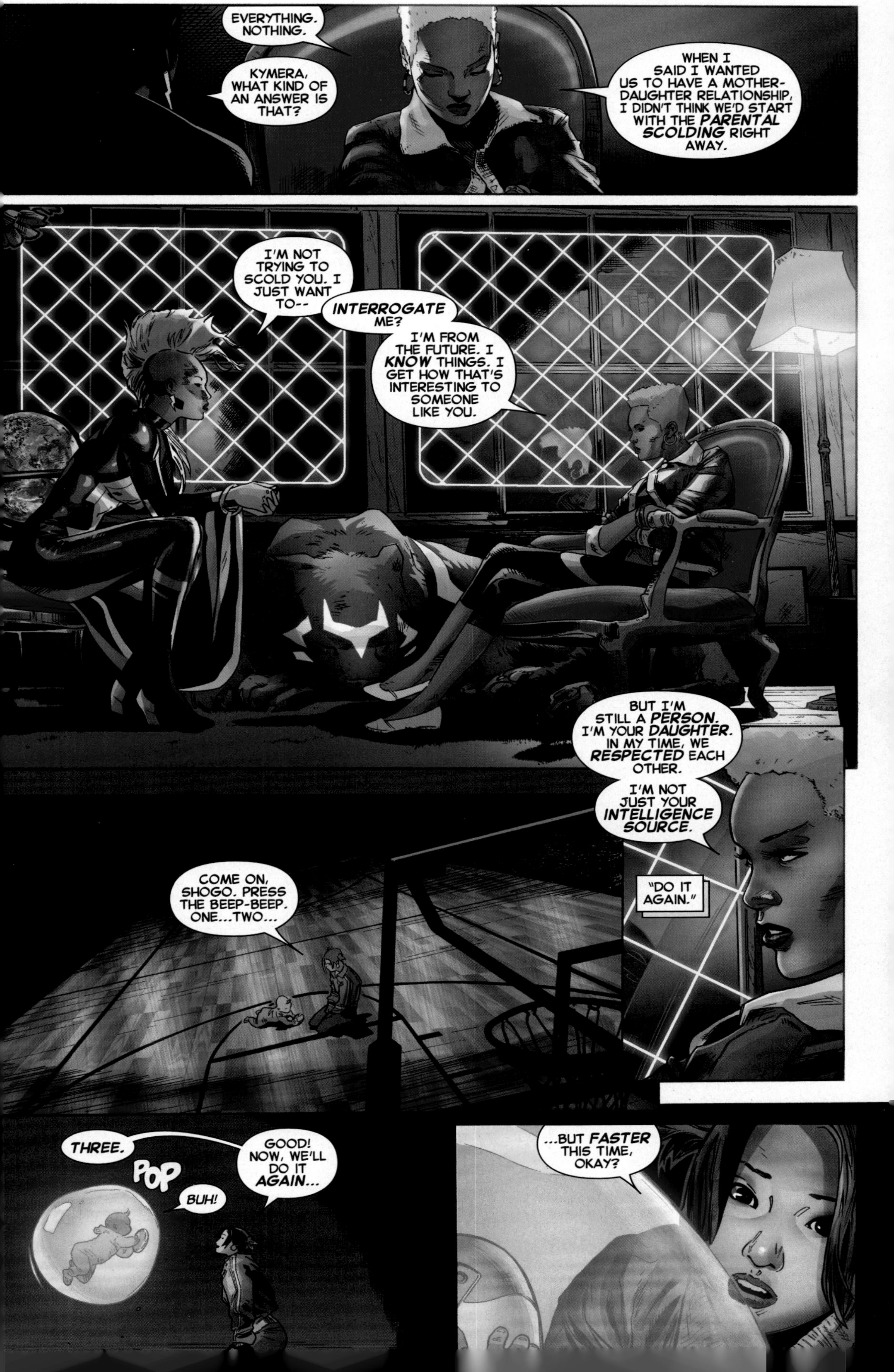
EVERYTHING. NOTHING.
KYMERA, WHAT KIND OF AN ANSWER IS THAT?
WHEN I SAID I WANTED US TO HAVE A MOTHER-DAUGHTER RELATIONSHIP, I DIDN'T THINK WE'D START WITH THE PARENTAL SCOLDING RIGHT AWAY.
I'M NOT TRYING TO SCOLD YOU. I JUST WANT TO--
INTERROGATE ME?
I'M FROM THE FUTURE. I KNOW THINGS. I GET HOW THAT'S INTERESTING TO SOMEONE LIKE YOU.
BUT I'M STILL A PERSON. I'M YOUR DAUGHTER. IN MY TIME, WE RESPECTED EACH OTHER.
I'M NOT JUST YOUR INTELLIGENCE SOURCE.
"DO IT AGAIN."
COME ON, SHOGO. PRESS THE BEEP-BEEP. ONE...TWO...
THREE.
GOOD! NOW, WE'LL DO IT AGAIN...
POP
BUH!
...BUT FASTER THIS TIME, OKAY?

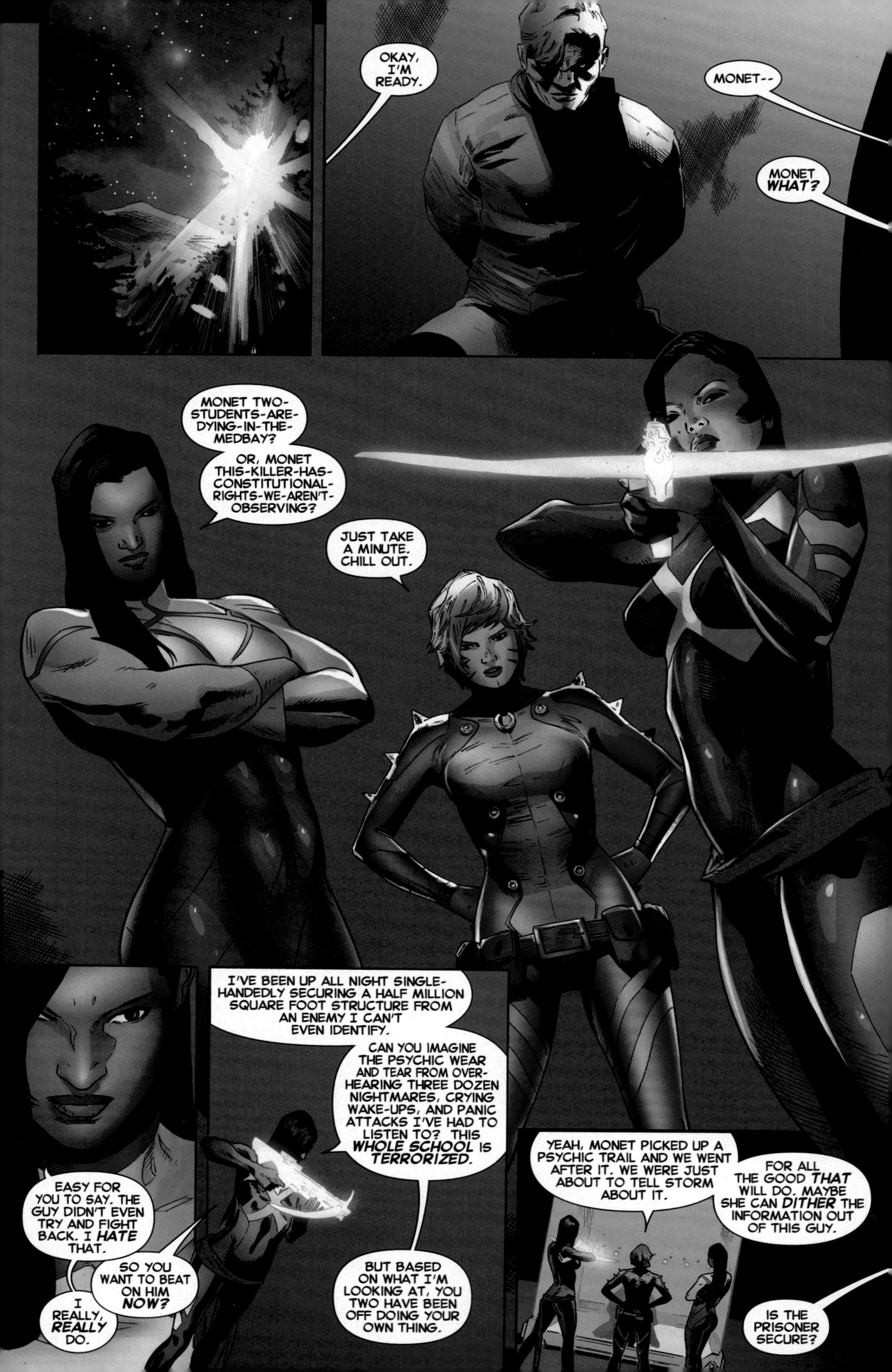
OKAY, I'M READY.
MONET--
MONET WHAT?
MONET TWO-STUDENTS-ARE-DYING-IN-THE-MEDBAY?
OR, MONET THIS-KILLER-HAS-CONSTITUTIONAL-RIGHTS-WE-AREN'T-OBSERVING?
JUST TAKE A MINUTE. CHILL OUT.
I'VE BEEN UP ALL NIGHT SINGLE-HANDEDLY SECURING A HALF MILLION SQUARE FOOT STRUCTURE FROM AN ENEMY I CAN'T EVEN IDENTIFY.
CAN YOU IMAGINE THE PSYCHIC WEAR AND TEAR FROM OVER-HEARING THREE DOZEN NIGHTMARES, CRYING WAKE-UPS, AND PANIC ATTACKS I'VE HAD TO LISTEN TO? THIS WHOLE SCHOOL IS TERRORIZED.
EASY FOR YOU TO SAY. THE GUY DIDN'T EVEN TRY AND FIGHT BACK. I HATE THAT.
SO YOU WANT TO BEAT ON HIM NOW?
I REALLY, REALLY DO.
BUT BASED ON WHAT I'M LOOKING AT, YOU TWO HAVE BEEN OFF DOING YOUR OWN THING.
YEAH, MONET PICKED UP A PSYCHIC TRAIL AND WE WENT AFTER IT. WE WERE JUST ABOUT TO TELL STORM ABOUT IT.
FOR ALL THE GOOD THAT WILL DO. MAYBE SHE CAN DITHER THE INFORMATION OUT OF THIS GUY.
IS THE PRISONER SECURE?

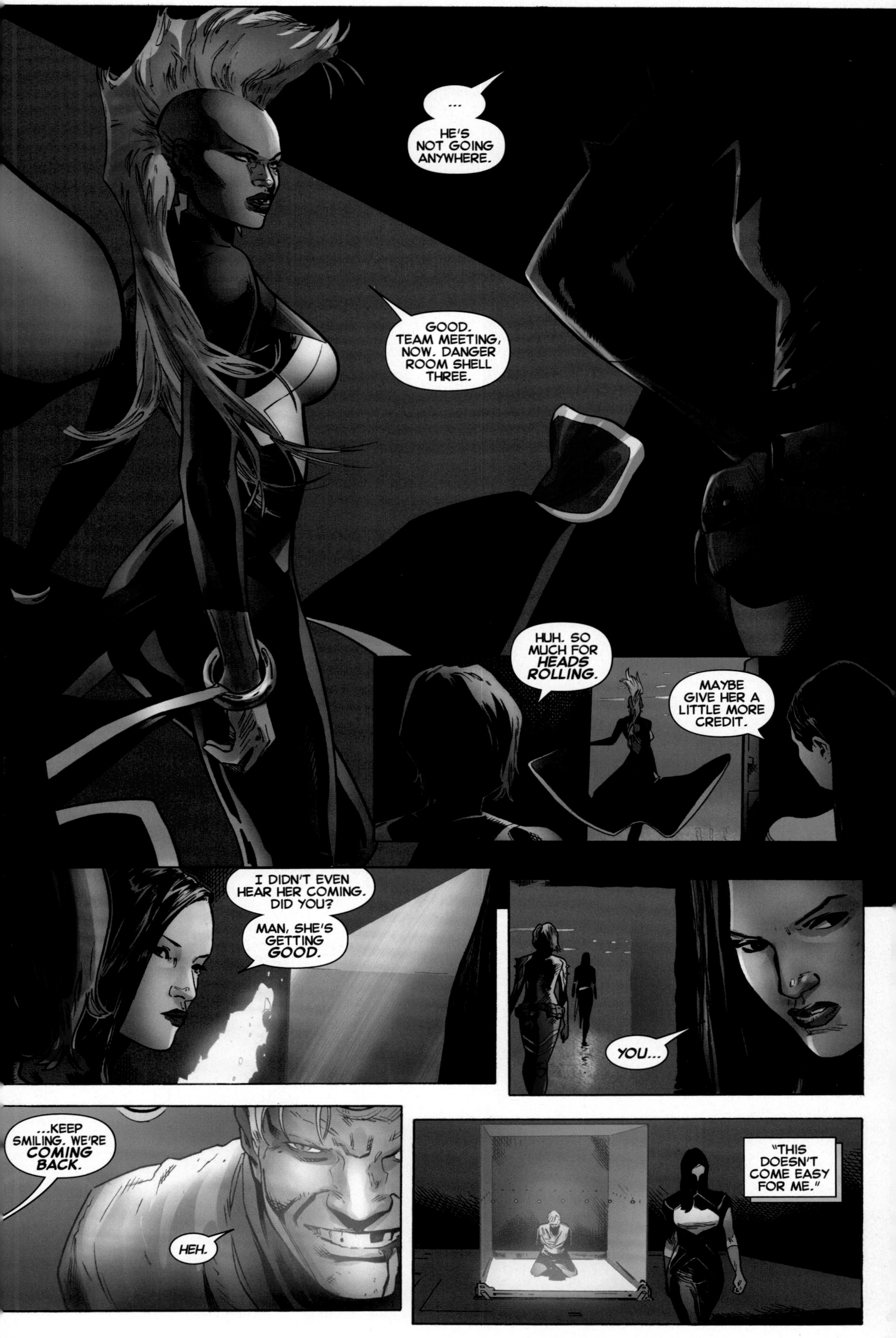
...
HE'S NOT GOING ANYWHERE.
GOOD. TEAM MEETING, NOW. DANGER ROOM SHELL THREE.
HUH. SO MUCH FOR HEADS ROLLING.
MAYBE GIVE HER A LITTLE MORE CREDIT.
I DIDN'T EVEN HEAR HER COMING. DID YOU?
MAN, SHE'S GETTING GOOD.
YOU...
...KEEP SMILING. WE'RE COMING BACK.
HEH.
"THIS DOESN'T COME EASY FOR ME."

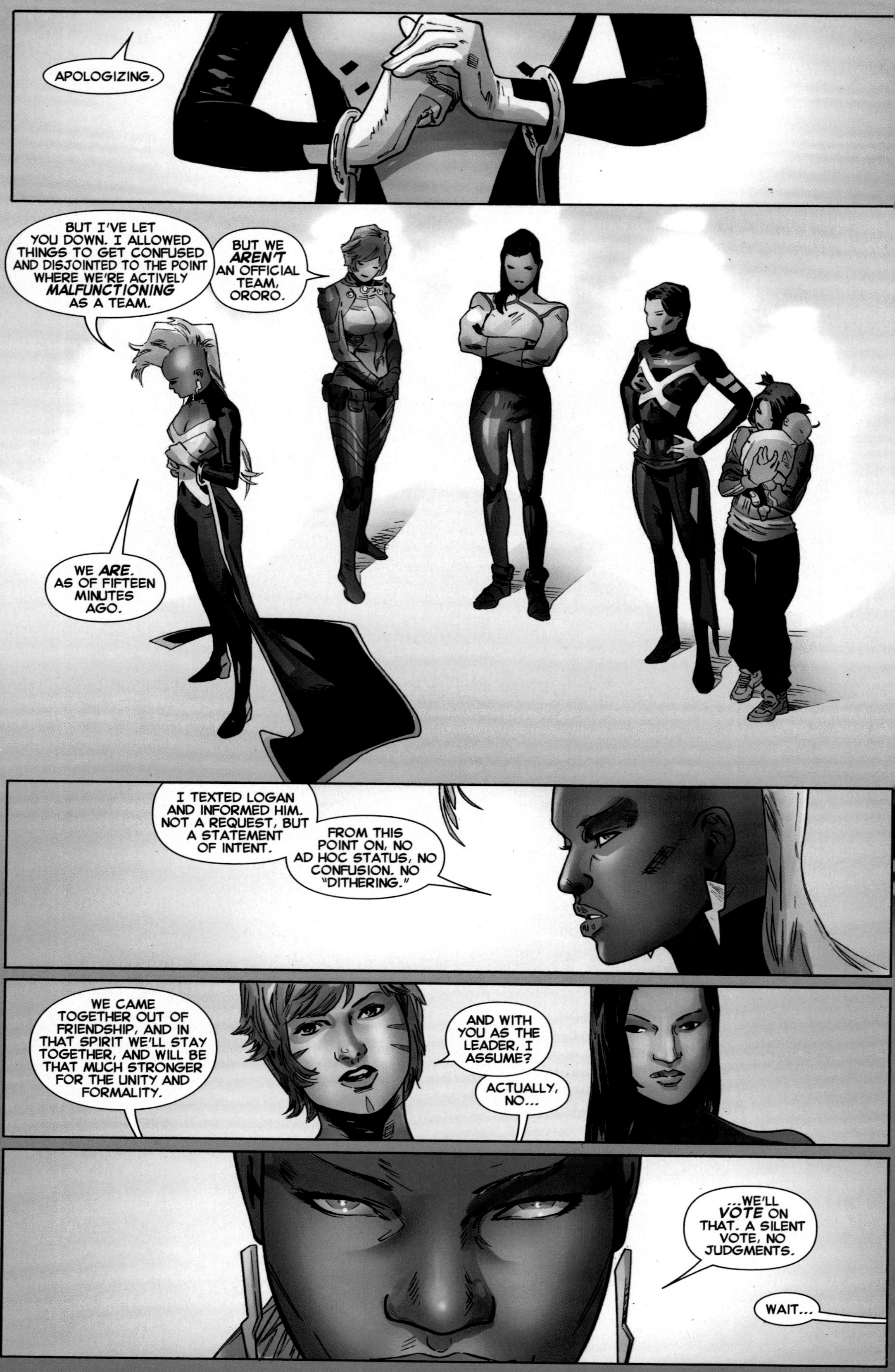
APOLOGIZING.
BUT I'VE LET YOU DOWN. I ALLOWED THINGS TO GET CONFUSED AND DISJOINTED TO THE POINT WHERE WE'RE ACTIVELY MALFUNCTIONING AS A TEAM.
BUT WE AREN'T AN OFFICIAL TEAM, ORORO.
WE ARE. AS OF FIFTEEN MINUTES AGO.
I TEXTED LOGAN AND INFORMED HIM. NOT A REQUEST, BUT A STATEMENT OF INTENT.
FROM THIS POINT ON, NO AD HOC STATUS, NO CONFUSION. NO "DITHERING."
WE CAME TOGETHER OUT OF FRIENDSHIP, AND IN THAT SPIRIT WE'LL STAY TOGETHER, AND WILL BE THAT MUCH STRONGER FOR THE UNITY AND FORMALITY.
AND WITH YOU AS THE LEADER, I ASSUME?
ACTUALLY, NO...
...WE'LL VOTE ON THAT. A SILENT VOTE, NO JUDGMENTS.
WAIT...

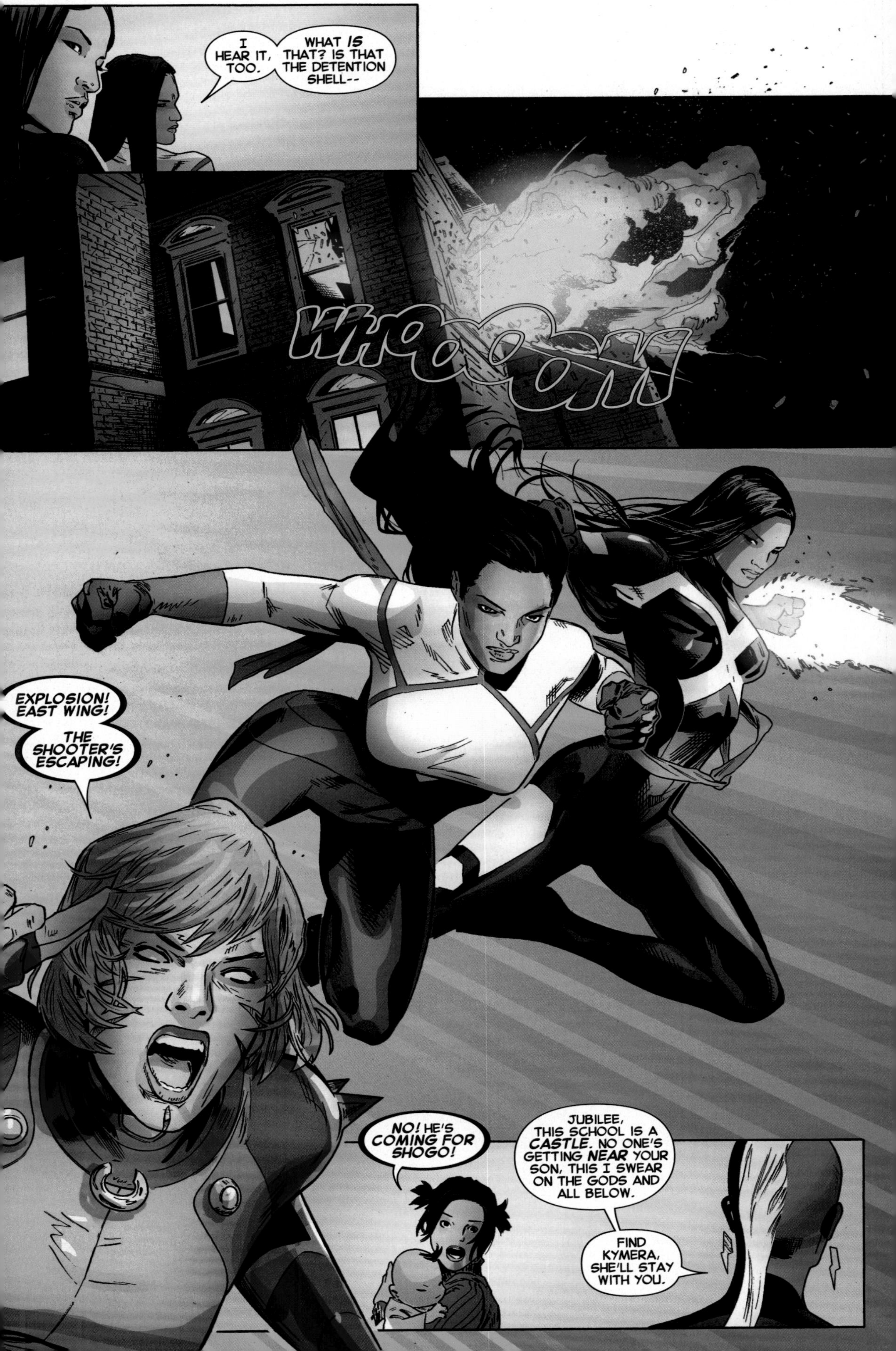
I HEAR IT, TOO.
WHAT IS THAT? IS THAT THE DETENTION SHELL--
WHOOOOM
EXPLOSION! EAST WING!
THE SHOOTER'S ESCAPING!
NO! HE'S COMING FOR SHOGO!
JUBILEE, THIS SCHOOL IS A CASTLE. NO ONE'S GETTING NEAR YOUR SON, THIS I SWEAR ON THE GODS AND ALL BELOW.
FIND KYMERA, SHE'LL STAY WITH YOU.

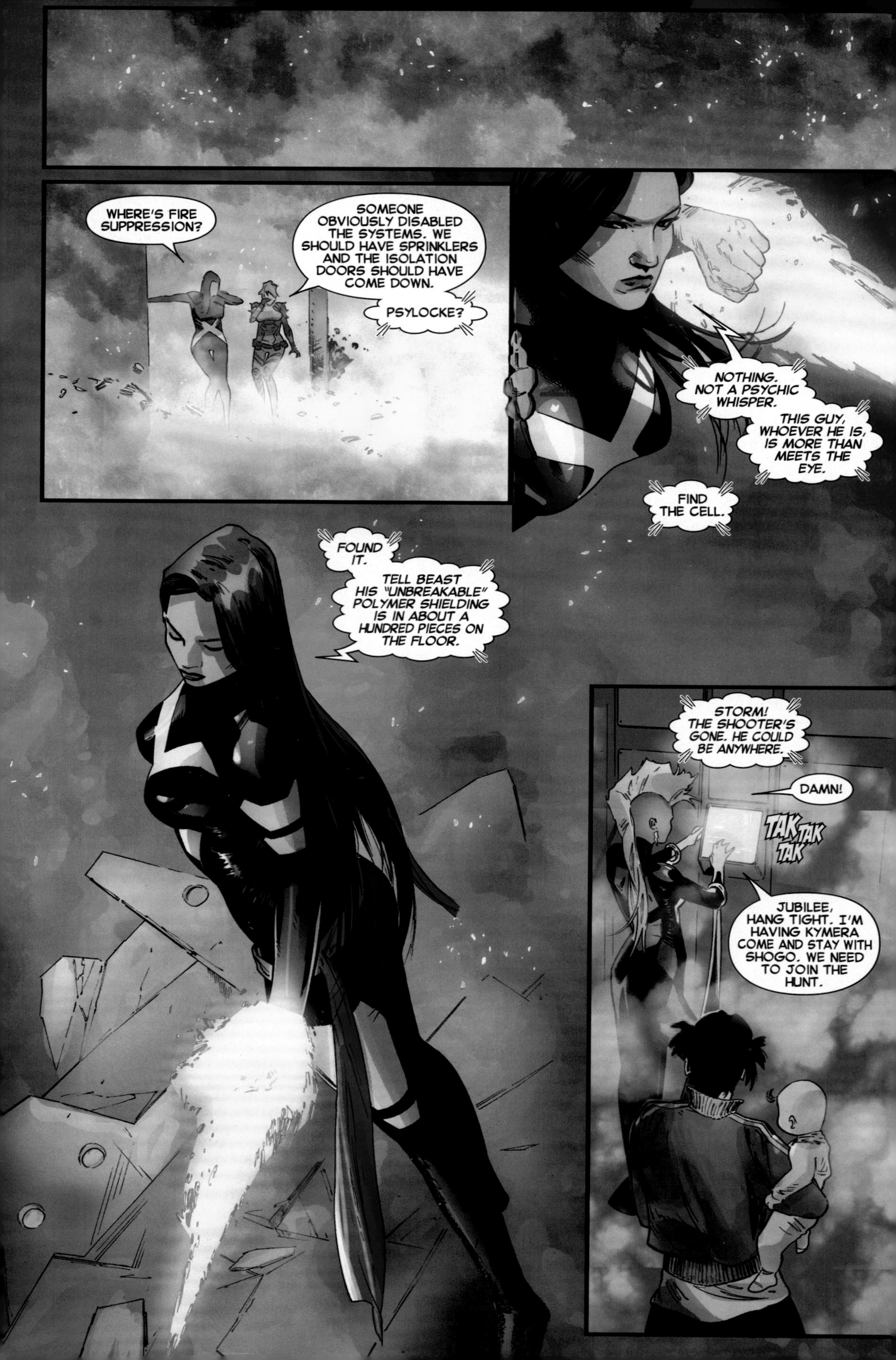
WHERE'S FIRE SUPPRESSION?
SOMEONE OBVIOUSLY DISABLED THE SYSTEMS. WE SHOULD HAVE SPRINKLERS AND THE ISOLATION DOORS SHOULD HAVE COME DOWN.
PSYLOCKE?
NOTHING. NOT A PSYCHIC WHISPER.
THIS GUY, WHOEVER HE IS, IS MORE THAN MEETS THE EYE.
FIND THE CELL.
FOUND IT.
TELL BEAST HIS "UNBREAKABLE" POLYMER SHIELDING IS IN ABOUT A HUNDRED PIECES ON THE FLOOR.
STORM! THE SHOOTER'S GONE. HE COULD BE ANYWHERE.
DAMN!
TAK TAK TAK
JUBILEE, HANG TIGHT. I'M HAVING KYMERA COME AND STAY WITH SHOGO. WE NEED TO JOIN THE HUNT.

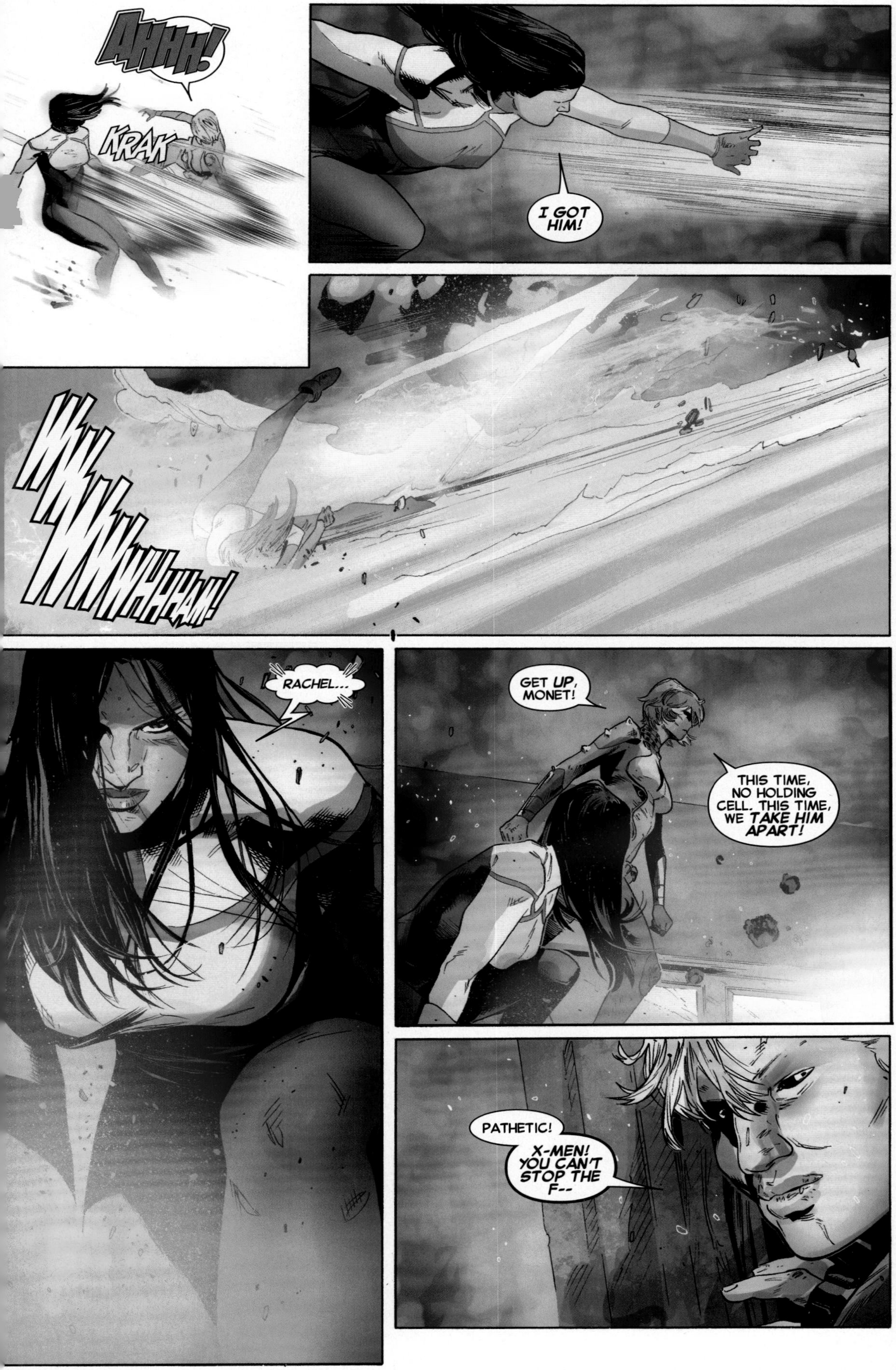
AHHH!
KRAK
I GOT HIM!
WWWHHAM!
RACHEL...
GET UP, MONET!
THIS TIME, NO HOLDING CELL. THIS TIME, WE TAKE HIM APART!
PATHETIC!
X-MEN! YOU CAN'T STOP THE F--

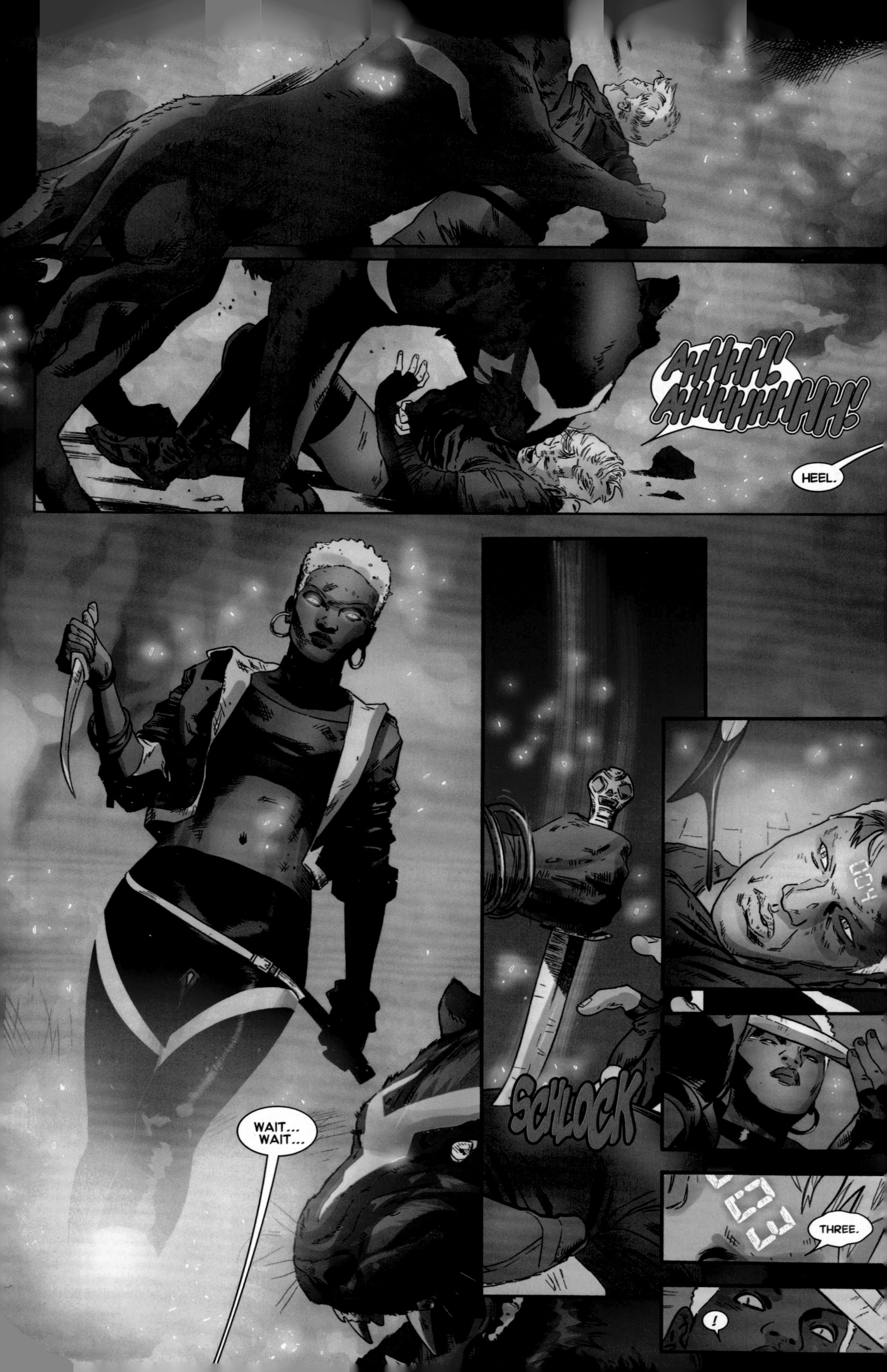
AHHHH! AHHHHHHHH!
HEEL.
WAIT... WAIT...
SCHLOCK
THREE.
!

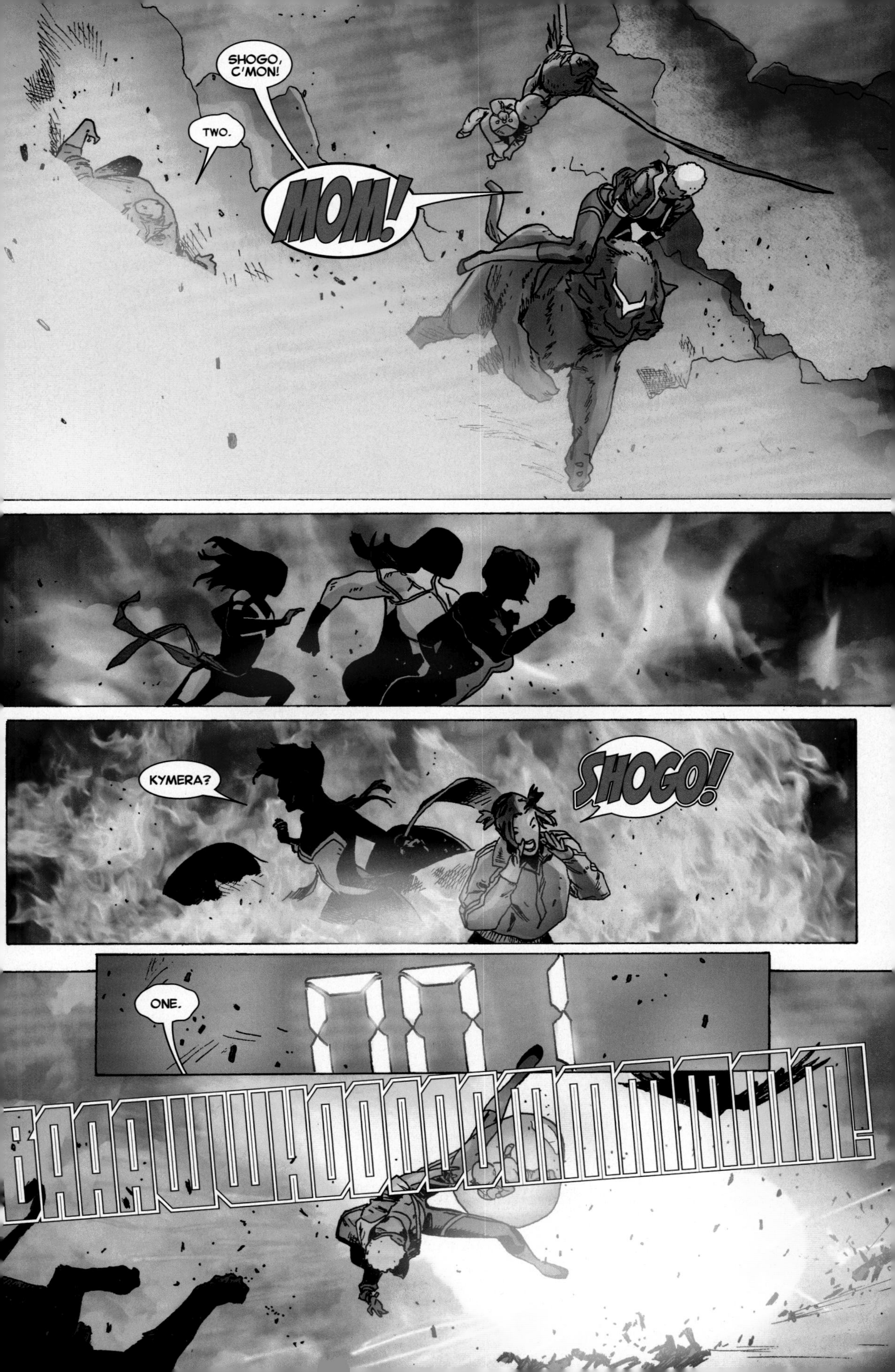
SHOGO, C'MON!
TWO.
MOM!
KYMERA?
SHOGO!
ONE.
BAAAUUWHOOOOOMMMMMMMM!

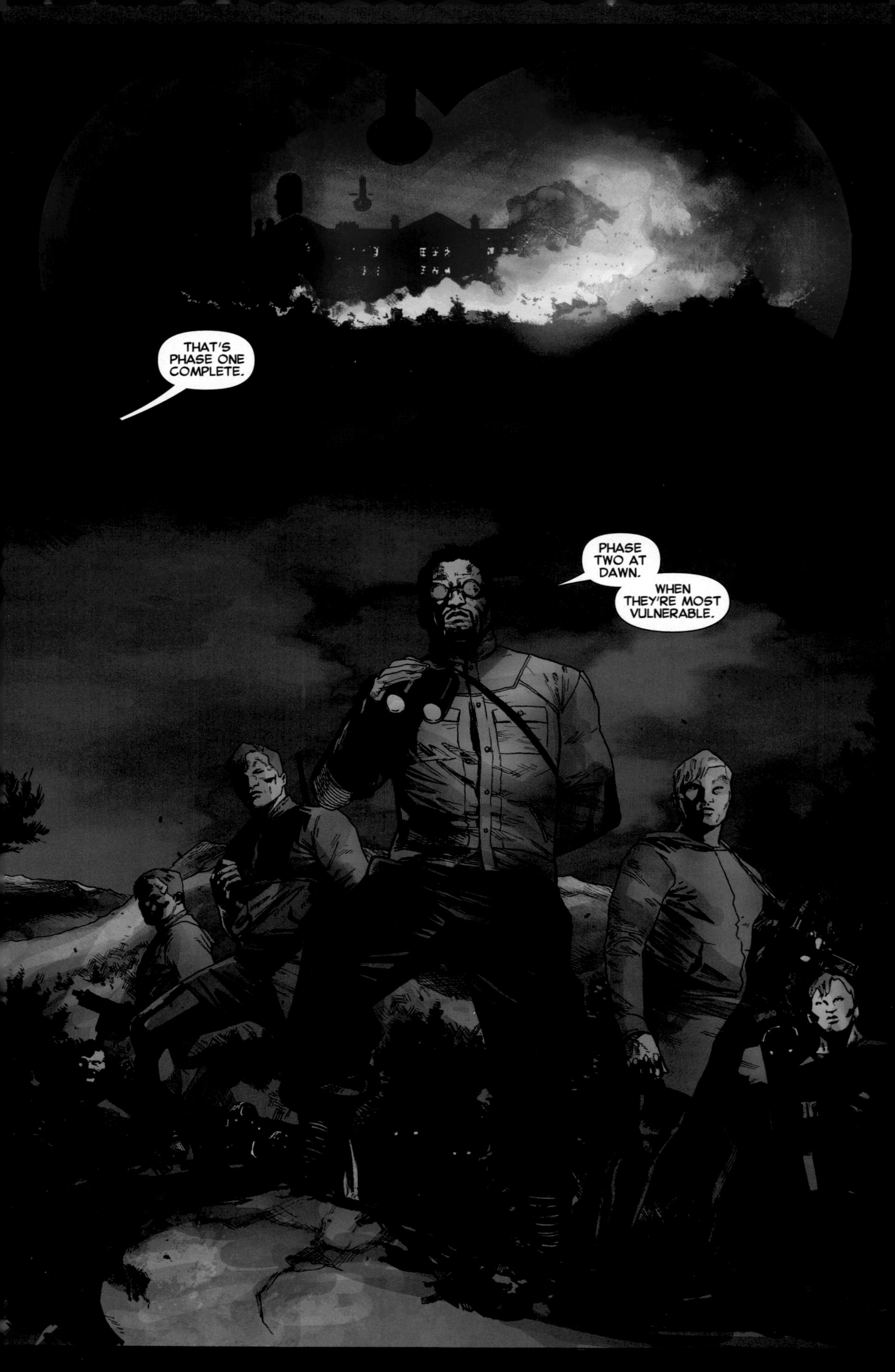
THAT'S PHASE ONE COMPLETE.
PHASE TWO AT DAWN.
WHEN THEY'RE MOST VULNERABLE.

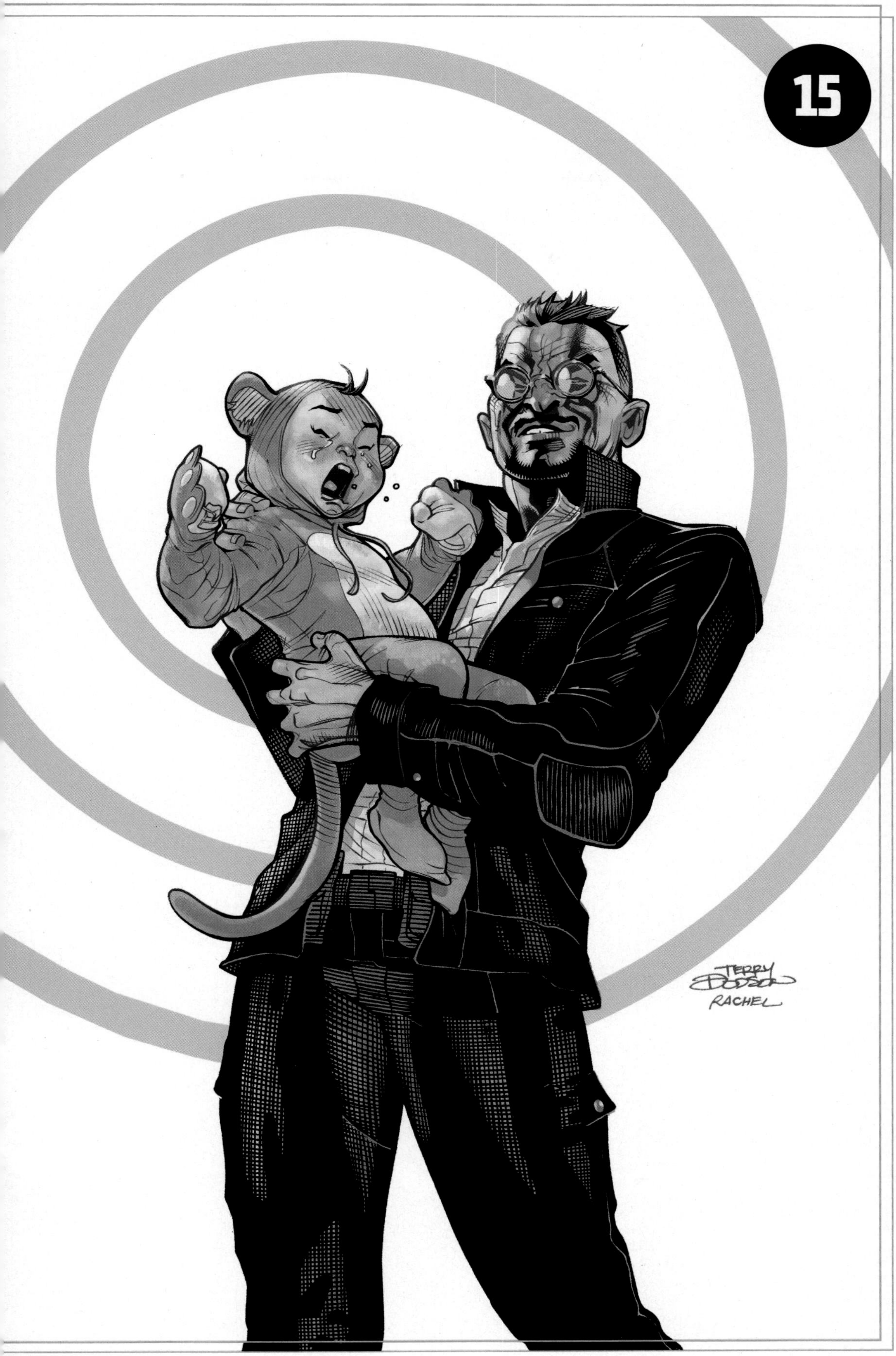
15
TERRY DODSON
RACHEL

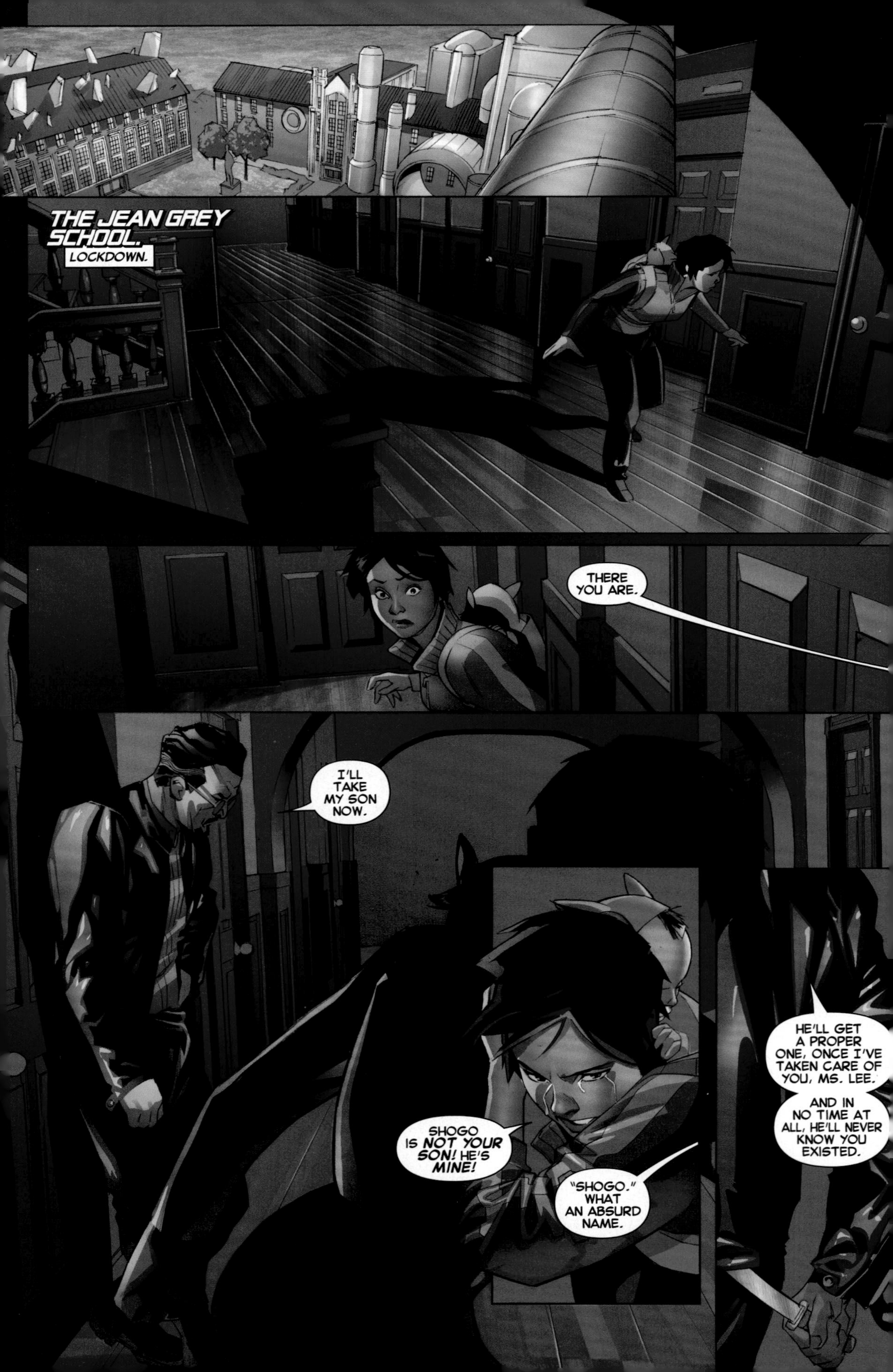
THE JEAN GREY SCHOOL.
LOCKDOWN.
THERE YOU ARE.
I'LL TAKE MY SON NOW.
SHOGO IS NOT YOUR SON! HE'S MINE!
"SHOGO." WHAT AN ABSURD NAME.
HE'LL GET A PROPER ONE, ONCE I'VE TAKEN CARE OF YOU, MS. LEE.
AND IN NO TIME AT ALL, HE'LL NEVER KNOW YOU EXISTED.

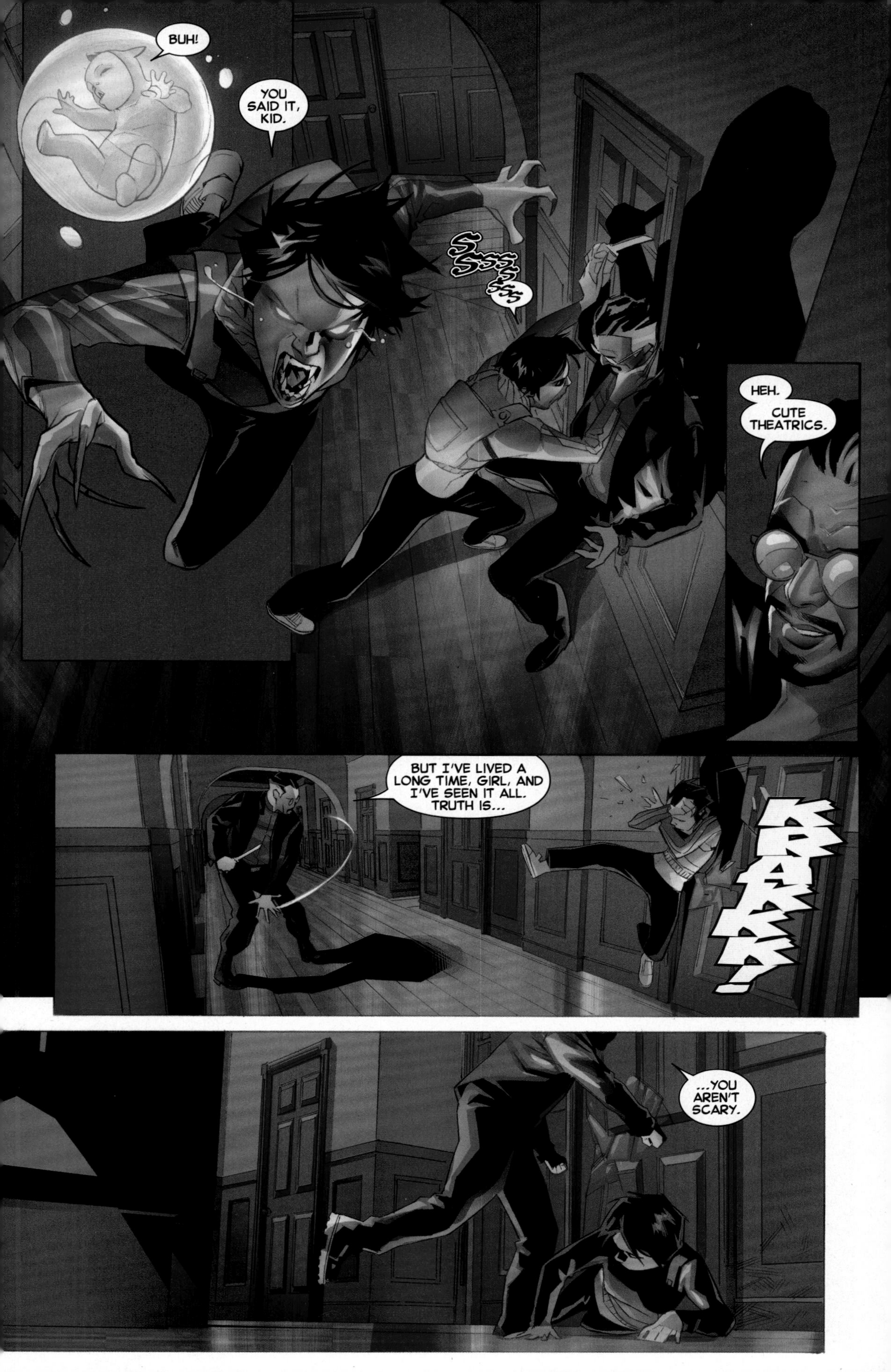
BUH!
YOU SAID IT, KID.
SSSSSSSS
HEH. CUTE THEATRICS.
BUT I'VE LIVED A LONG TIME, GIRL, AND I'VE SEEN IT ALL. TRUTH IS...
KRAKK!
...YOU AREN'T SCARY.

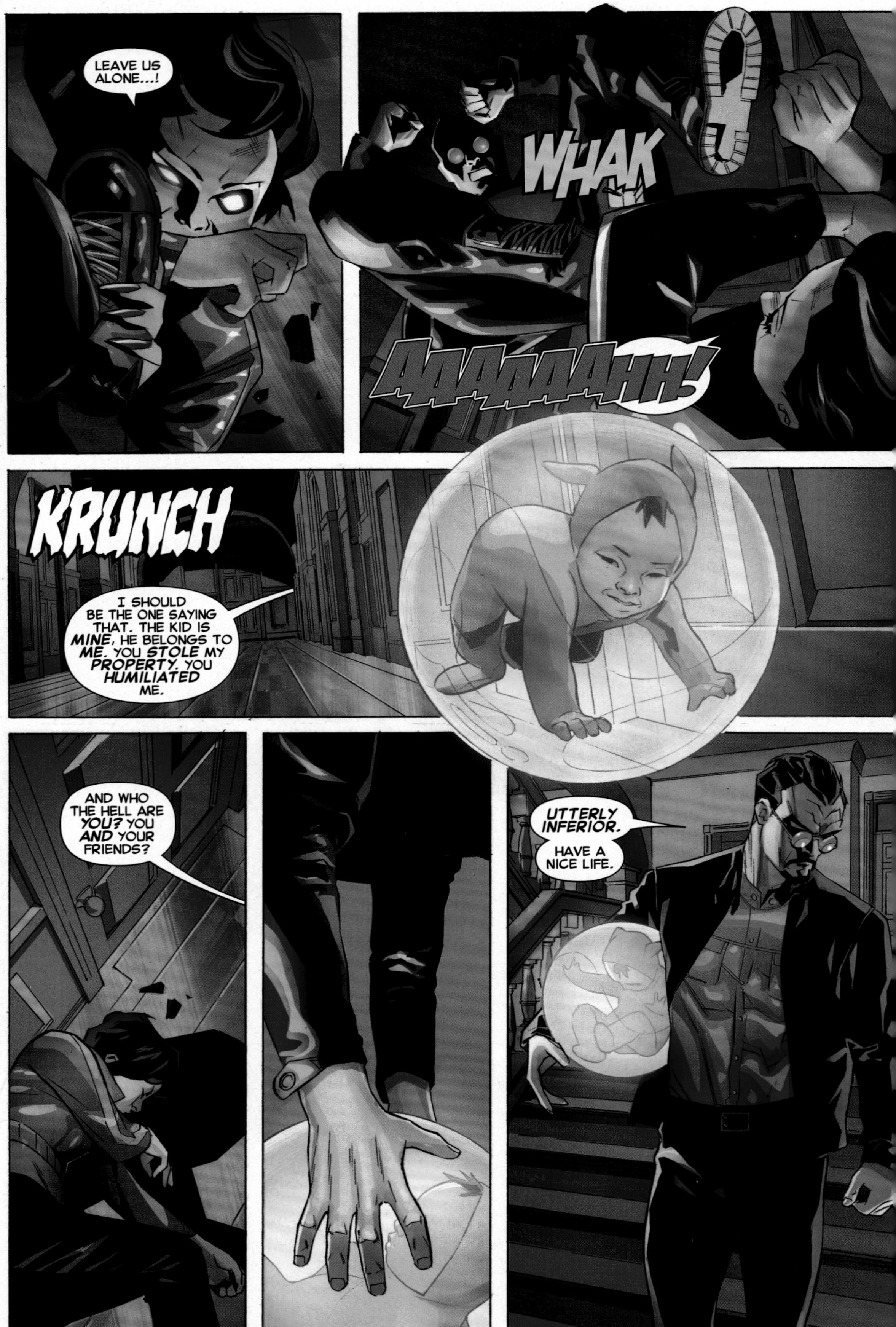
LEAVE US ALONE...!
WHAK
AAAAAAAHH!
KRUNCH
I SHOULD BE THE ONE SAYING THAT. THE KID IS MINE, HE BELONGS TO ME. YOU STOLE MY PROPERTY. YOU HUMILIATED ME.
AND WHO THE HELL ARE YOU? YOU AND YOUR FRIENDS?
UTTERLY INFERIOR.
HAVE A NICE LIFE.

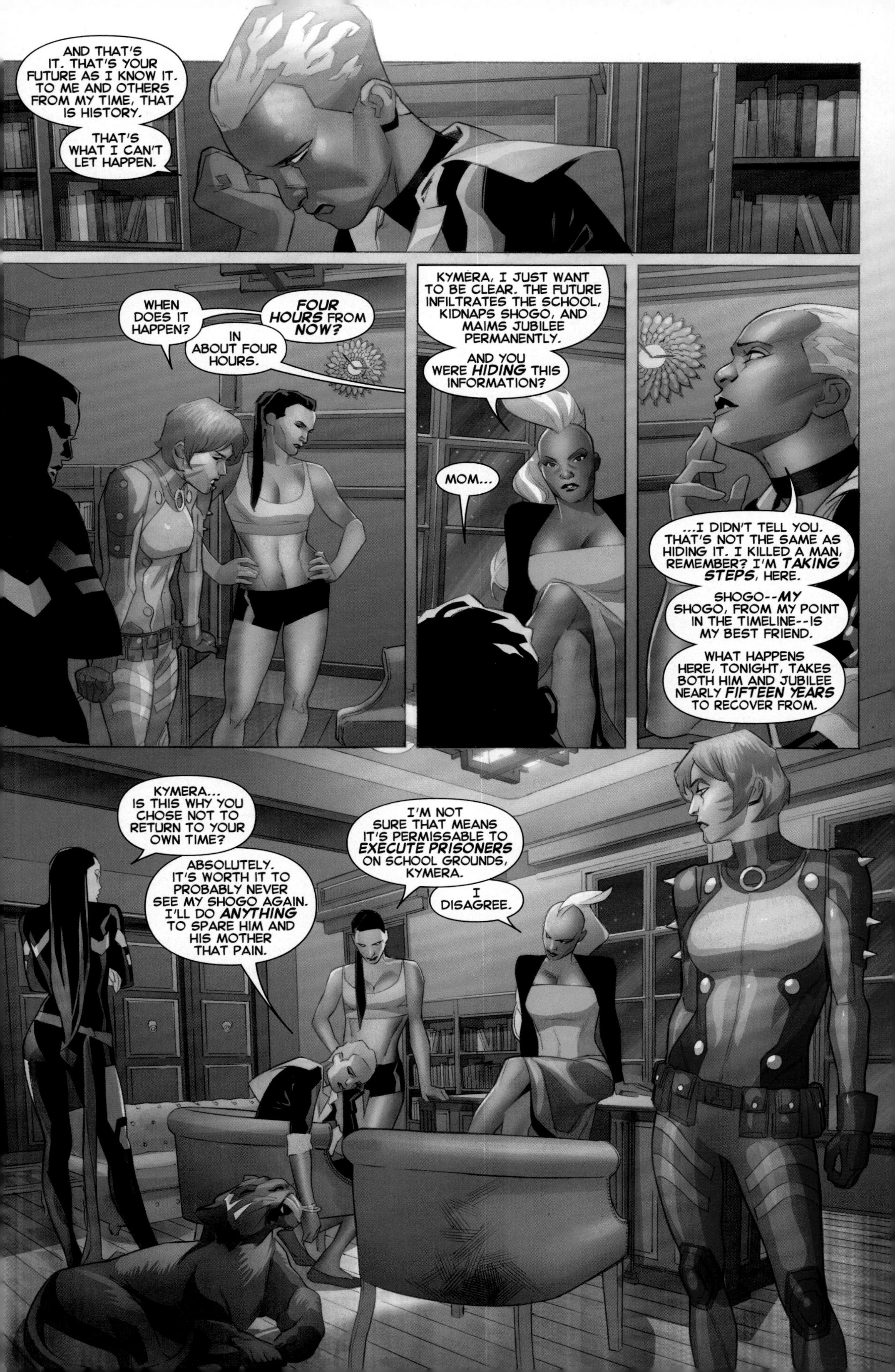
AND THAT'S IT. THAT'S YOUR FUTURE AS I KNOW IT. TO ME AND OTHERS FROM MY TIME, THAT IS HISTORY.
THAT'S WHAT I CAN'T LET HAPPEN.
WHEN DOES IT HAPPEN?
FOUR HOURS FROM NOW?
IN ABOUT FOUR HOURS.
KYMERA, I JUST WANT TO BE CLEAR. THE FUTURE INFILTRATES THE SCHOOL, KIDNAPS SHOGO, AND MAIMS JUBILEE PERMANENTLY.
AND YOU WERE HIDING THIS INFORMATION?
MOM...
...I DIDN'T TELL YOU. THAT'S NOT THE SAME AS HIDING IT. I KILLED A MAN, REMEMBER? I'M TAKING STEPS, HERE.
SHOGO--MY SHOGO, FROM MY POINT IN THE TIMELINE--IS MY BEST FRIEND.
WHAT HAPPENS HERE, TONIGHT, TAKES BOTH HIM AND JUBILEE NEARLY FIFTEEN YEARS TO RECOVER FROM.
KYMERA... IS THIS WHY YOU CHOSE NOT TO RETURN TO YOUR OWN TIME?
ABSOLUTELY. IT'S WORTH IT TO PROBABLY NEVER SEE MY SHOGO AGAIN. I'LL DO ANYTHING TO SPARE HIM AND HIS MOTHER THAT PAIN.
I'M NOT SURE THAT MEANS IT'S PERMISSABLE TO EXECUTE PRISONERS ON SCHOOL GROUNDS, KYMERA.
I DISAGREE.

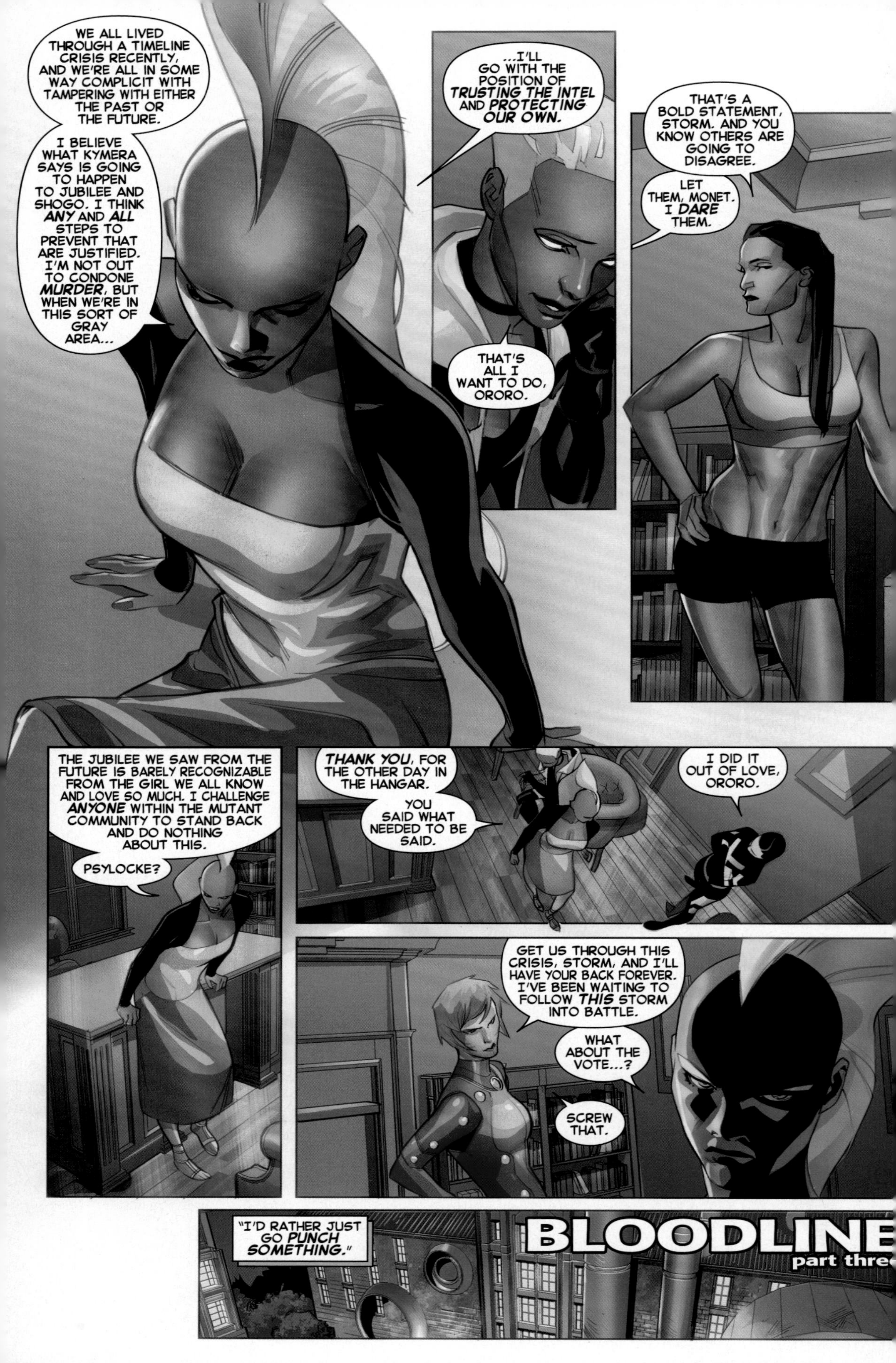
WE ALL LIVED THROUGH A TIMELINE CRISIS RECENTLY, AND WE'RE ALL IN SOME WAY COMPLICIT WITH TAMPERING WITH EITHER THE PAST OR THE FUTURE.
I BELIEVE WHAT KYMERA SAYS IS GOING TO HAPPEN TO JUBILEE AND SHOGO. I THINK ANY AND ALL STEPS TO PREVENT THAT ARE JUSTIFIED. I'M NOT OUT TO CONDONE MURDER, BUT WHEN WE'RE IN THIS SORT OF GRAY AREA...
...I'LL GO WITH THE POSITION OF TRUSTING THE INTEL AND PROTECTING OUR OWN.
THAT'S ALL I WANT TO DO, ORORO.
THAT'S A BOLD STATEMENT, STORM. AND YOU KNOW OTHERS ARE GOING TO DISAGREE.
LET THEM, MONET. I DARE THEM.
THE JUBILEE WE SAW FROM THE FUTURE IS BARELY RECOGNIZABLE FROM THE GIRL WE ALL KNOW AND LOVE SO MUCH. I CHALLENGE ANYONE WITHIN THE MUTANT COMMUNITY TO STAND BACK AND DO NOTHING ABOUT THIS.
PSYLOCKE?
THANK YOU, FOR THE OTHER DAY IN THE HANGAR.
YOU SAID WHAT NEEDED TO BE SAID.
I DID IT OUT OF LOVE, ORORO.
GET US THROUGH THIS CRISIS, STORM, AND I'LL HAVE YOUR BACK FOREVER. I'VE BEEN WAITING TO FOLLOW THIS STORM INTO BATTLE.
WHAT ABOUT THE VOTE...?
SCREW THAT.
"I'D RATHER JUST GO PUNCH SOMETHING."
BLOODLINE
part thre

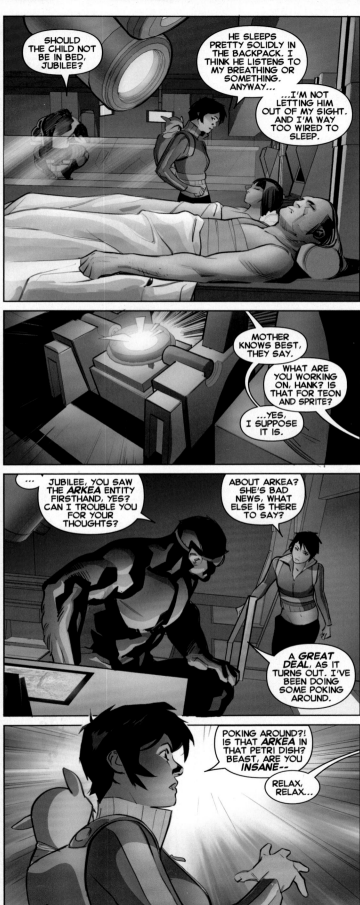

SHOULD THE CHILD NOT BE IN BED, JUBILEE?

HE SLEEPS PRETTY SOLIDLY IN THE BACKPACK. I THINK HE LISTENS TO MY BREATHING OR SOMETHING. ANYWAY...

...I'M NOT LETTING HIM OUT OF MY SIGHT. AND I'M WAY TOO WIRED TO SLEEP.

MOTHER KNOWS BEST, THEY SAY.

WHAT ARE YOU WORKING ON, HANK? IS THAT FOR TEON AND SPRITE?

...YES, I SUPPOSE IT IS.

... JUBILEE, YOU SAW THE *ARKEA* ENTITY FIRSTHAND, YES? CAN I TROUBLE YOU FOR YOUR THOUGHTS?

ABOUT ARKEA? SHE'S BAD NEWS, WHAT ELSE IS THERE TO SAY?

A *GREAT DEAL*, AS IT TURNS OUT. I'VE BEEN DOING SOME POKING AROUND.

POKING AROUND?! IS THAT *ARKEA* IN THAT PETRI DISH? BEAST, ARE YOU *INSANE*--

RELAX, RELAX...

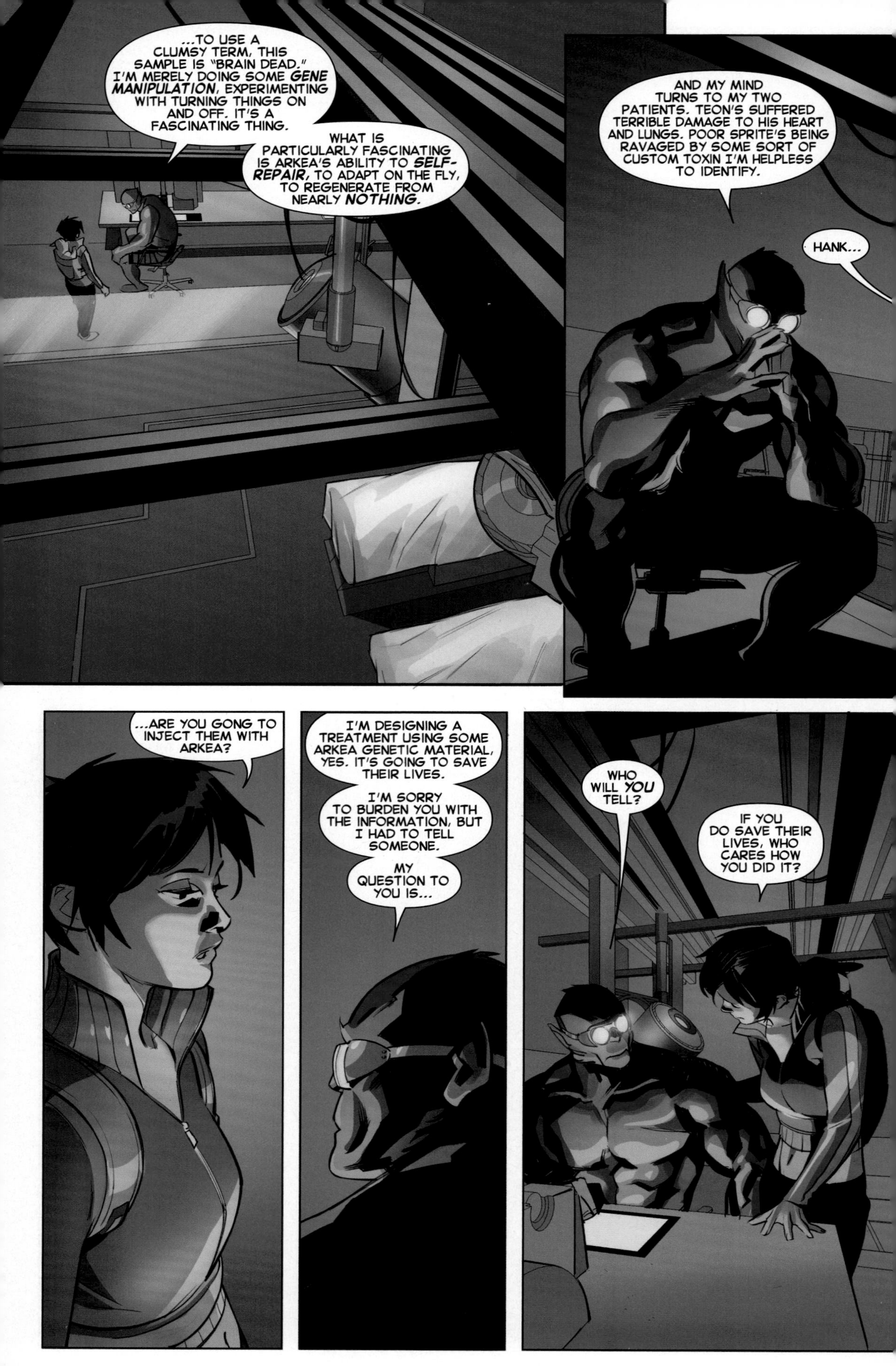
...TO USE A CLUMSY TERM, THIS SAMPLE IS "BRAIN DEAD." I'M MERELY DOING SOME GENE MANIPULATION, EXPERIMENTING WITH TURNING THINGS ON AND OFF. IT'S A FASCINATING THING.
WHAT IS PARTICULARLY FASCINATING IS ARKEA'S ABILITY TO SELF-REPAIR, TO ADAPT ON THE FLY, TO REGENERATE FROM NEARLY NOTHING.
AND MY MIND TURNS TO MY TWO PATIENTS. TEON'S SUFFERED TERRIBLE DAMAGE TO HIS HEART AND LUNGS. POOR SPRITE'S BEING RAVAGED BY SOME SORT OF CUSTOM TOXIN I'M HELPLESS TO IDENTIFY.
HANK...
...ARE YOU GONG TO INJECT THEM WITH ARKEA?
I'M DESIGNING A TREATMENT USING SOME ARKEA GENETIC MATERIAL, YES. IT'S GOING TO SAVE THEIR LIVES.
I'M SORRY TO BURDEN YOU WITH THE INFORMATION, BUT I HAD TO TELL SOMEONE.
MY QUESTION TO YOU IS...
WHO WILL YOU TELL?
IF YOU DO SAVE THEIR LIVES, WHO CARES HOW YOU DID IT?

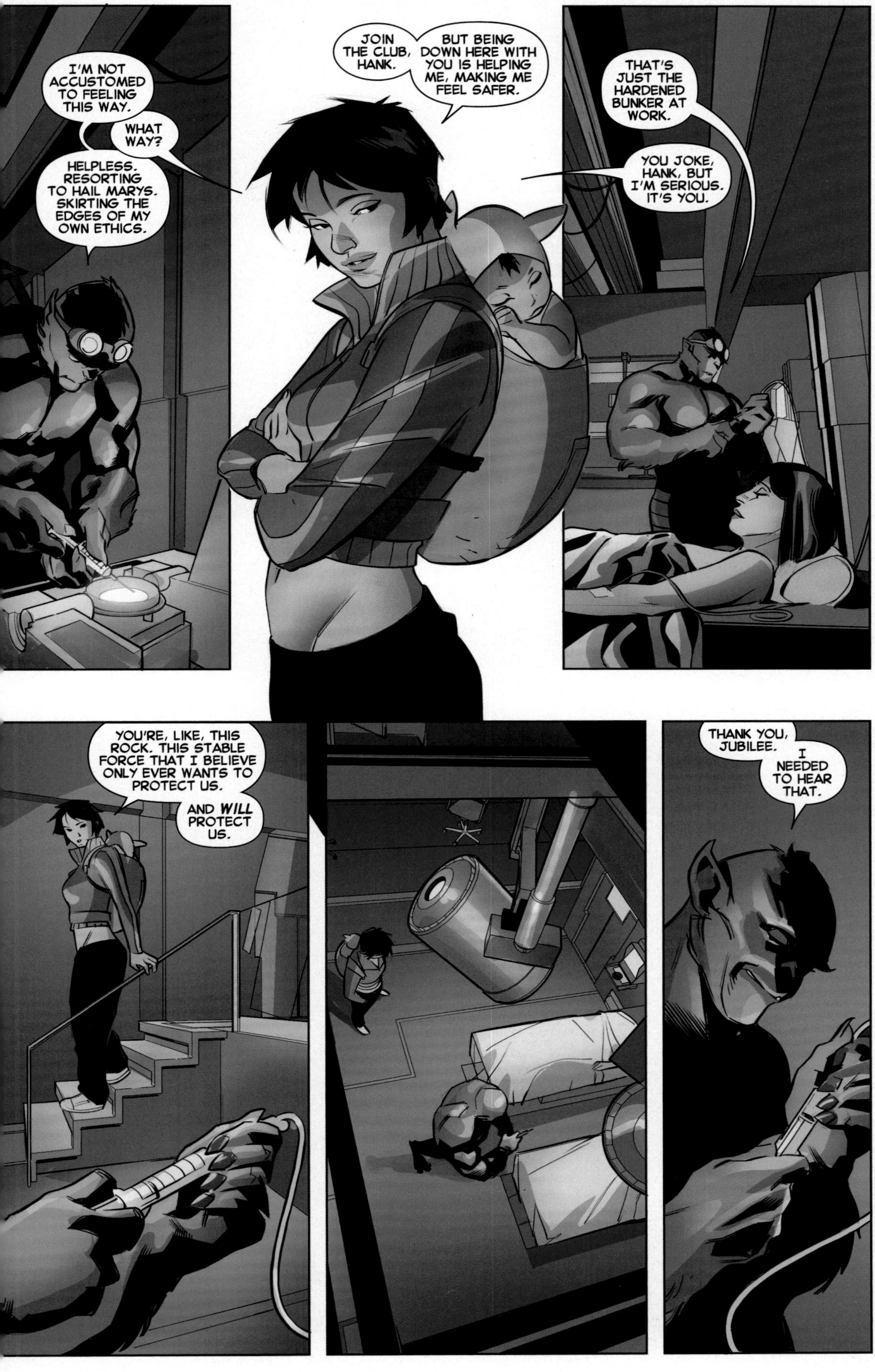
I'M NOT ACCUSTOMED TO FEELING THIS WAY.
WHAT WAY?
HELPLESS. RESORTING TO HAIL MARYS. SKIRTING THE EDGES OF MY OWN ETHICS.
JOIN THE CLUB, HANK.
BUT BEING DOWN HERE WITH YOU IS HELPING ME, MAKING ME FEEL SAFER.
THAT'S JUST THE HARDENED BUNKER AT WORK.
YOU JOKE, HANK, BUT I'M SERIOUS. IT'S YOU.
YOU'RE, LIKE, THIS ROCK. THIS STABLE FORCE THAT I BELIEVE ONLY EVER WANTS TO PROTECT US.
AND *WILL* PROTECT US.
THANK YOU, JUBILEE.
I NEEDED TO HEAR THAT.

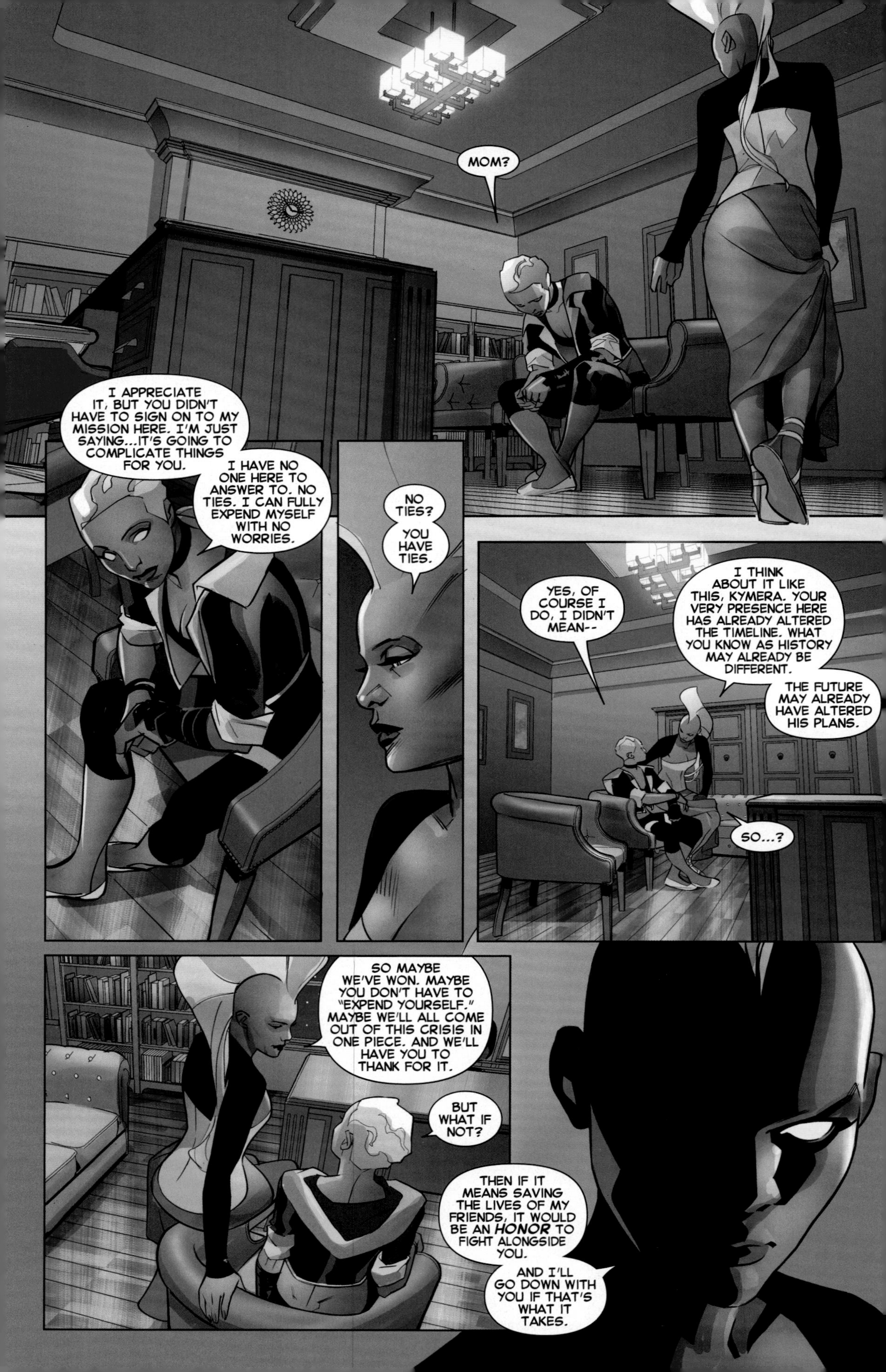
MOM?
I APPRECIATE IT, BUT YOU DIDN'T HAVE TO SIGN ON TO MY MISSION HERE. I'M JUST SAYING...IT'S GOING TO COMPLICATE THINGS FOR YOU.
I HAVE NO ONE HERE TO ANSWER TO. NO TIES. I CAN FULLY EXPEND MYSELF WITH NO WORRIES.
NO TIES?
YOU HAVE TIES.
YES, OF COURSE I DO, I DIDN'T MEAN--
I THINK ABOUT IT LIKE THIS, KYMERA. YOUR VERY PRESENCE HERE HAS ALREADY ALTERED THE TIMELINE. WHAT YOU KNOW AS HISTORY MAY ALREADY BE DIFFERENT.
THE FUTURE MAY ALREADY HAVE ALTERED HIS PLANS.
SO...?
SO MAYBE WE'VE WON. MAYBE YOU DON'T HAVE TO "EXPEND YOURSELF." MAYBE WE'LL ALL COME OUT OF THIS CRISIS IN ONE PIECE. AND WE'LL HAVE YOU TO THANK FOR IT.
BUT WHAT IF NOT?
THEN IF IT MEANS SAVING THE LIVES OF MY FRIENDS, IT WOULD BE AN *HONOR* TO FIGHT ALONGSIDE YOU.
AND I'LL GO DOWN WITH YOU IF THAT'S WHAT IT TAKES.

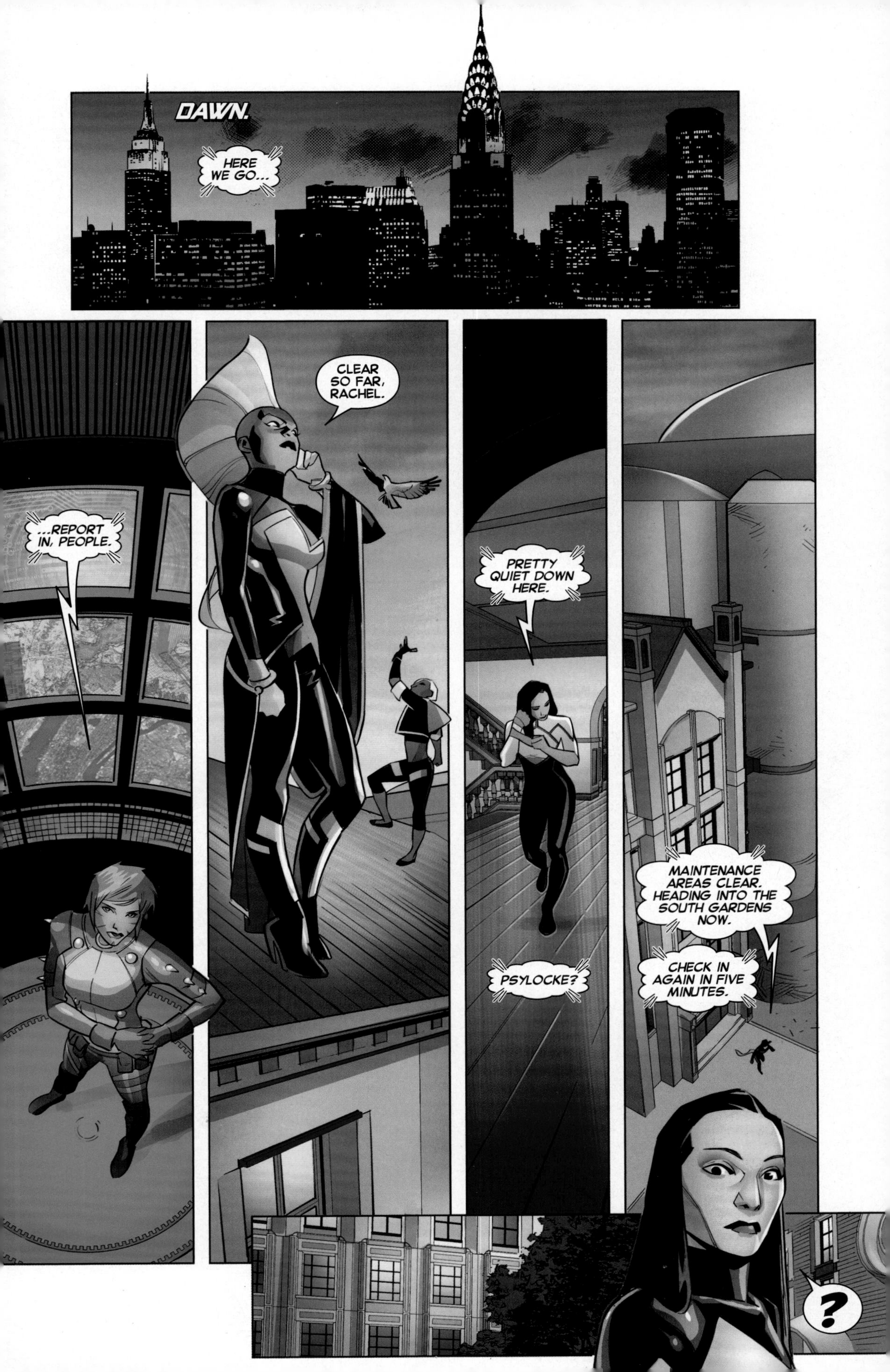
DAWN.
HERE WE GO...
...REPORT IN, PEOPLE.
CLEAR SO FAR, RACHEL.
PRETTY QUIET DOWN HERE.
PSYLOCKE?
MAINTENANCE AREAS CLEAR. HEADING INTO THE SOUTH GARDENS NOW.
CHECK IN AGAIN IN FIVE MINUTES.
?

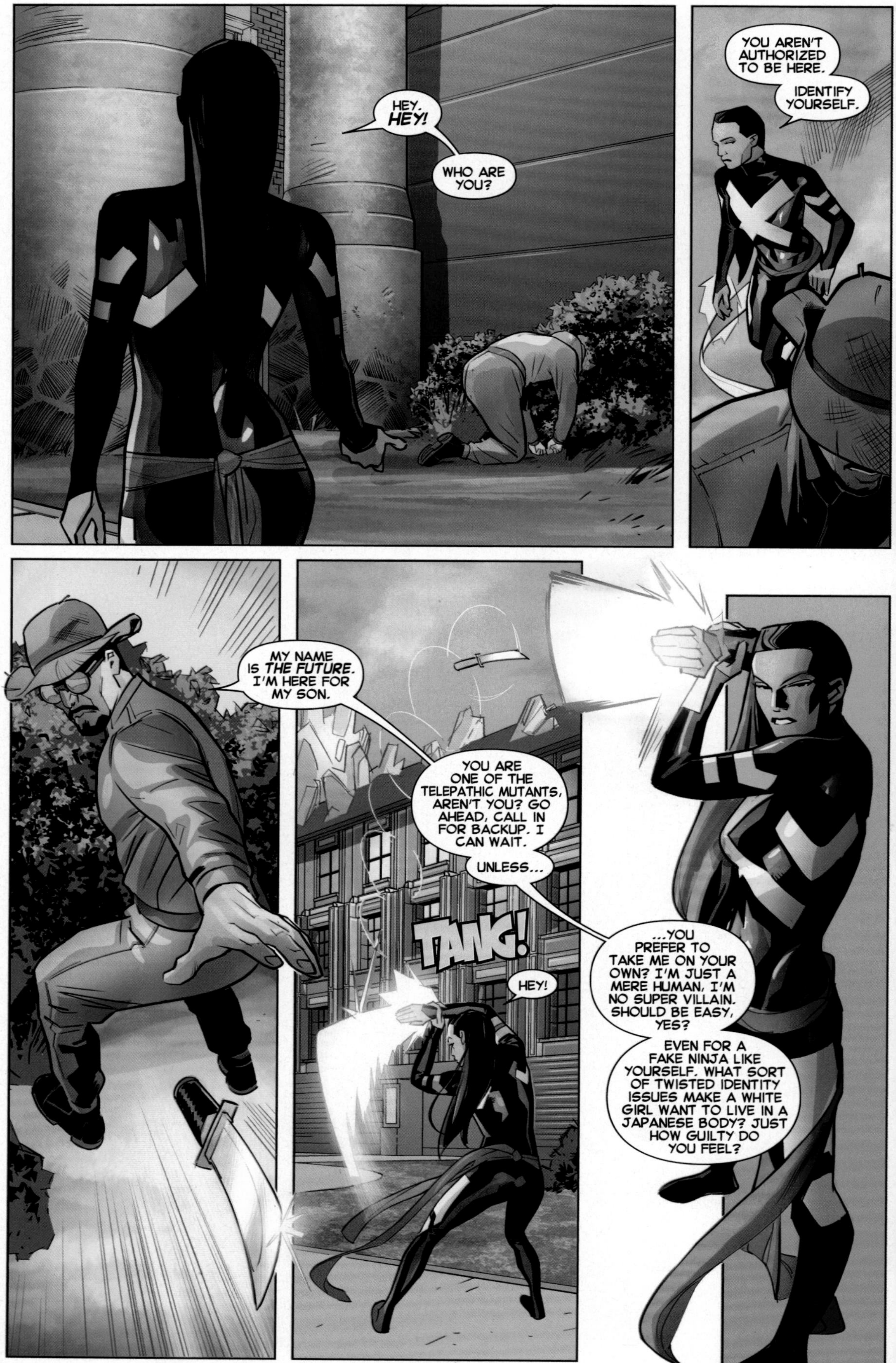
HEY. HEY!
WHO ARE YOU?
YOU AREN'T AUTHORIZED TO BE HERE.
IDENTIFY YOURSELF.
MY NAME IS THE FUTURE. I'M HERE FOR MY SON.
YOU ARE ONE OF THE TELEPATHIC MUTANTS, AREN'T YOU? GO AHEAD, CALL IN FOR BACKUP. I CAN WAIT.
UNLESS...
TANG!
HEY!
...YOU PREFER TO TAKE ME ON YOUR OWN? I'M JUST A MERE HUMAN, I'M NO SUPER VILLAIN. SHOULD BE EASY, YES?
EVEN FOR A FAKE NINJA LIKE YOURSELF. WHAT SORT OF TWISTED IDENTITY ISSUES MAKE A WHITE GIRL WANT TO LIVE IN A JAPANESE BODY? JUST HOW GUILTY DO YOU FEEL?

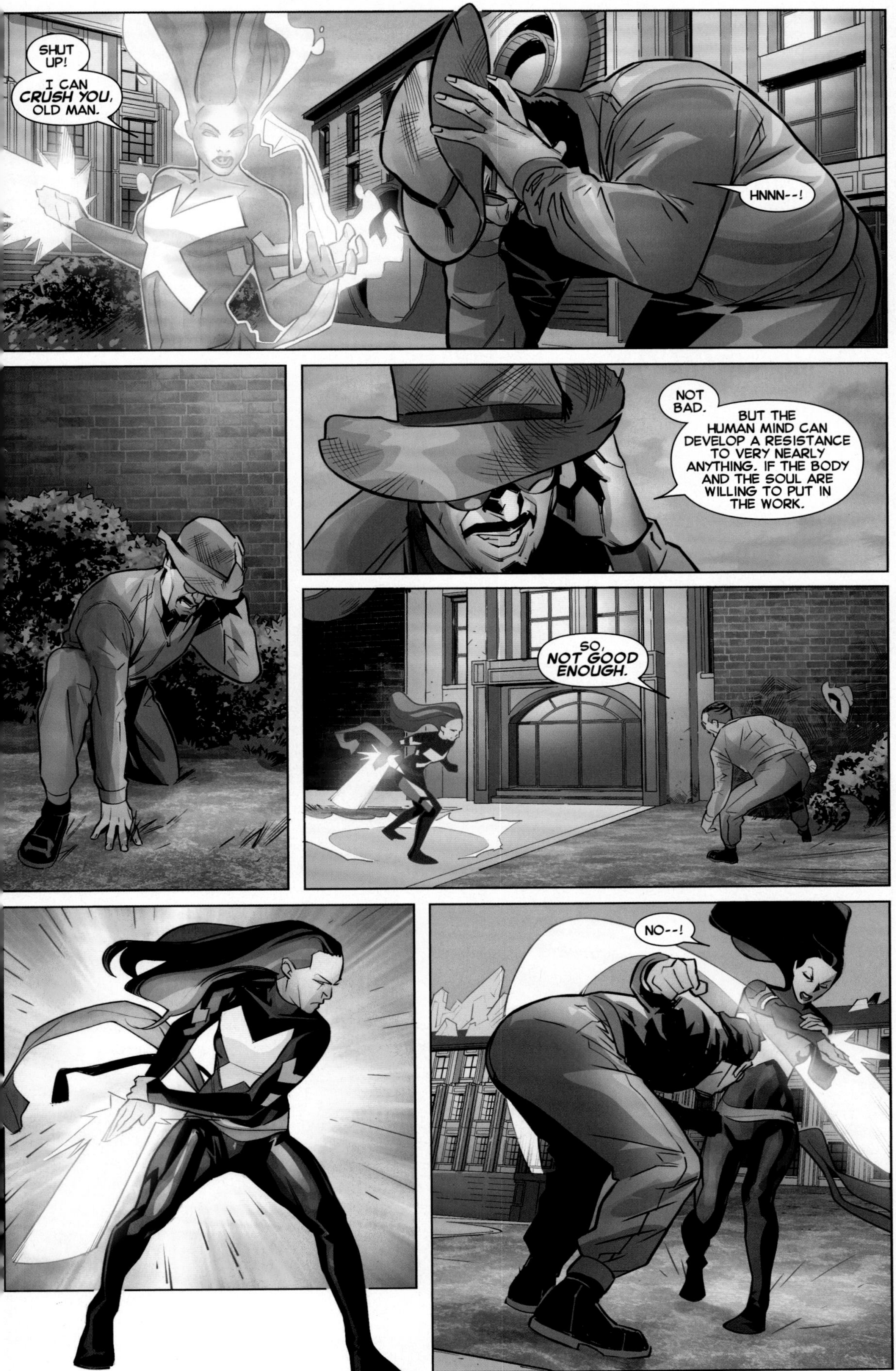
SHUT UP!
I CAN CRUSH YOU, OLD MAN.
HNNN--!
NOT BAD.
BUT THE HUMAN MIND CAN DEVELOP A RESISTANCE TO VERY NEARLY ANYTHING. IF THE BODY AND THE SOUL ARE WILLING TO PUT IN THE WORK.
SO, NOT GOOD ENOUGH.
NO--!

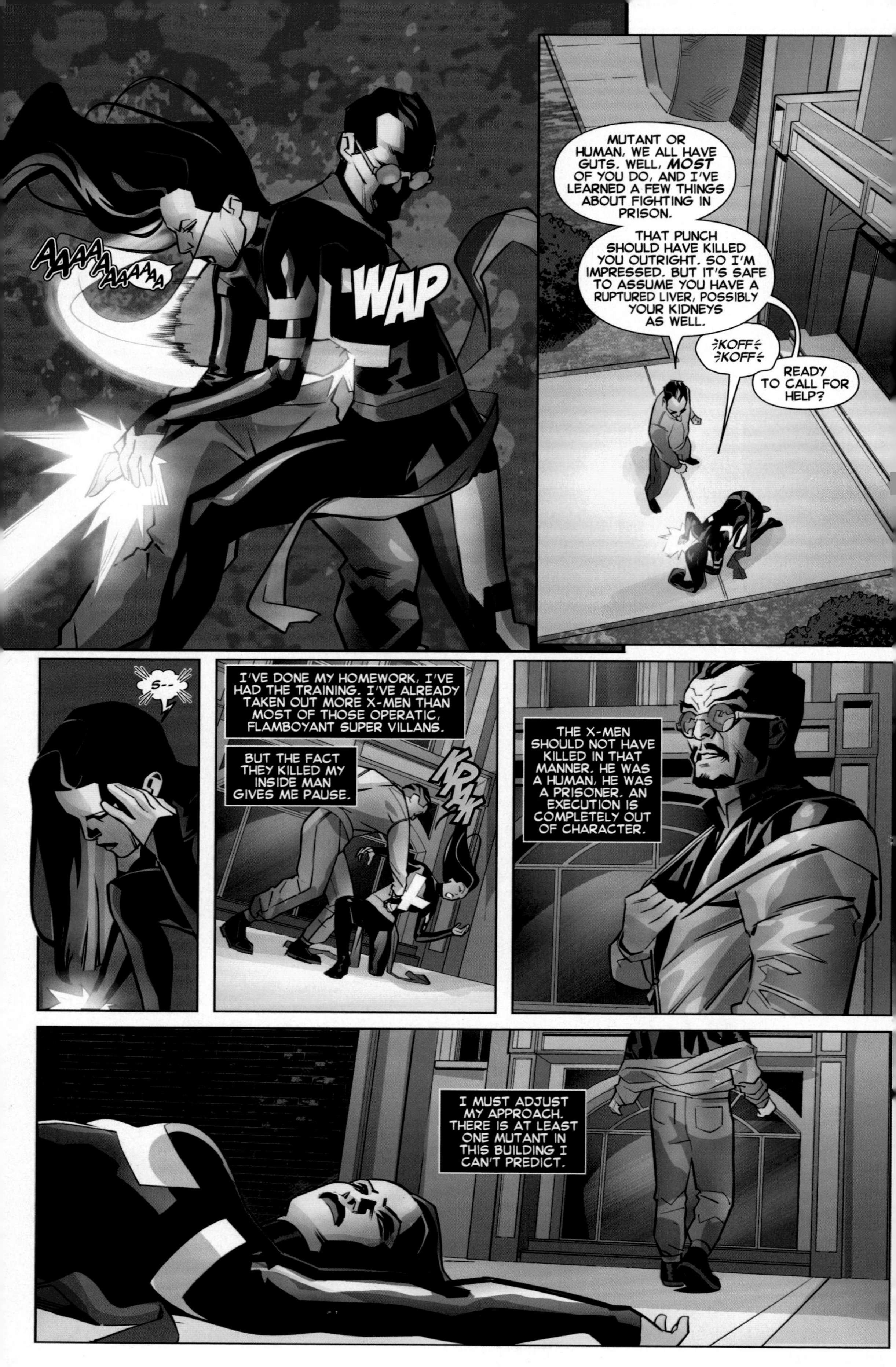
AAAAAAAAAAAA
'WAP
MUTANT OR HUMAN, WE ALL HAVE GUTS. WELL, MOST OF YOU DO, AND I'VE LEARNED A FEW THINGS ABOUT FIGHTING IN PRISON.
THAT PUNCH SHOULD HAVE KILLED YOU OUTRIGHT. SO I'M IMPRESSED. BUT IT'S SAFE TO ASSUME YOU HAVE A RUPTURED LIVER, POSSIBLY YOUR KIDNEYS AS WELL.
KOFF KOFF
READY TO CALL FOR HELP?
S--
I'VE DONE MY HOMEWORK, I'VE HAD THE TRAINING. I'VE ALREADY TAKEN OUT MORE X-MEN THAN MOST OF THOSE OPERATIC, FLAMBOYANT SUPER VILLANS.
BUT THE FACT THEY KILLED MY INSIDE MAN GIVES ME PAUSE.
KRAK
THE X-MEN SHOULD NOT HAVE KILLED IN THAT MANNER. HE WAS A HUMAN, HE WAS A PRISONER. AN EXECUTION IS COMPLETELY OUT OF CHARACTER.
I MUST ADJUST MY APPROACH. THERE IS AT LEAST ONE MUTANT IN THIS BUILDING I CAN'T PREDICT.

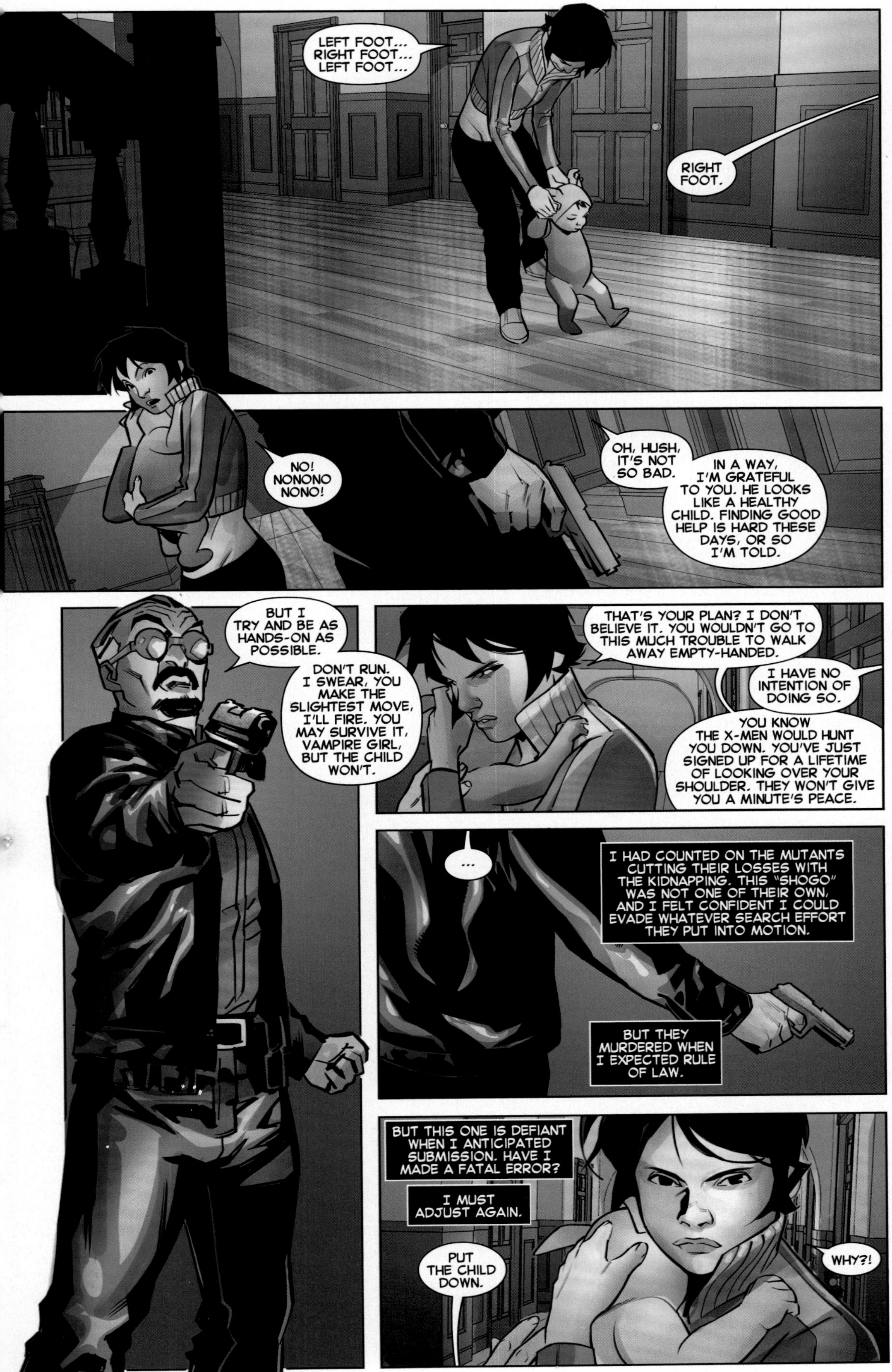
LEFT FOOT... RIGHT FOOT... LEFT FOOT...
RIGHT FOOT.
NO! NONONO NONO!
OH, HUSH, IT'S NOT SO BAD.
IN A WAY, I'M GRATEFUL TO YOU. HE LOOKS LIKE A HEALTHY CHILD. FINDING GOOD HELP IS HARD THESE DAYS, OR SO I'M TOLD.
BUT I TRY AND BE AS HANDS-ON AS POSSIBLE.
DON'T RUN. I SWEAR, YOU MAKE THE SLIGHTEST MOVE, I'LL FIRE. YOU MAY SURVIVE IT, VAMPIRE GIRL, BUT THE CHILD WON'T.
THAT'S YOUR PLAN? I DON'T BELIEVE IT. YOU WOULDN'T GO TO THIS MUCH TROUBLE TO WALK AWAY EMPTY-HANDED.
I HAVE NO INTENTION OF DOING SO.
YOU KNOW THE X-MEN WOULD HUNT YOU DOWN. YOU'VE JUST SIGNED UP FOR A LIFETIME OF LOOKING OVER YOUR SHOULDER. THEY WON'T GIVE YOU A MINUTE'S PEACE.
...
I HAD COUNTED ON THE MUTANTS CUTTING THEIR LOSSES WITH THE KIDNAPPING. THIS "SHOGO" WAS NOT ONE OF THEIR OWN, AND I FELT CONFIDENT I COULD EVADE WHATEVER SEARCH EFFORT THEY PUT INTO MOTION.
BUT THEY MURDERED WHEN I EXPECTED RULE OF LAW.
BUT THIS ONE IS DEFIANT WHEN I ANTICIPATED SUBMISSION. HAVE I MADE A FATAL ERROR?
I MUST ADJUST AGAIN.
PUT THE CHILD DOWN.
WHY?!

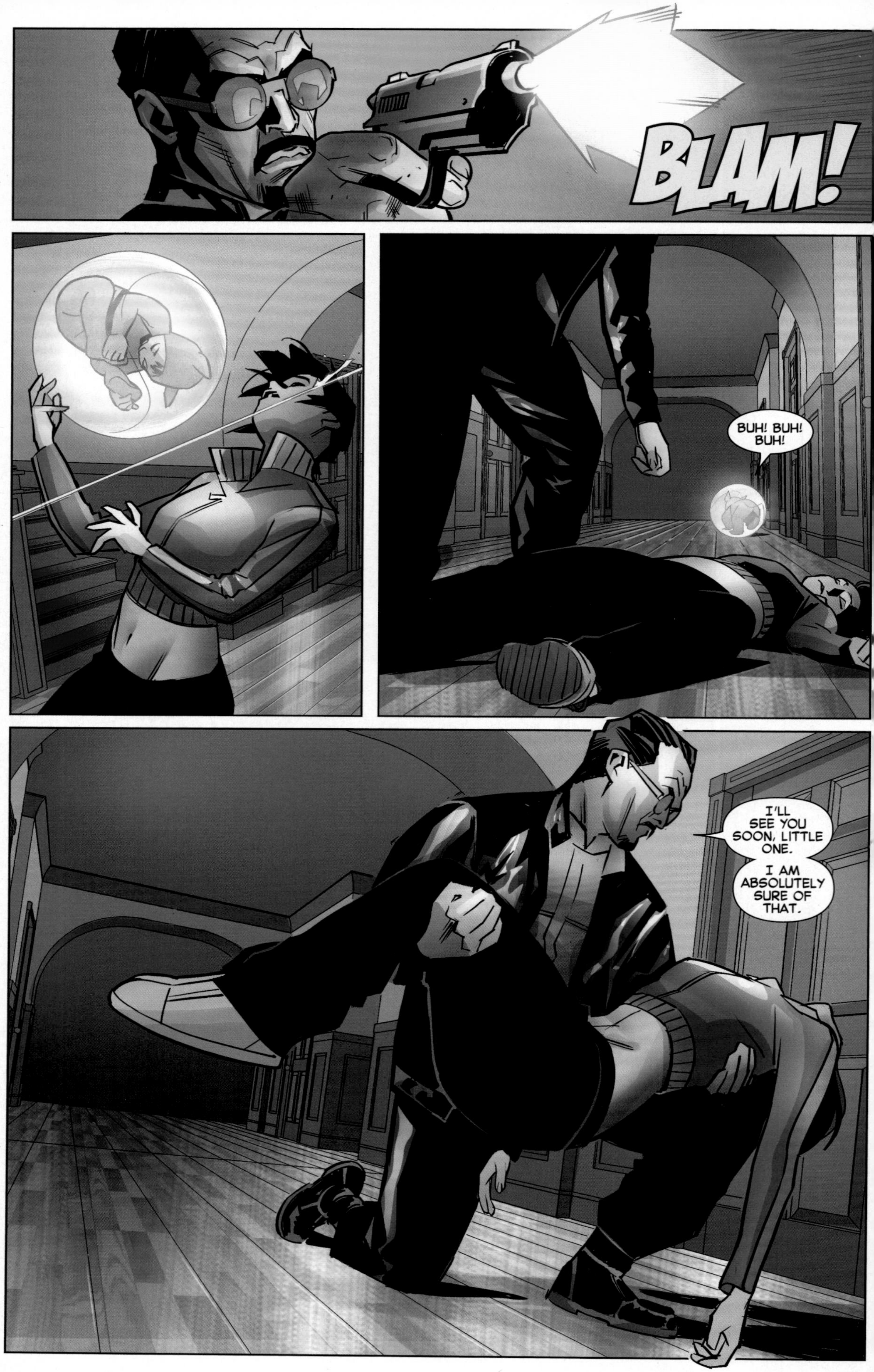
BLAM!
BUH! BUH! BUH!
I'LL SEE YOU SOON, LITTLE ONE.
I AM ABSOLUTELY SURE OF THAT.

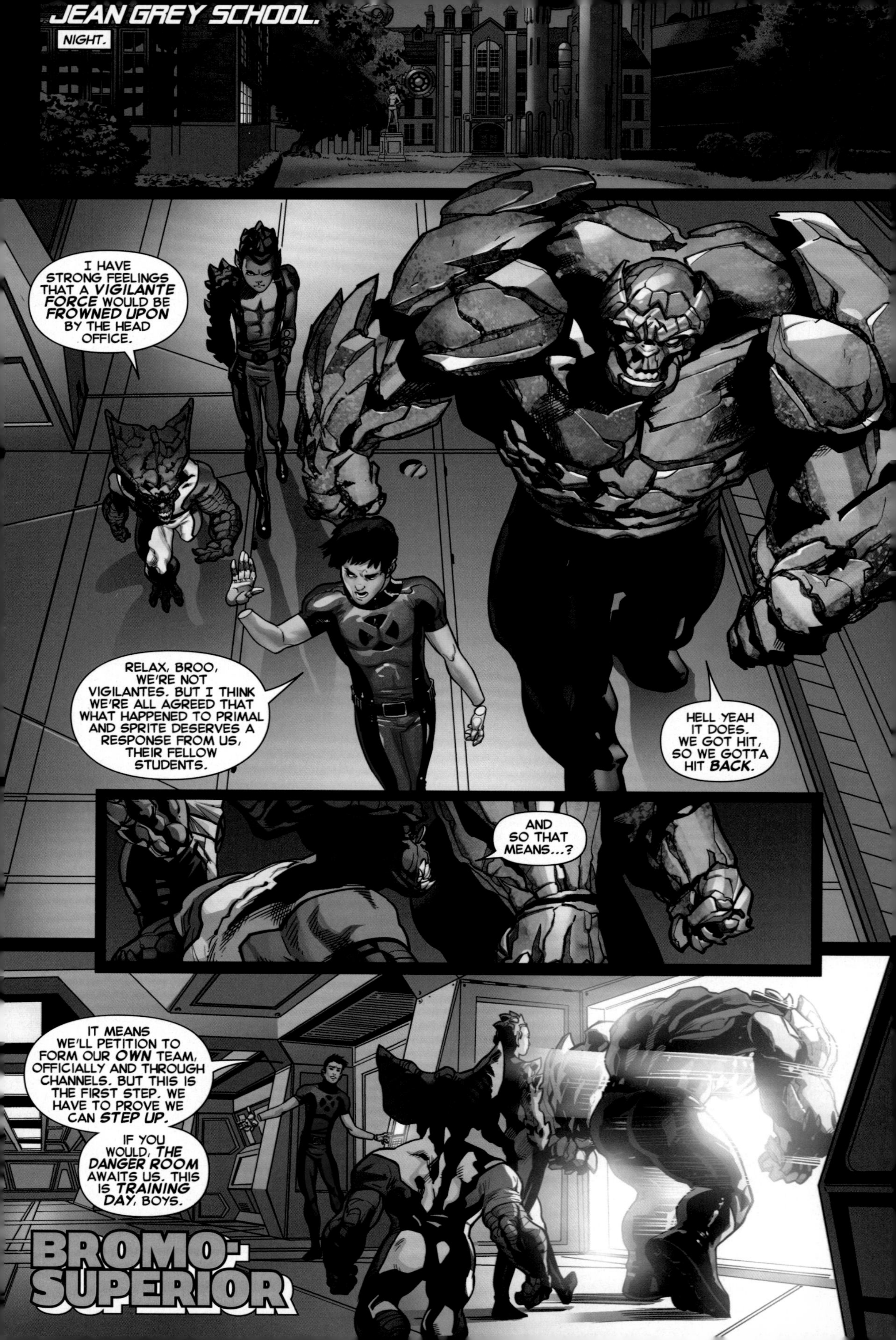
JEAN GREY SCHOOL.
NIGHT.
I HAVE STRONG FEELINGS THAT A VIGILANTE FORCE WOULD BE FROWNED UPON BY THE HEAD OFFICE.
RELAX, BROO, WE'RE NOT VIGILANTES. BUT I THINK WE'RE ALL AGREED THAT WHAT HAPPENED TO PRIMAL AND SPRITE DESERVES A RESPONSE FROM US, THEIR FELLOW STUDENTS.
HELL YEAH IT DOES. WE GOT HIT, SO WE GOTTA HIT BACK.
AND SO THAT MEANS...?
IT MEANS WE'LL PETITION TO FORM OUR OWN TEAM, OFFICIALLY AND THROUGH CHANNELS. BUT THIS IS THE FIRST STEP. WE HAVE TO PROVE WE CAN STEP UP.
IF YOU WOULD, THE DANGER ROOM AWAITS US. THIS IS TRAINING DAY, BOYS.
BROMO-SUPERIOR

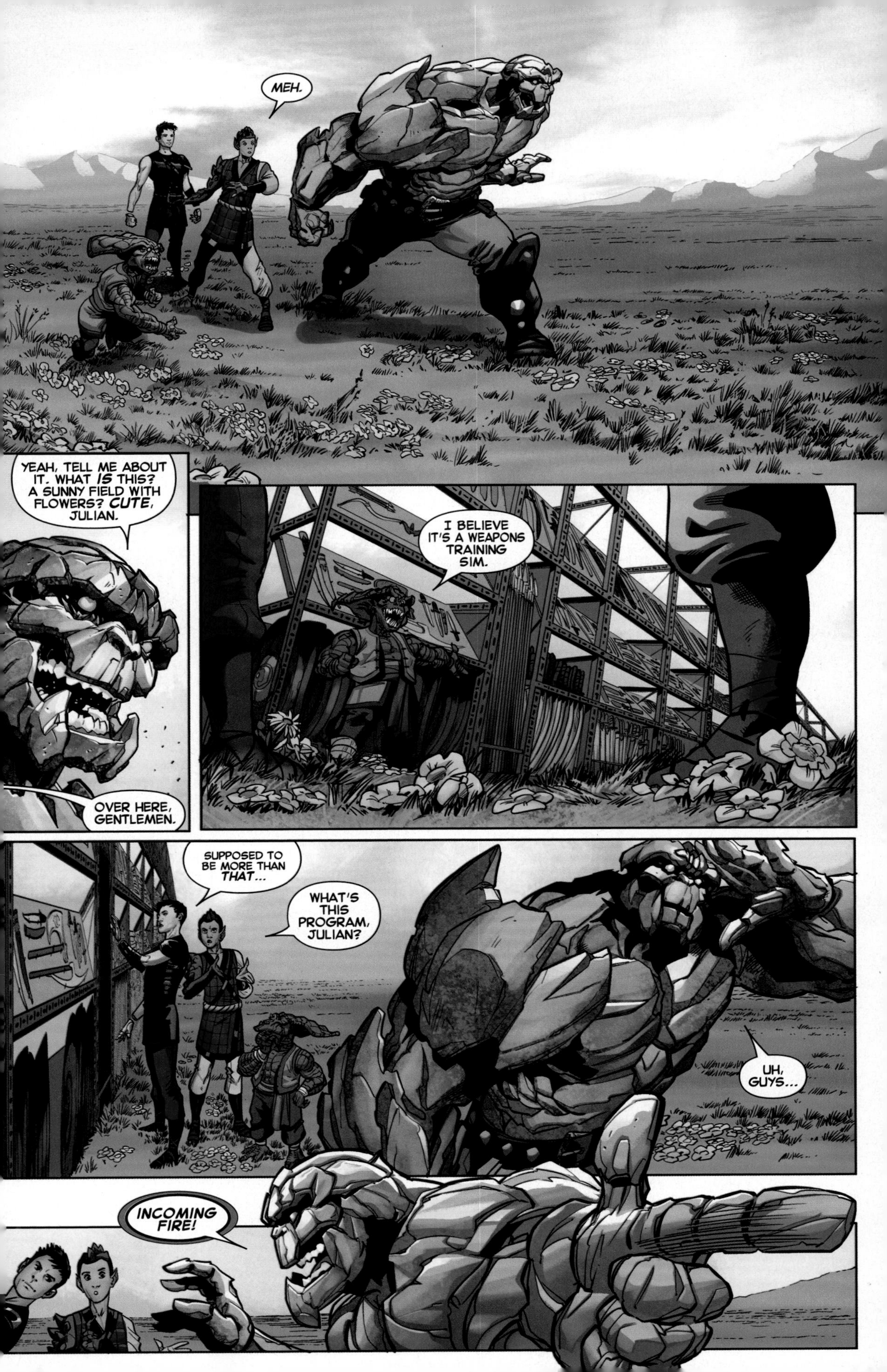
MEH.
YEAH, TELL ME ABOUT IT. WHAT *IS* THIS? A SUNNY FIELD WITH FLOWERS? *CUTE*, JULIAN.
OVER HERE, GENTLEMEN.
I BELIEVE IT'S A WEAPONS TRAINING SIM.
SUPPOSED TO BE MORE THAN *THAT*...
WHAT'S THIS PROGRAM, JULIAN?
UH, GUYS...
INCOMING FIRE!

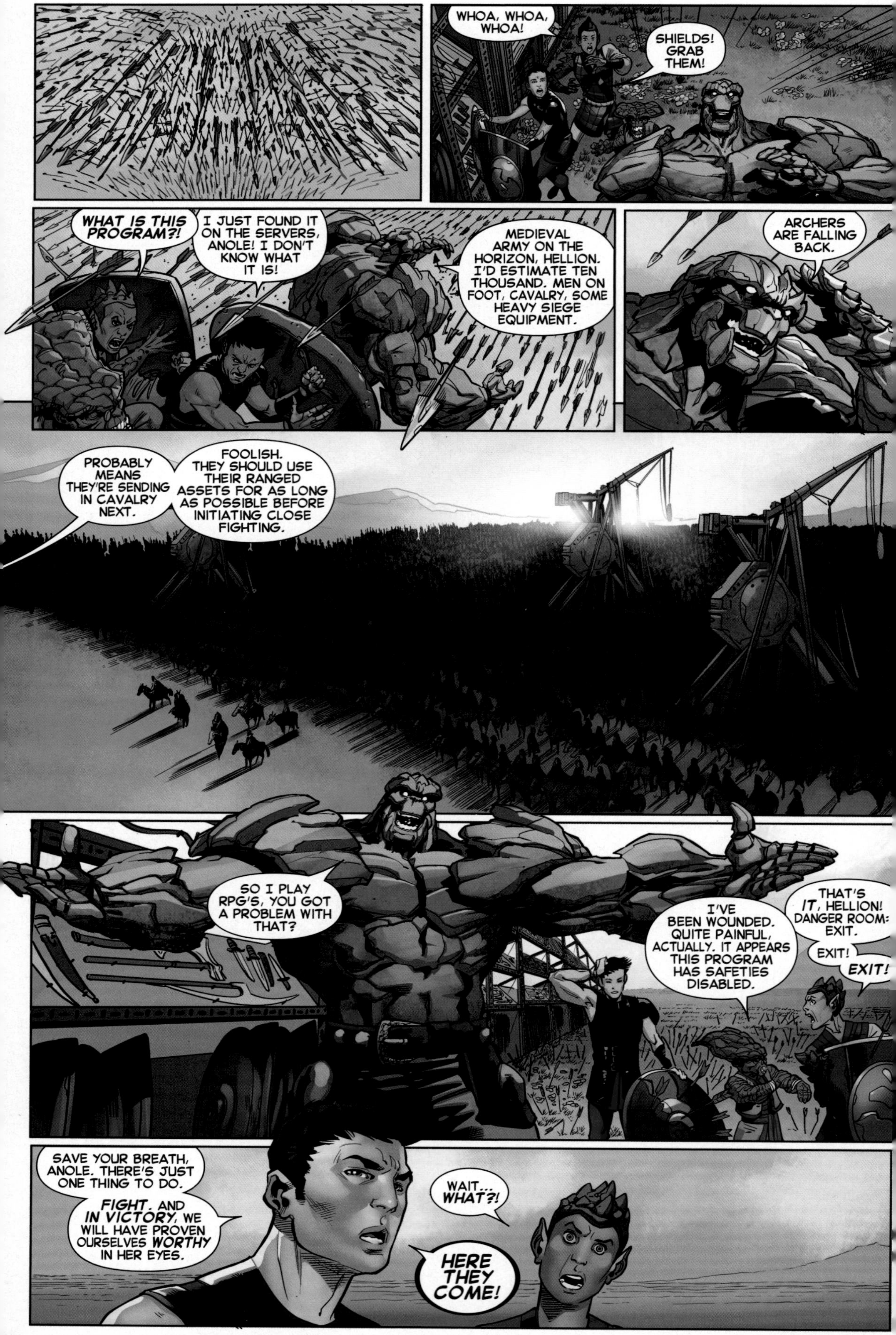
WHOA, WHOA, WHOA!
SHIELDS! GRAB THEM!
WHAT IS THIS PROGRAM?!
I JUST FOUND IT ON THE SERVERS, ANOLE! I DON'T KNOW WHAT IT IS!
MEDIEVAL ARMY ON THE HORIZON, HELLION. I'D ESTIMATE TEN THOUSAND. MEN ON FOOT, CAVALRY, SOME HEAVY SIEGE EQUIPMENT.
ARCHERS ARE FALLING BACK.
PROBABLY MEANS THEY'RE SENDING IN CAVALRY NEXT.
FOOLISH. THEY SHOULD USE THEIR RANGED ASSETS FOR AS LONG AS POSSIBLE BEFORE INITIATING CLOSE FIGHTING.
SO I PLAY RPG'S, YOU GOT A PROBLEM WITH THAT?
I'VE BEEN WOUNDED. QUITE PAINFUL, ACTUALLY. IT APPEARS THIS PROGRAM HAS SAFETIES DISABLED.
THAT'S IT, HELLION! DANGER ROOM: EXIT.
EXIT!
EXIT!
SAVE YOUR BREATH, ANOLE. THERE'S JUST ONE THING TO DO.
FIGHT. AND IN VICTORY, WE WILL HAVE PROVEN OURSELVES WORTHY IN HER EYES.
WAIT... WHAT?!
HERE THEY COME!

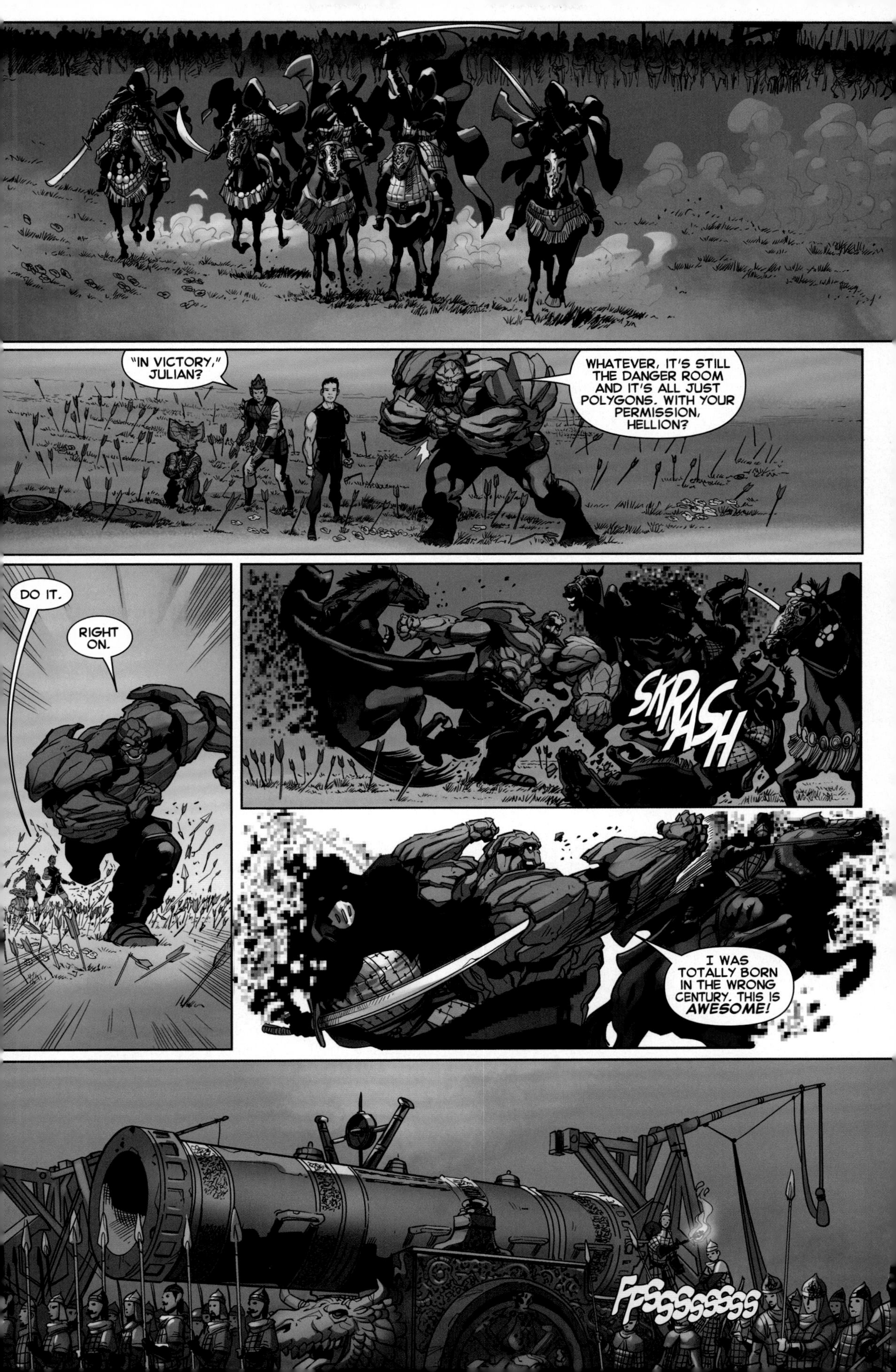

"IN VICTORY," JULIAN?
WHATEVER, IT'S STILL THE DANGER ROOM AND IT'S ALL JUST POLYGONS. WITH YOUR PERMISSION, HELLION?
DO IT.
RIGHT ON.
SKRASH
I WAS TOTALLY BORN IN THE WRONG CENTURY. THIS IS AWESOME!
FFSSSSSSSS

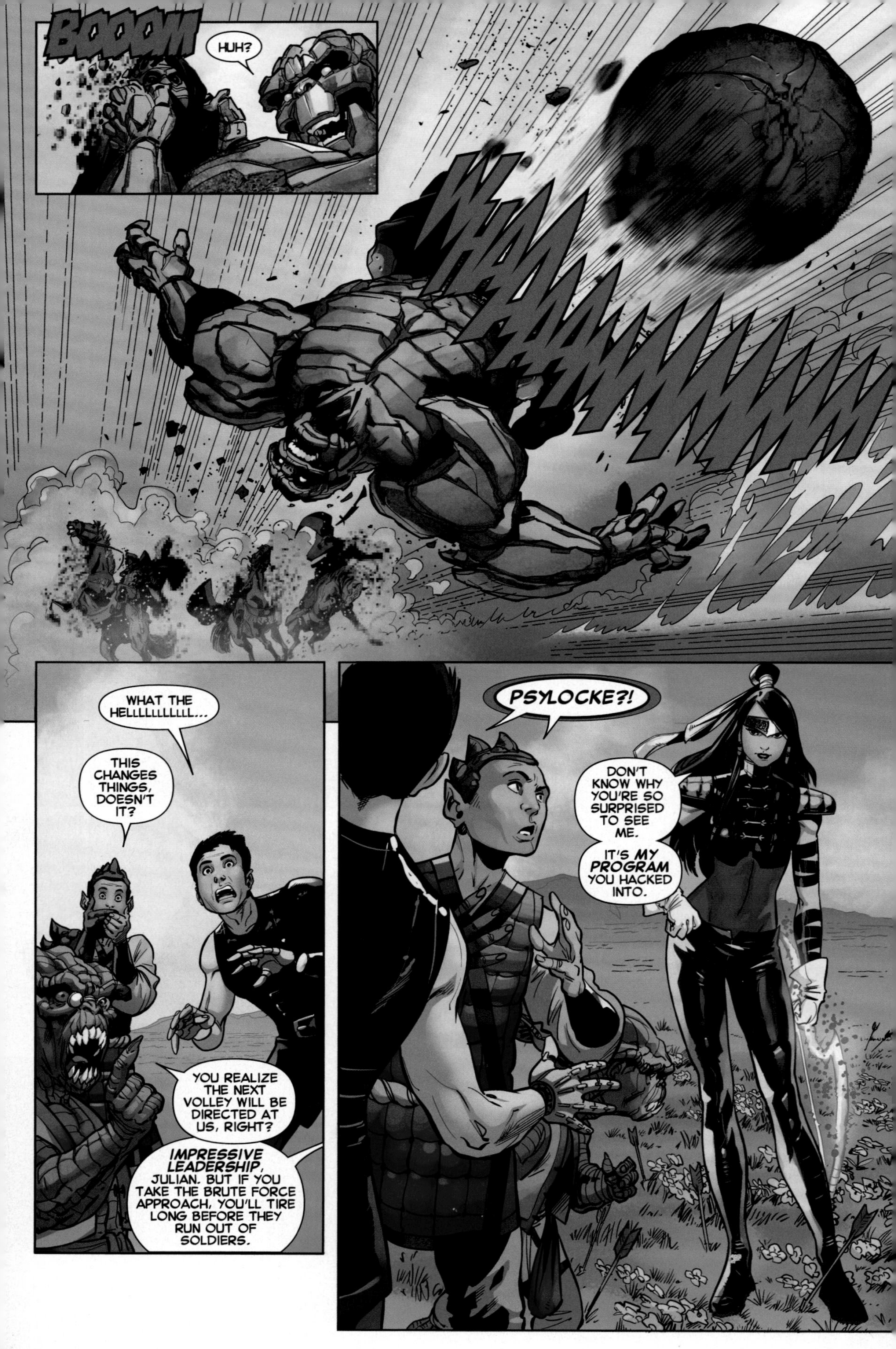
BOOOM
HUH?
WHAAAAAMMMMMM
WHAT THE HELLLLLLLLLLL...
THIS CHANGES THINGS, DOESN'T IT?
YOU REALIZE THE NEXT VOLLEY WILL BE DIRECTED AT US, RIGHT?
IMPRESSIVE LEADERSHIP, JULIAN. BUT IF YOU TAKE THE BRUTE FORCE APPROACH, YOU'LL TIRE LONG BEFORE THEY RUN OUT OF SOLDIERS.
PSYLOCKE?!
DON'T KNOW WHY YOU'RE SO SURPRISED TO SEE ME.
IT'S MY PROGRAM YOU HACKED INTO.

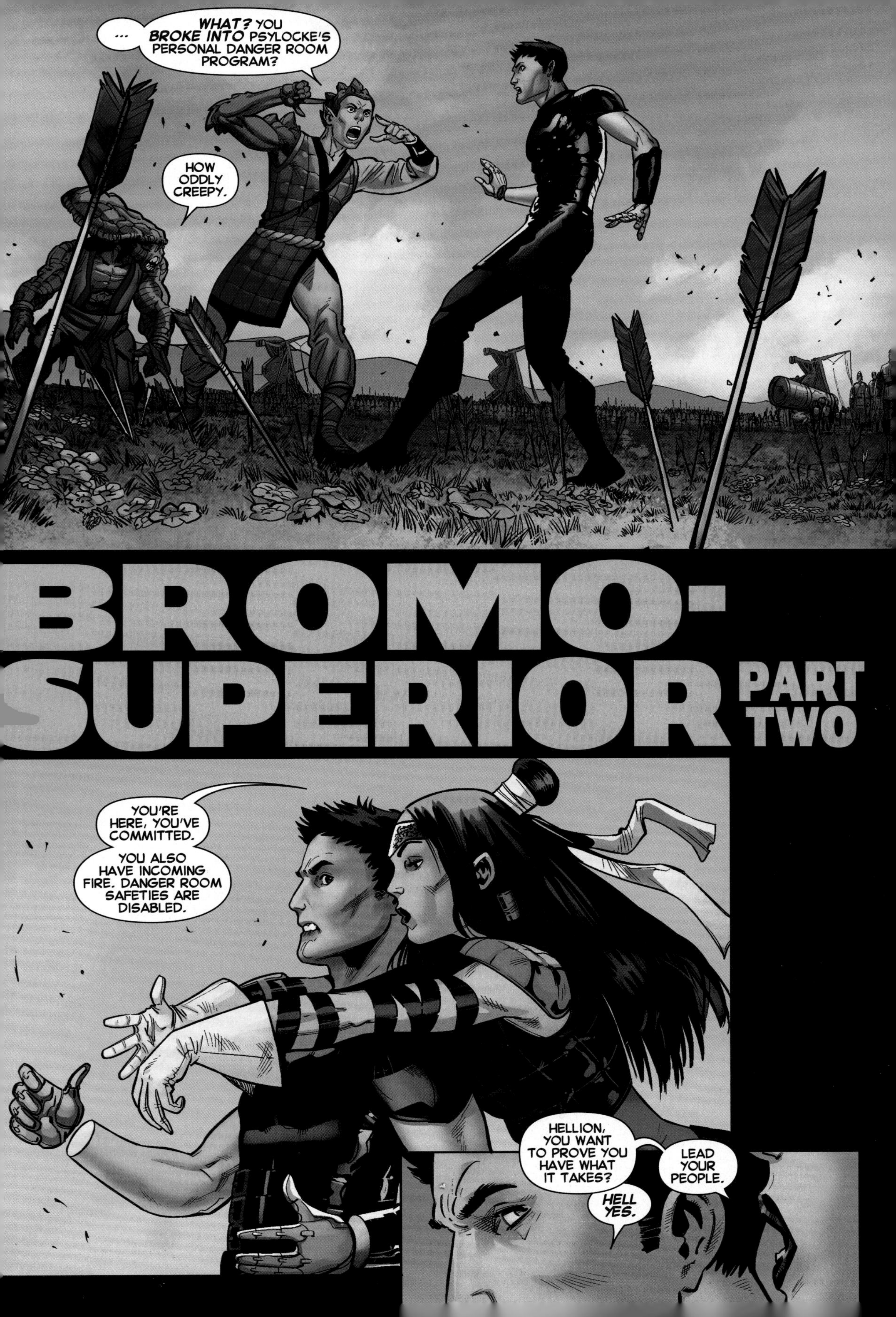
... WHAT? YOU BROKE INTO PSYLOCKE'S PERSONAL DANGER ROOM PROGRAM?
HOW ODDLY CREEPY.
BROMO-SUPERIOR PART TWO
YOU'RE HERE, YOU'VE COMMITTED.
YOU ALSO HAVE INCOMING FIRE. DANGER ROOM SAFETIES ARE DISABLED.
HELLION, YOU WANT TO PROVE YOU HAVE WHAT IT TAKES?
LEAD YOUR PEOPLE.
HELL YES.

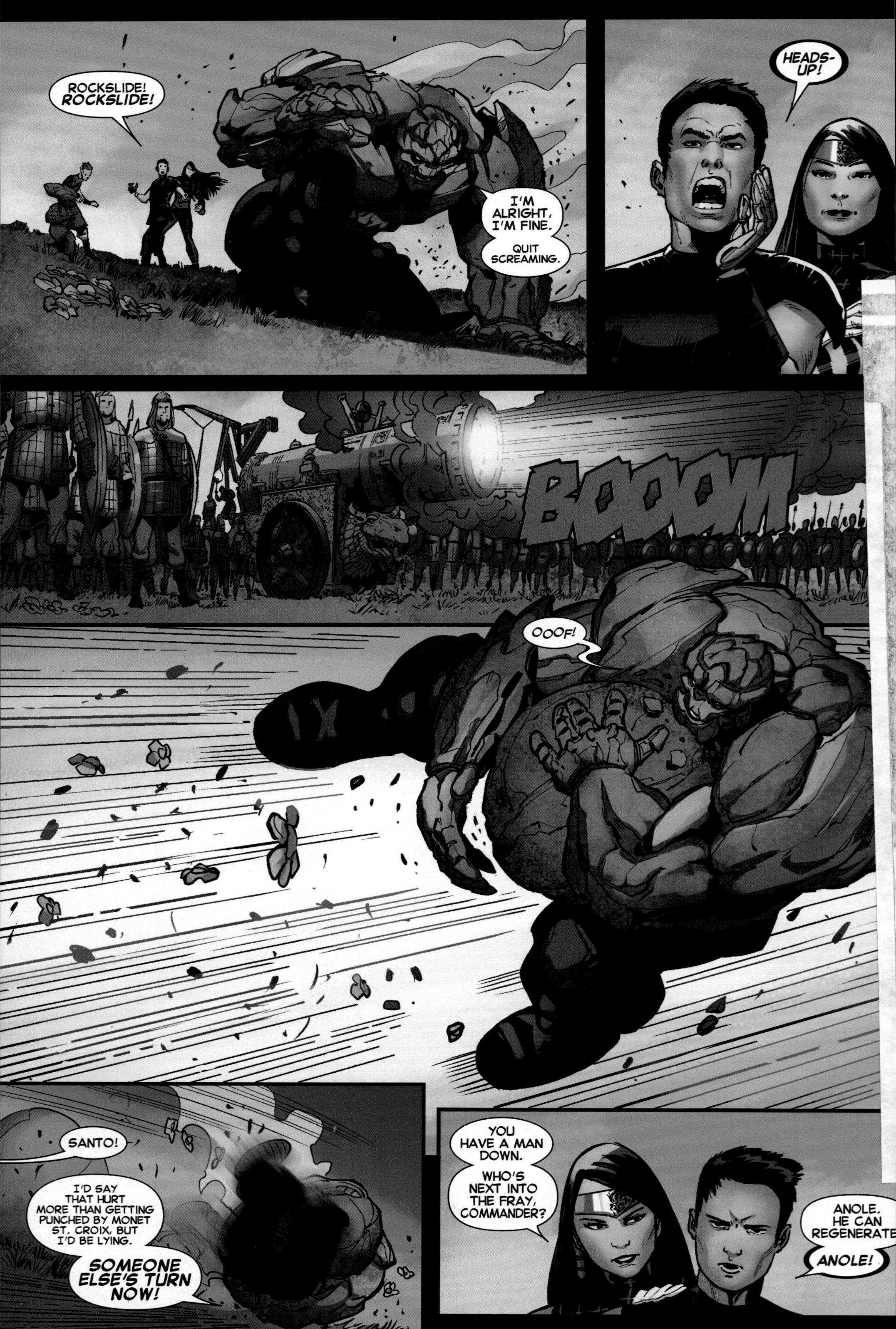
ROCKSLIDE! ROCKSLIDE!
I'M ALRIGHT, I'M FINE.
QUIT SCREAMING.
HEADS-UP!
BOOOM
OOOF!
SANTO!
I'D SAY THAT HURT MORE THAN GETTING PUNCHED BY MONET ST. CROIX, BUT I'D BE LYING.
SOMEONE ELSE'S TURN NOW!
YOU HAVE A MAN DOWN.
WHO'S NEXT INTO THE FRAY, COMMANDER?
ANOLE. HE CAN REGENERATE
ANOLE!

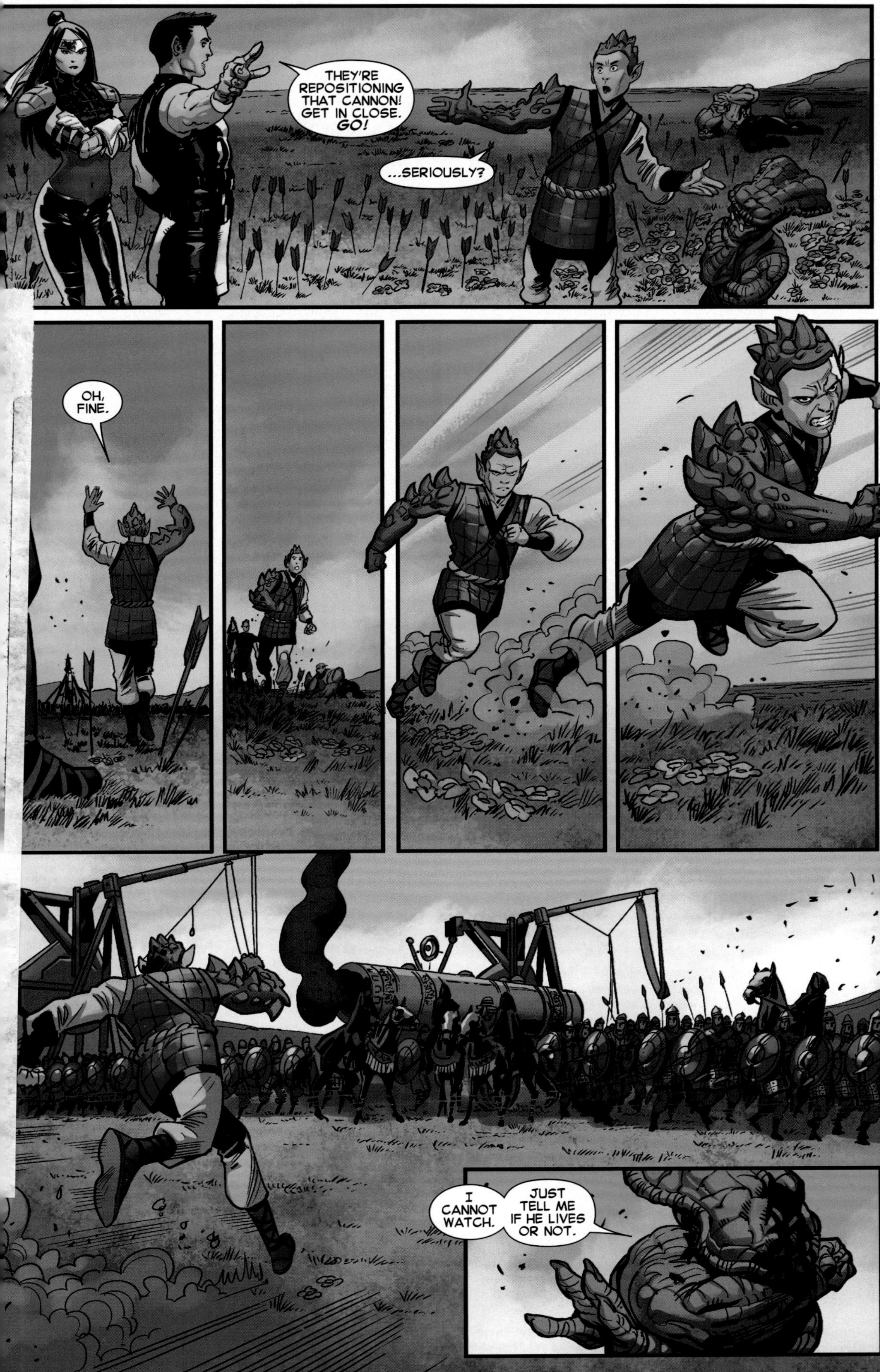
THEY'RE REPOSITIONING THAT CANNON! GET IN CLOSE. GO!
...SERIOUSLY?
OH, FINE.
I CANNOT WATCH.
JUST TELL ME IF HE LIVES OR NOT.

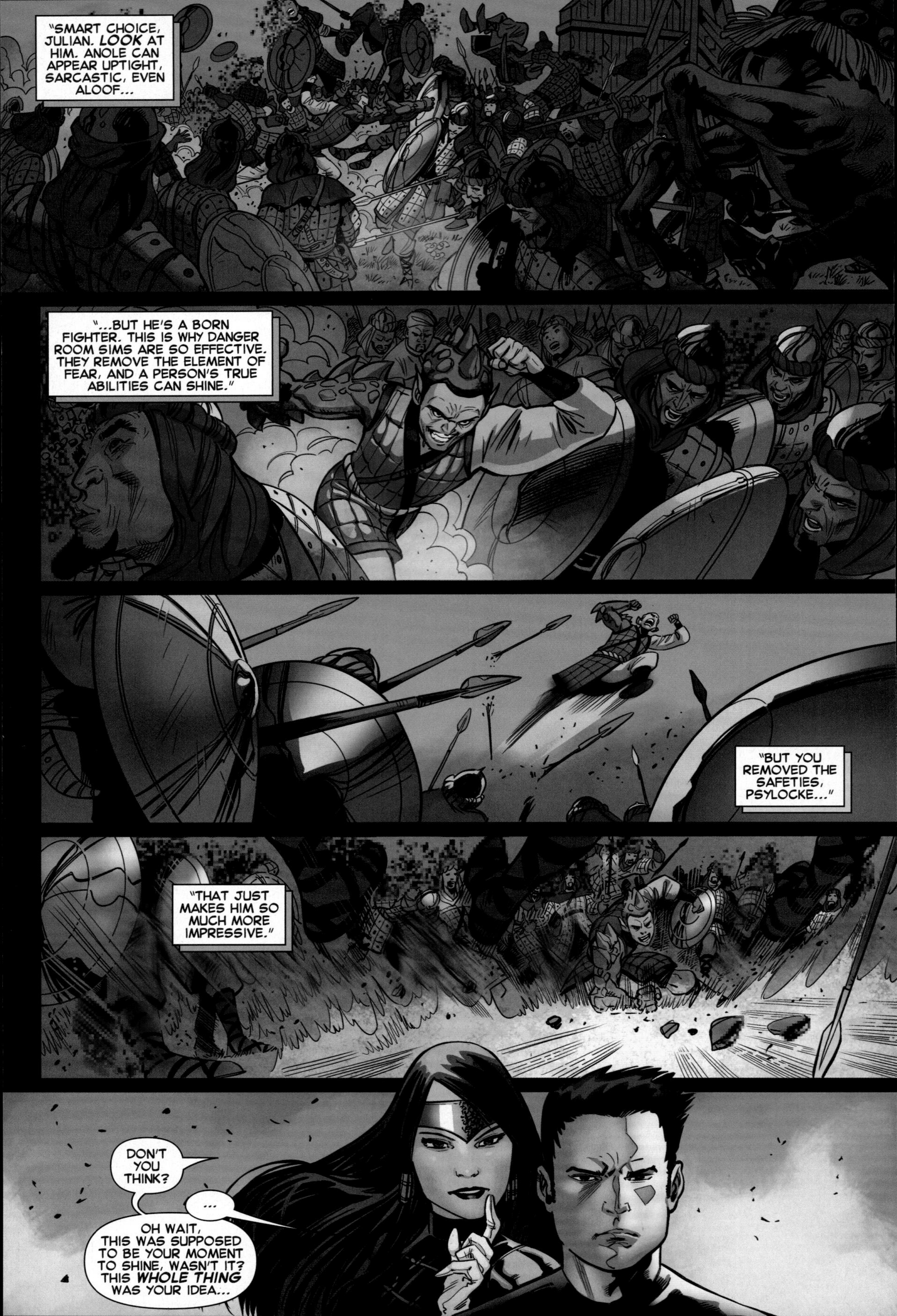
"SMART CHOICE, JULIAN. LOOK AT HIM. ANOLE CAN APPEAR UPTIGHT, SARCASTIC, EVEN ALOOF...
"...BUT HE'S A BORN FIGHTER. THIS IS WHY DANGER ROOM SIMS ARE SO EFFECTIVE. THEY REMOVE THE ELEMENT OF FEAR, AND A PERSON'S TRUE ABILITIES CAN SHINE."
"BUT YOU REMOVED THE SAFETIES, PSYLOCKE..."
"THAT JUST MAKES HIM SO MUCH MORE IMPRESSIVE."
DON'T YOU THINK?
...
OH WAIT, THIS WAS SUPPOSED TO BE YOUR MOMENT TO SHINE, WASN'T IT? THIS WHOLE THING WAS YOUR IDEA...

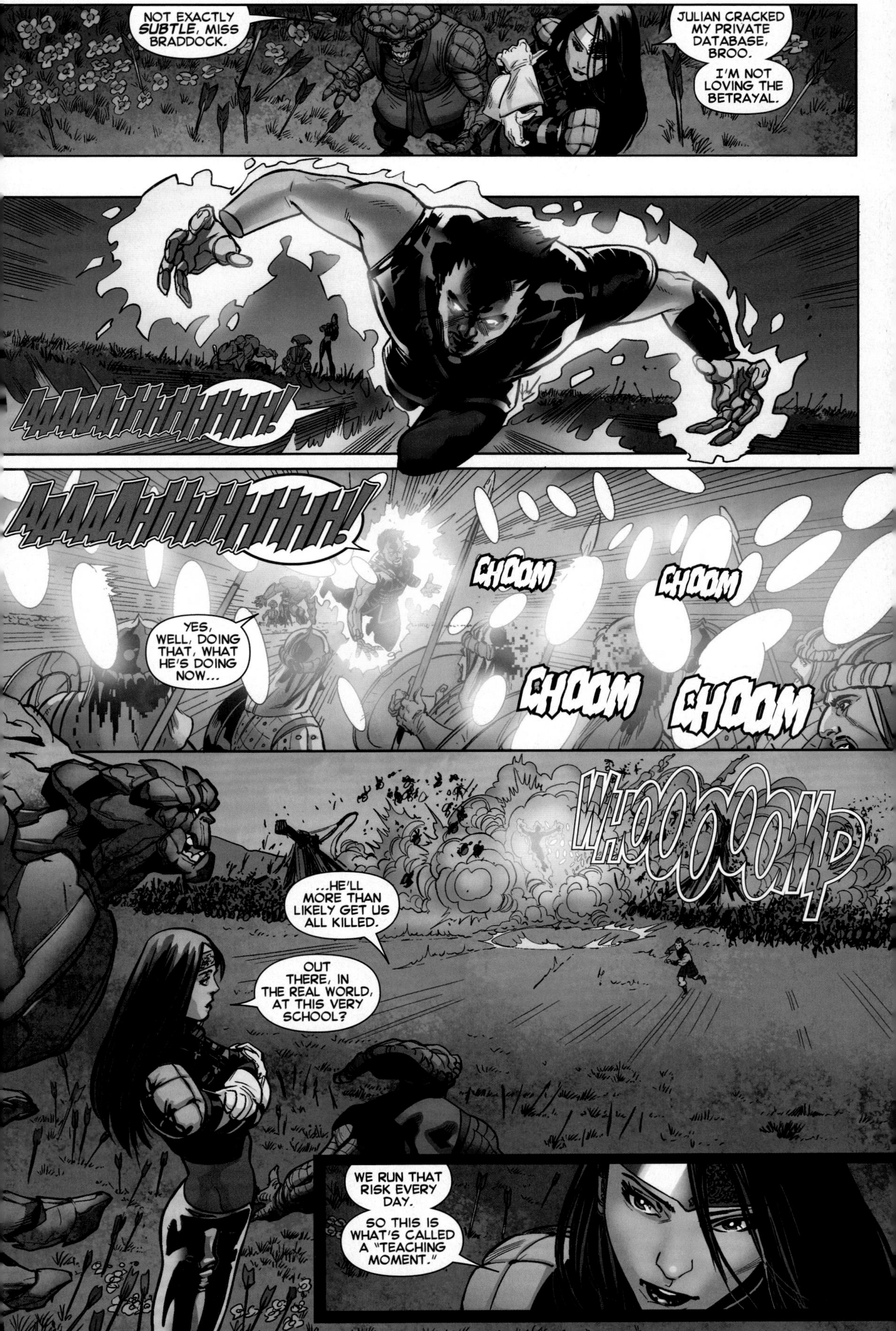

NOT EXACTLY SUBTLE, MISS BRADDOCK.
JULIAN CRACKED MY PRIVATE DATABASE, BROO.
I'M NOT LOVING THE BETRAYAL.
AAAAAHHHHHHH!
AAAAAHHHHHHH!
CHOOM
CHOOM
YES, WELL, DOING THAT, WHAT HE'S DOING NOW...
CHOOM
CHOOM
WHOOOOOOMP
...HE'LL MORE THAN LIKELY GET US ALL KILLED.
OUT THERE, IN THE REAL WORLD, AT THIS VERY SCHOOL?
WE RUN THAT RISK EVERY DAY.
SO THIS IS WHAT'S CALLED A "TEACHING MOMENT."

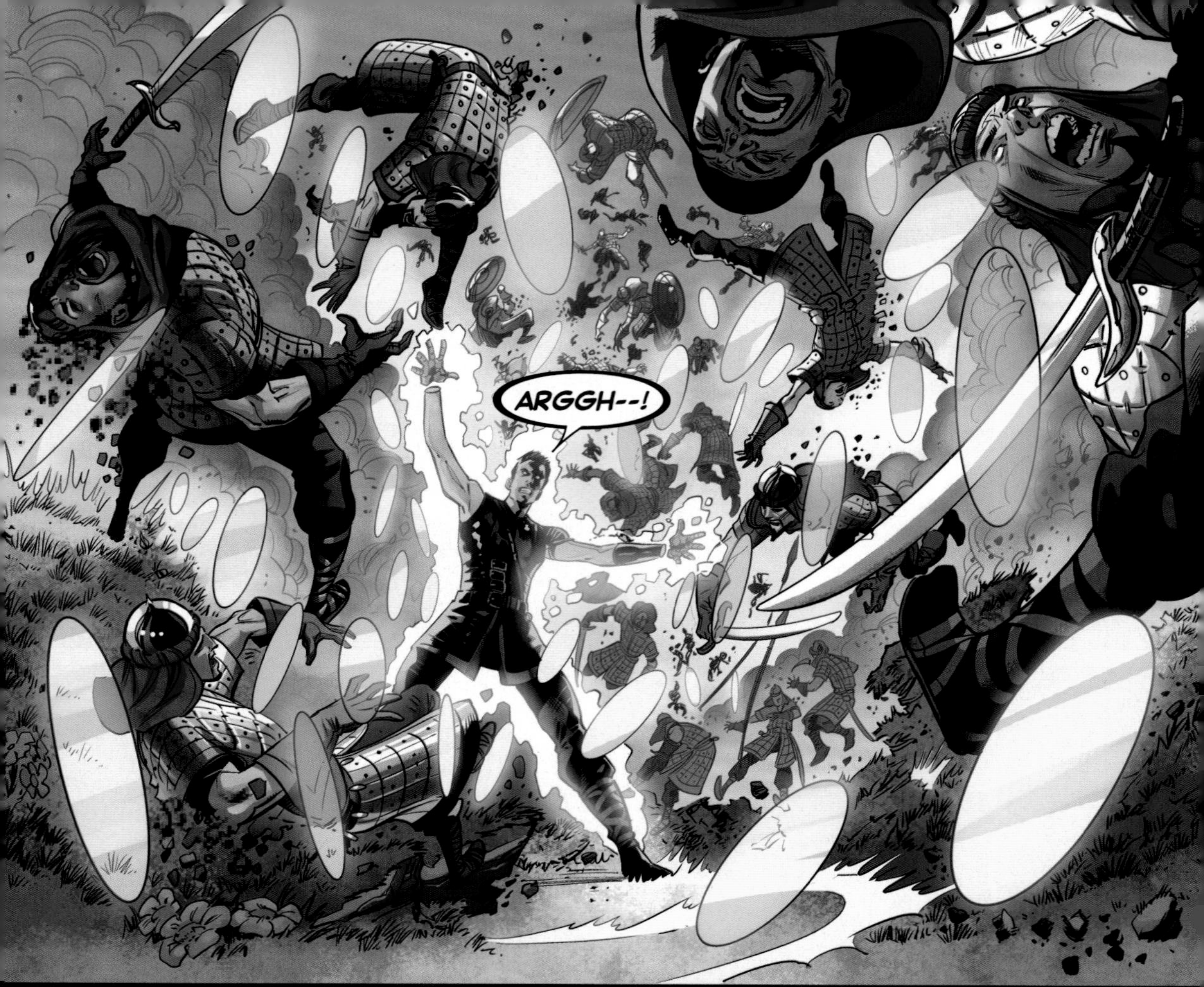
ARGGH--!

BROMO-SUPERIOR PART THREE

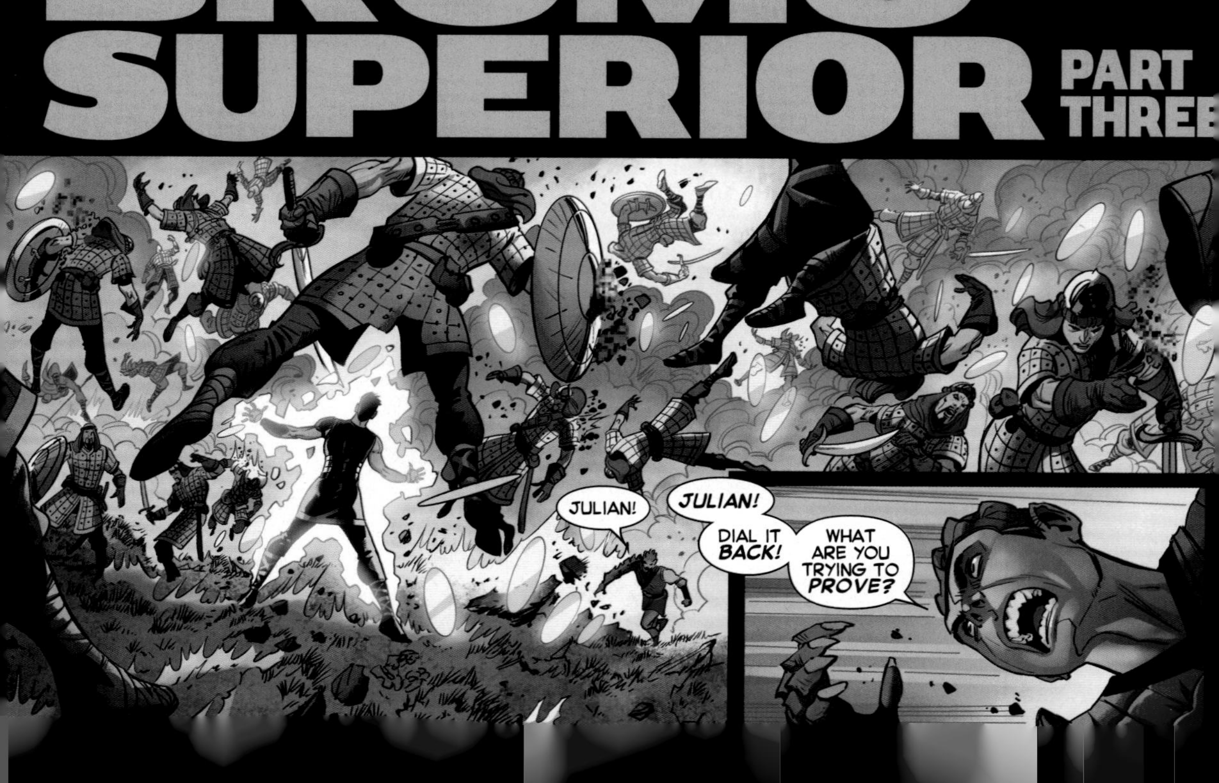
JULIAN!
JULIAN!
DIAL IT BACK!
WHAT ARE YOU TRYING TO PROVE?

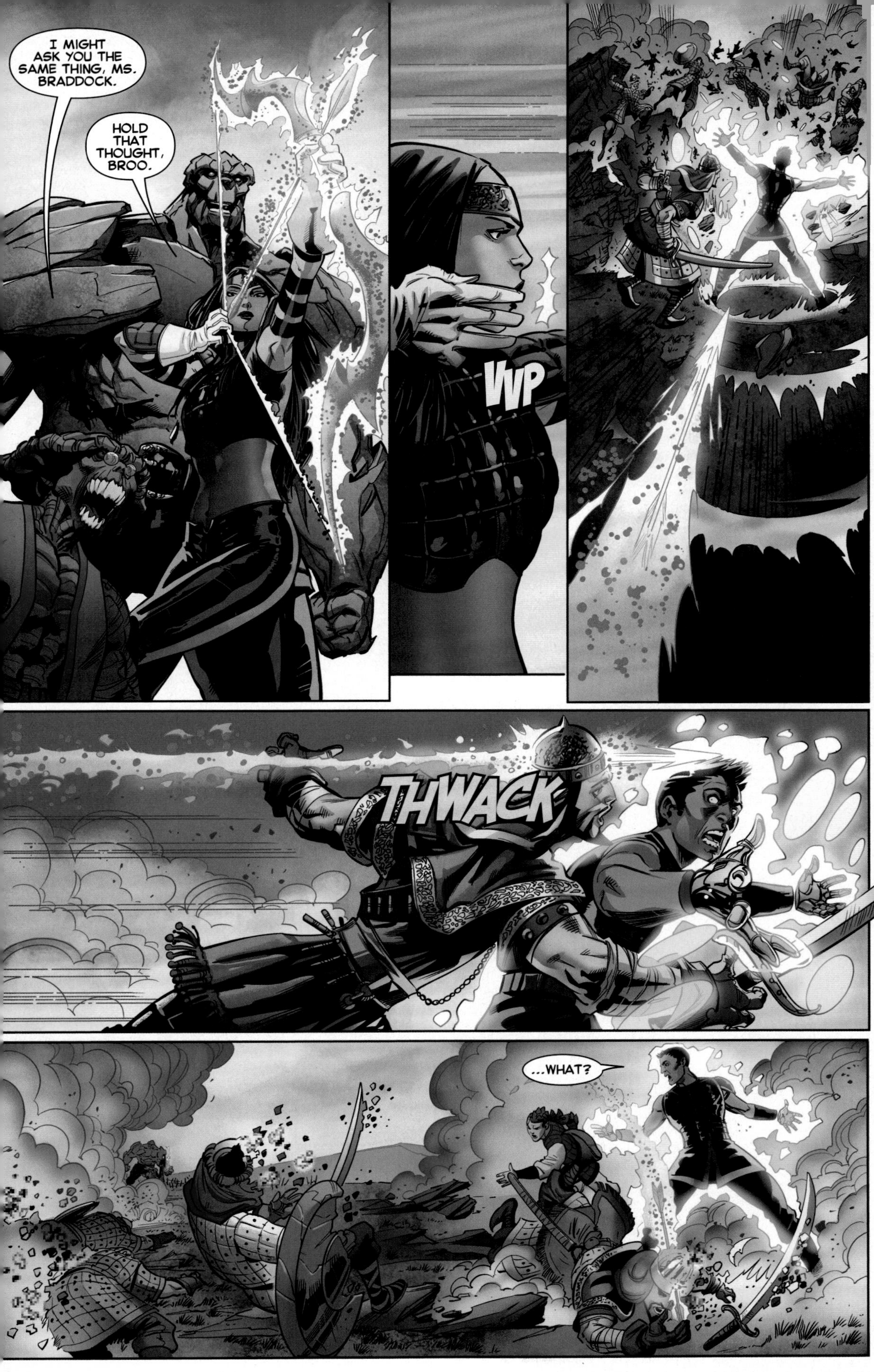
I MIGHT ASK YOU THE SAME THING, MS. BRADDOCK.
HOLD THAT THOUGHT, BROO.
VVP
THWACK
...WHAT?

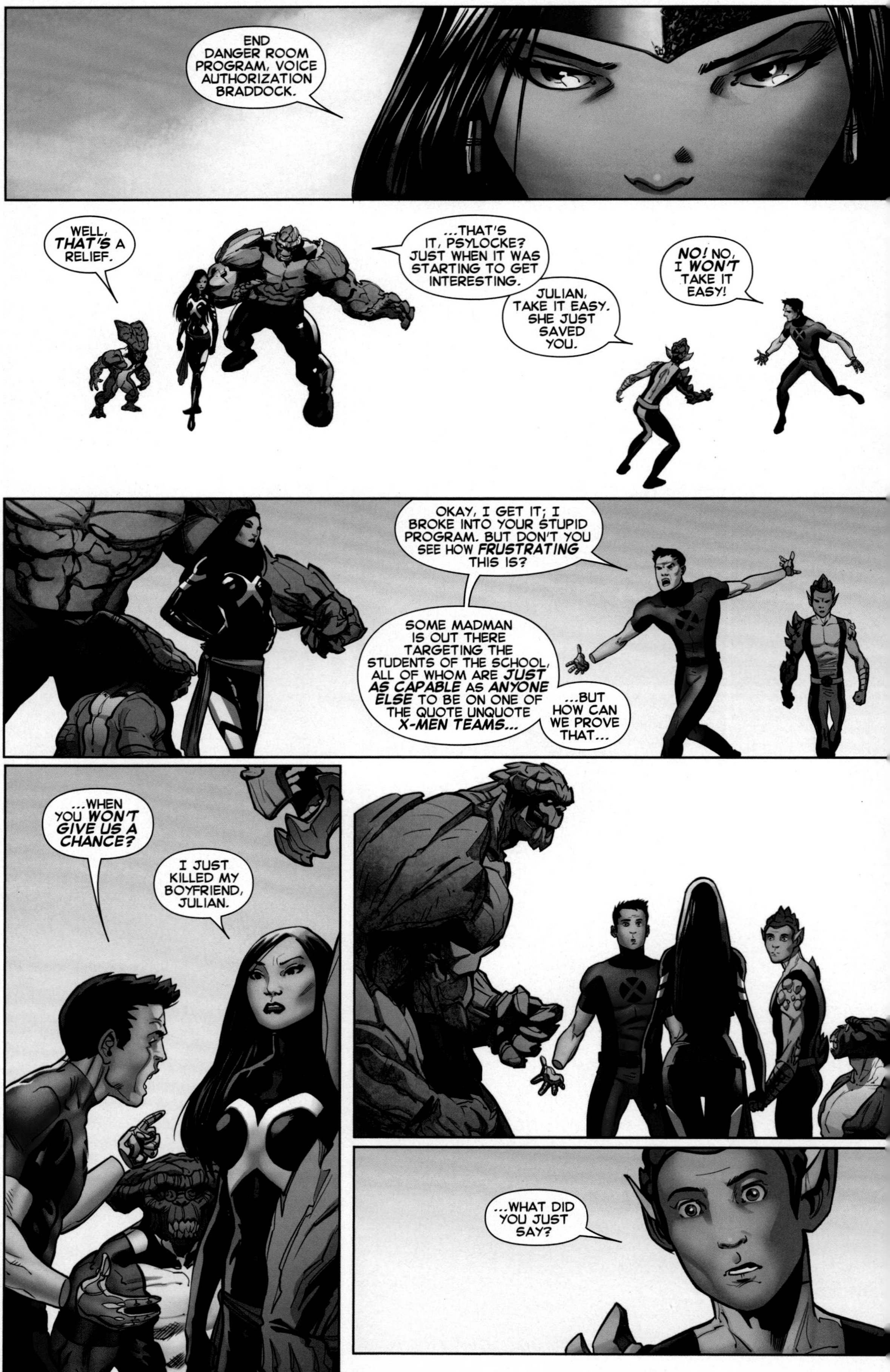
END DANGER ROOM PROGRAM, VOICE AUTHORIZATION BRADDOCK.
WELL, THAT'S A RELIEF.
...THAT'S IT, PSYLOCKE? JUST WHEN IT WAS STARTING TO GET INTERESTING.
JULIAN, TAKE IT EASY. SHE JUST SAVED YOU.
NO! NO, I WON'T TAKE IT EASY!
OKAY, I GET IT; I BROKE INTO YOUR STUPID PROGRAM. BUT DON'T YOU SEE HOW FRUSTRATING THIS IS?
SOME MADMAN IS OUT THERE TARGETING THE STUDENTS OF THE SCHOOL, ALL OF WHOM ARE JUST AS CAPABLE AS ANYONE ELSE TO BE ON ONE OF THE QUOTE UNQUOTE X-MEN TEAMS...
...BUT HOW CAN WE PROVE THAT...
...WHEN YOU WON'T GIVE US A CHANCE?
I JUST KILLED MY BOYFRIEND, JULIAN.
...WHAT DID YOU JUST SAY?

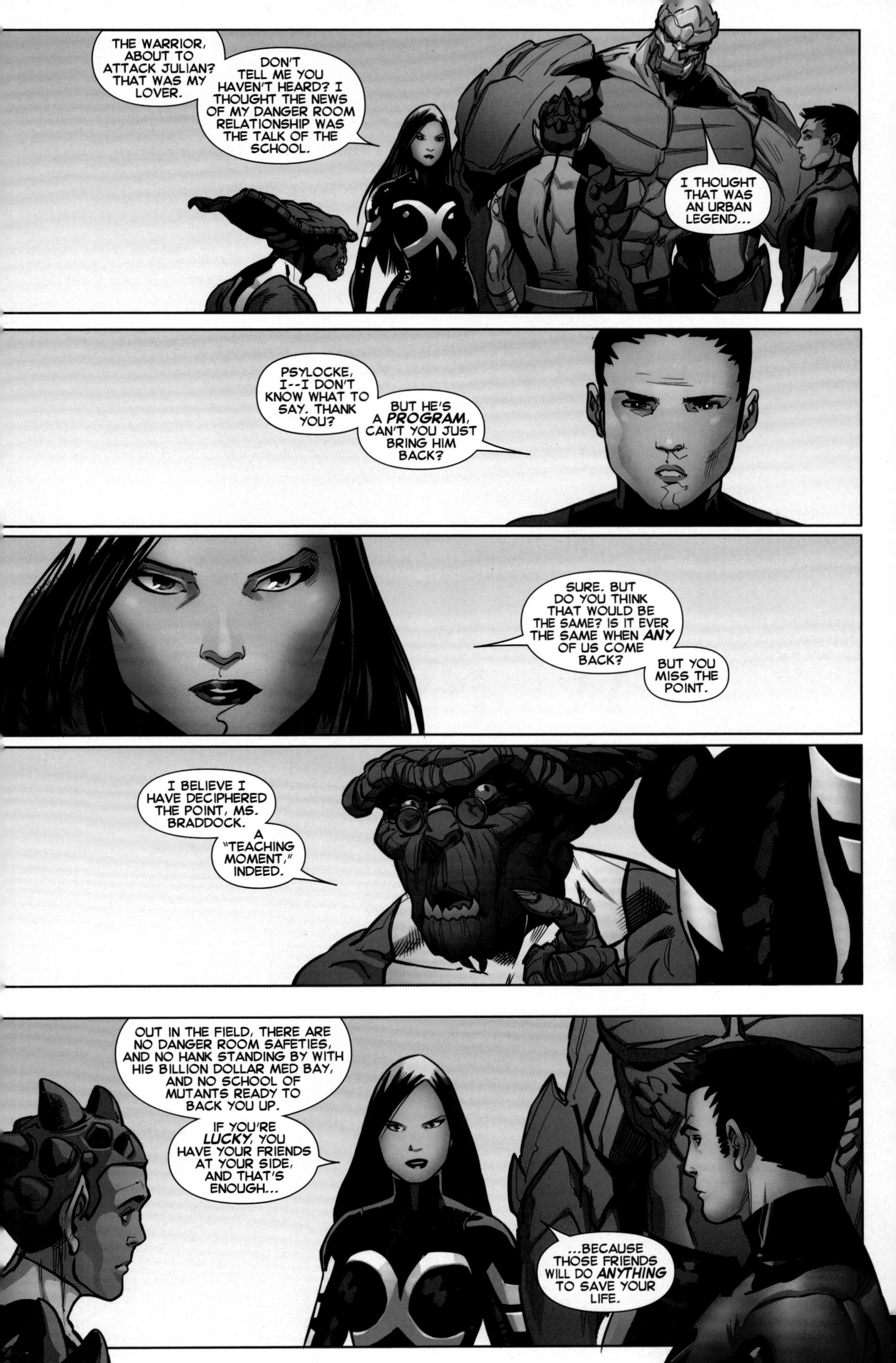
THE WARRIOR, ABOUT TO ATTACK JULIAN? THAT WAS MY LOVER.
DON'T TELL ME YOU HAVEN'T HEARD? I THOUGHT THE NEWS OF MY DANGER ROOM RELATIONSHIP WAS THE TALK OF THE SCHOOL.
I THOUGHT THAT WAS AN URBAN LEGEND...
PSYLOCKE, I--I DON'T KNOW WHAT TO SAY. THANK YOU?
BUT HE'S A PROGRAM, CAN'T YOU JUST BRING HIM BACK?
SURE. BUT DO YOU THINK THAT WOULD BE THE SAME? IS IT EVER THE SAME WHEN ANY OF US COME BACK?
BUT YOU MISS THE POINT.
I BELIEVE I HAVE DECIPHERED THE POINT, MS. BRADDOCK.
A "TEACHING MOMENT," INDEED.
OUT IN THE FIELD, THERE ARE NO DANGER ROOM SAFETIES, AND NO HANK STANDING BY WITH HIS BILLION DOLLAR MED BAY, AND NO SCHOOL OF MUTANTS READY TO BACK YOU UP.
IF YOU'RE LUCKY, YOU HAVE YOUR FRIENDS AT YOUR SIDE, AND THAT'S ENOUGH...
...BECAUSE THOSE FRIENDS WILL DO ANYTHING TO SAVE YOUR LIFE.

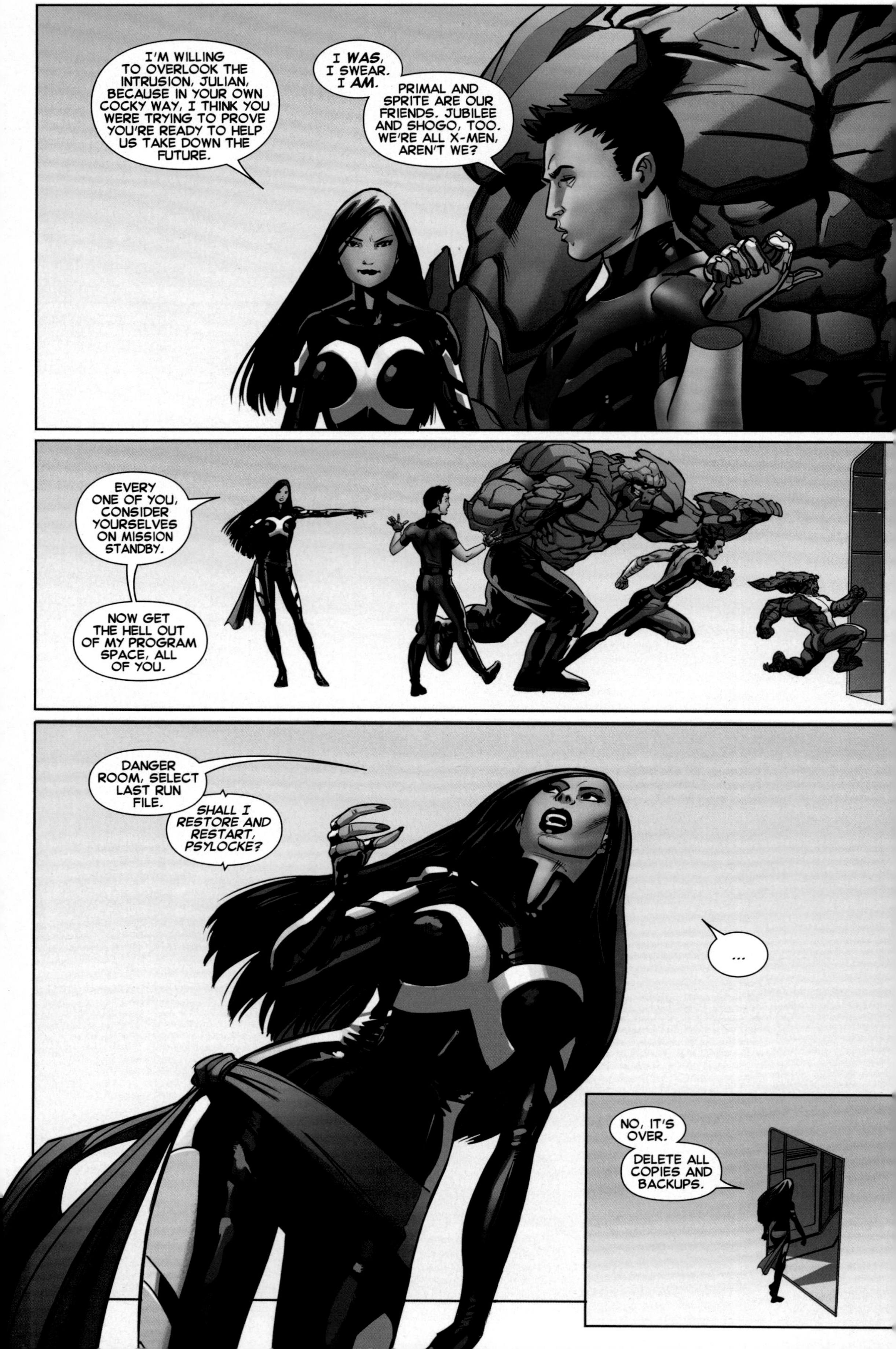
I'M WILLING TO OVERLOOK THE INTRUSION, JULIAN, BECAUSE IN YOUR OWN COCKY WAY, I THINK YOU WERE TRYING TO PROVE YOU'RE READY TO HELP US TAKE DOWN THE FUTURE.
I WAS, I SWEAR. I AM.
PRIMAL AND SPRITE ARE OUR FRIENDS. JUBILEE AND SHOGO, TOO. WE'RE ALL X-MEN, AREN'T WE?
EVERY ONE OF YOU, CONSIDER YOURSELVES ON MISSION STANDBY.
NOW GET THE HELL OUT OF MY PROGRAM SPACE, ALL OF YOU.
DANGER ROOM, SELECT LAST RUN FILE.
SHALL I RESTORE AND RESTART, PSYLOCKE?
...
NO, IT'S OVER.
DELETE ALL COPIES AND BACKUPS.

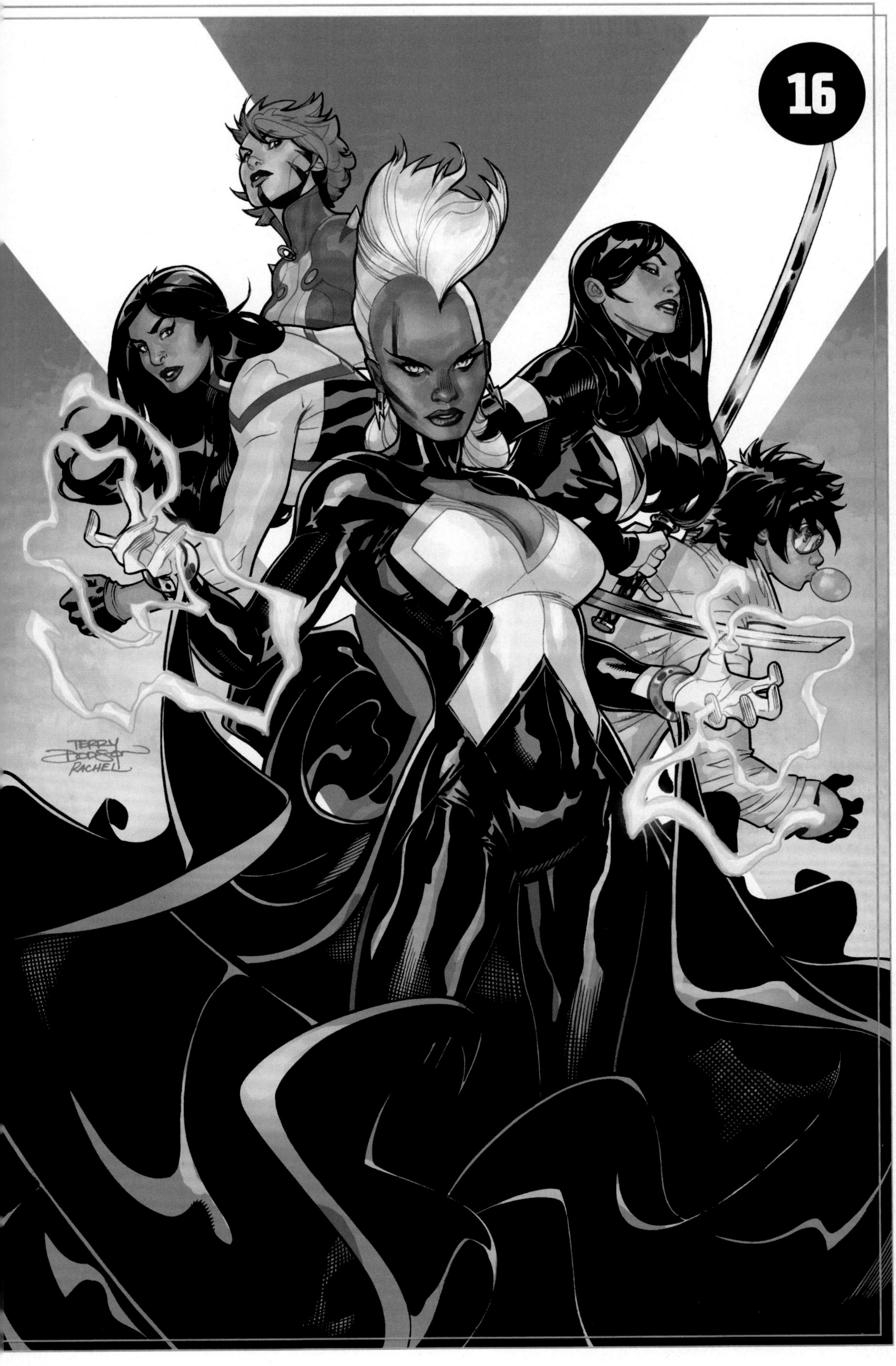
16
TERRY DODSON
RACHEL

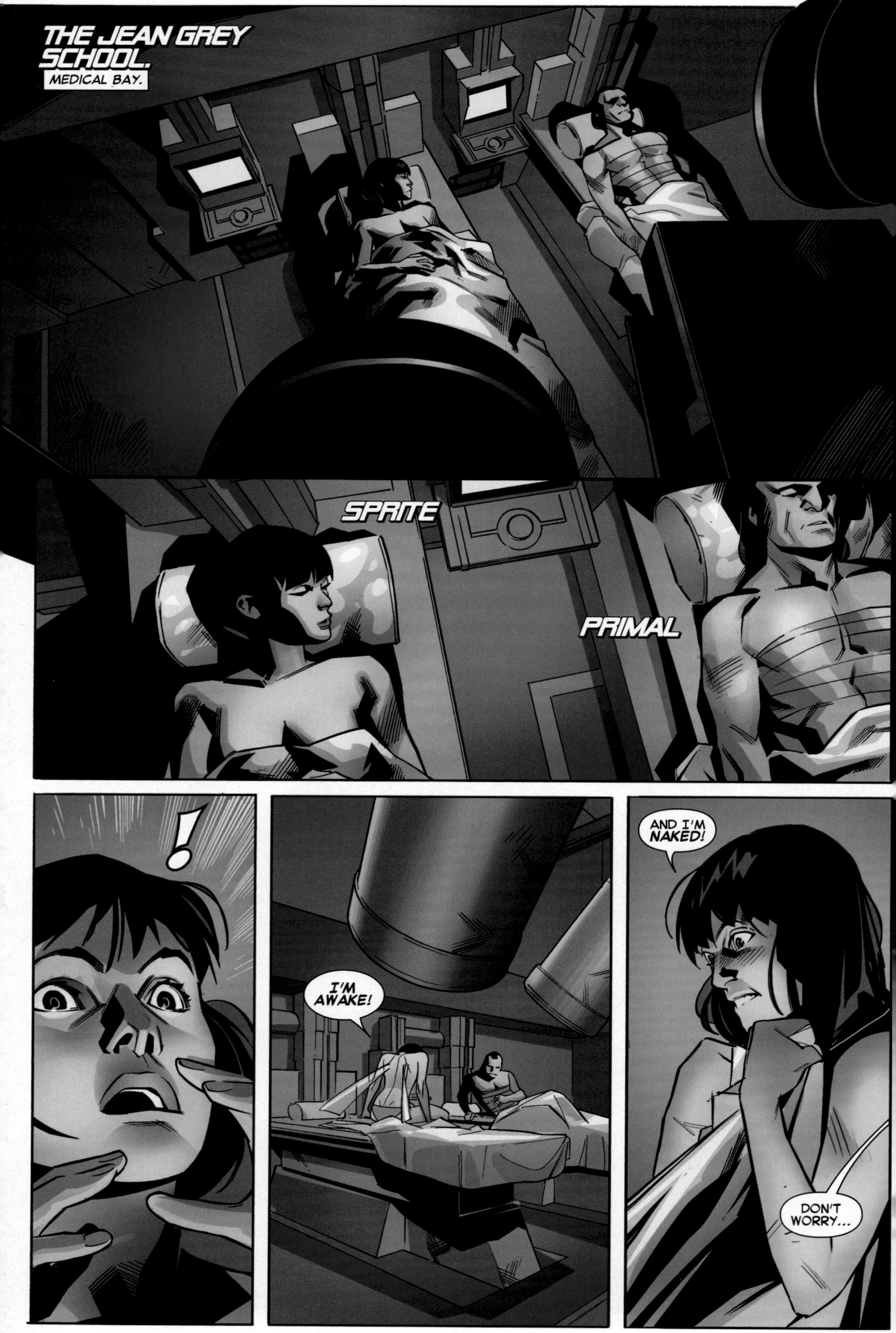
THE JEAN GREY SCHOOL.
MEDICAL BAY.
SPRITE
PRIMAL
!
I'M AWAKE!
AND I'M NAKED!
DON'T WORRY...

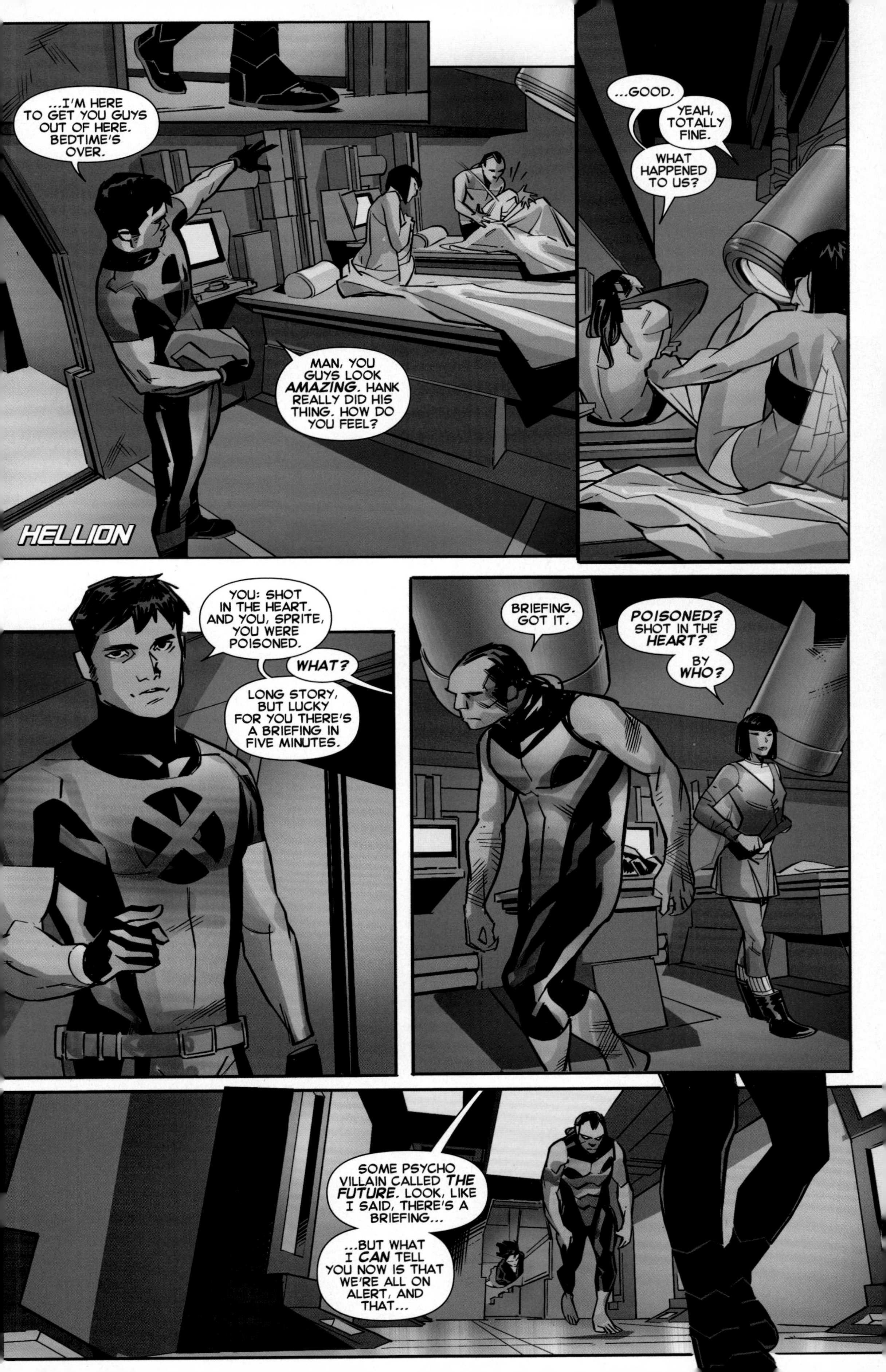
...I'M HERE TO GET YOU GUYS OUT OF HERE. BEDTIME'S OVER.
HELLION
MAN, YOU GUYS LOOK AMAZING. HANK REALLY DID HIS THING. HOW DO YOU FEEL?
...GOOD.
YEAH, TOTALLY FINE.
WHAT HAPPENED TO US?
YOU: SHOT IN THE HEART. AND YOU, SPRITE, YOU WERE POISONED.
WHAT?
LONG STORY, BUT LUCKY FOR YOU THERE'S A BRIEFING IN FIVE MINUTES.
BRIEFING. GOT IT.
POISONED? SHOT IN THE HEART?
BY WHO?
SOME PSYCHO VILLAIN CALLED THE FUTURE. LOOK, LIKE I SAID, THERE'S A BRIEFING...
...BUT WHAT I CAN TELL YOU NOW IS THAT WE'RE ALL ON ALERT, AND THAT...

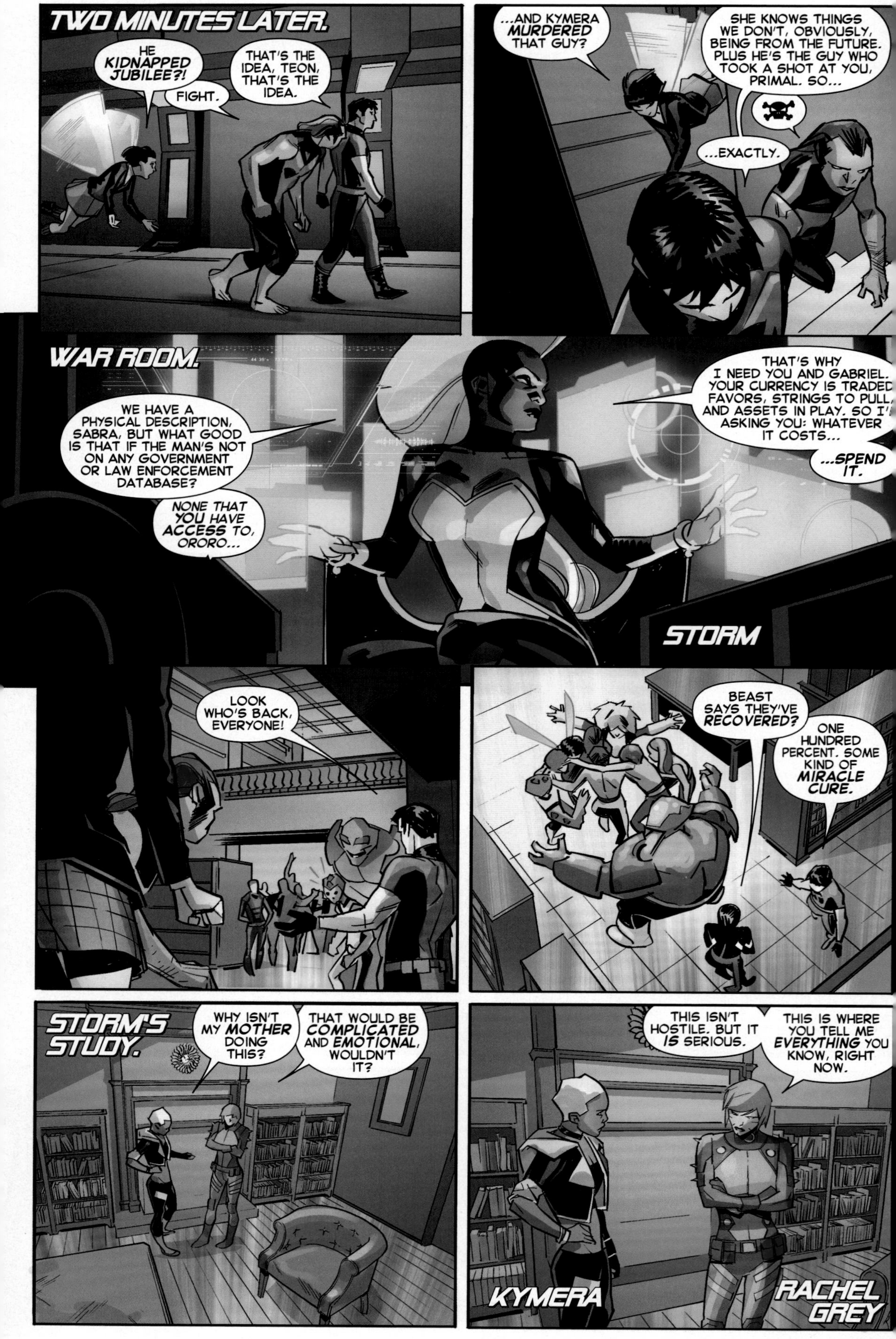
TWO MINUTES LATER.
HE KIDNAPPED JUBILEE?!
FIGHT.
THAT'S THE IDEA, TEON, THAT'S THE IDEA.
...AND KYMERA MURDERED THAT GUY?
SHE KNOWS THINGS WE DON'T, OBVIOUSLY, BEING FROM THE FUTURE. PLUS HE'S THE GUY WHO TOOK A SHOT AT YOU, PRIMAL. SO...
...EXACTLY.
WAR ROOM.
WE HAVE A PHYSICAL DESCRIPTION, SABRA, BUT WHAT GOOD IS THAT IF THE MAN'S NOT ON ANY GOVERNMENT OR LAW ENFORCEMENT DATABASE?
NONE THAT YOU HAVE ACCESS TO, ORORO...
THAT'S WHY I NEED YOU AND GABRIEL. YOUR CURRENCY IS TRADED FAVORS, STRINGS TO PULL, AND ASSETS IN PLAY. SO I'M ASKING YOU: WHATEVER IT COSTS...
...SPEND IT.
STORM
LOOK WHO'S BACK, EVERYONE!
BEAST SAYS THEY'VE RECOVERED?
ONE HUNDRED PERCENT. SOME KIND OF MIRACLE CURE.
STORM'S STUDY.
WHY ISN'T MY MOTHER DOING THIS?
THAT WOULD BE COMPLICATED AND EMOTIONAL, WOULDN'T IT?
THIS ISN'T HOSTILE. BUT IT IS SERIOUS.
THIS IS WHERE YOU TELL ME EVERYTHING YOU KNOW, RIGHT NOW.
KYMERA
RACHEL GREY

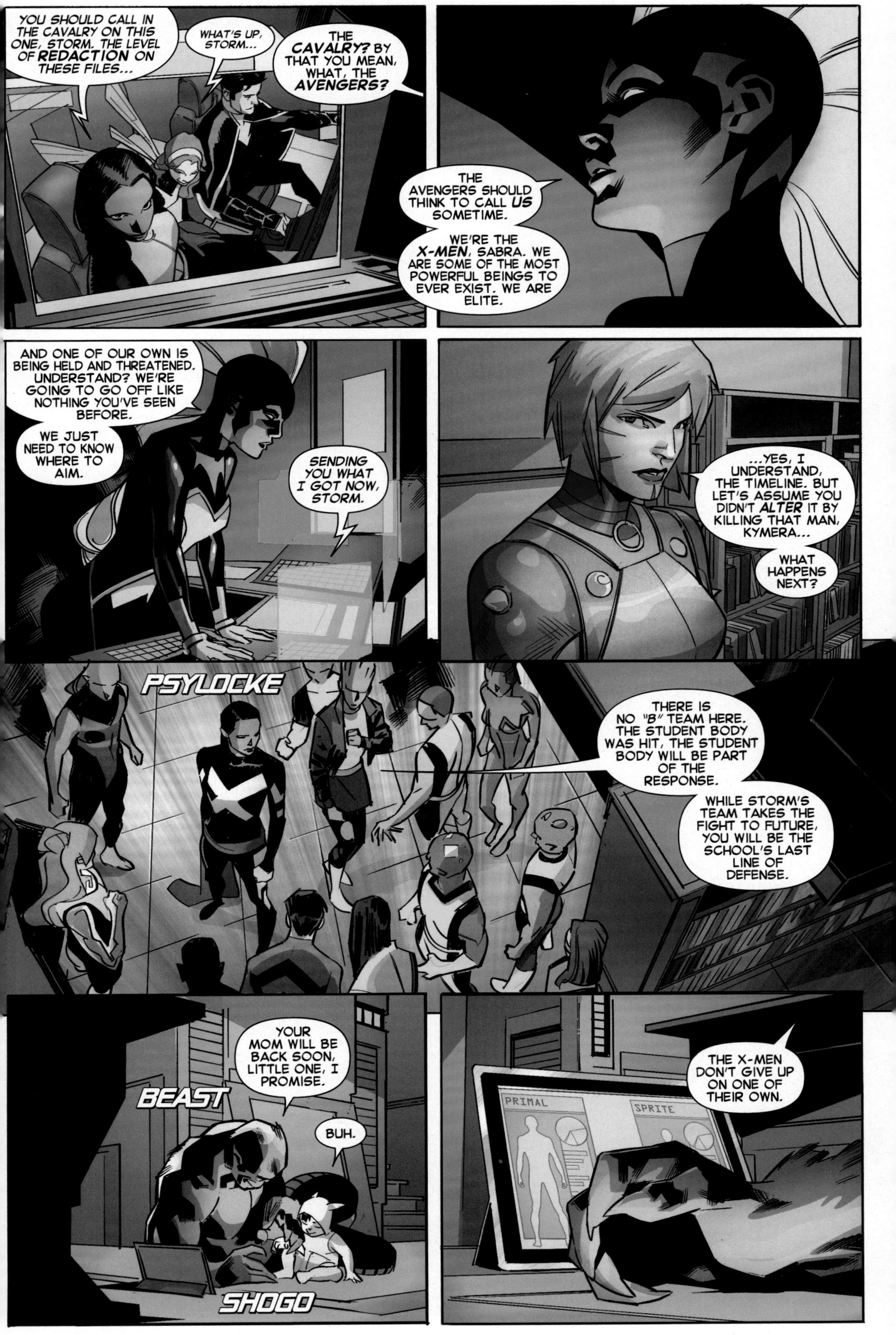
YOU SHOULD CALL IN THE CAVALRY ON THIS ONE, STORM. THE LEVEL OF REDACTION ON THESE FILES...
WHAT'S UP, STORM...
THE CAVALRY? BY THAT YOU MEAN, WHAT, THE AVENGERS?
THE AVENGERS SHOULD THINK TO CALL US SOMETIME.
WE'RE THE X-MEN, SABRA. WE ARE SOME OF THE MOST POWERFUL BEINGS TO EVER EXIST. WE ARE ELITE.
AND ONE OF OUR OWN IS BEING HELD AND THREATENED. UNDERSTAND? WE'RE GOING TO GO OFF LIKE NOTHING YOU'VE SEEN BEFORE.
WE JUST NEED TO KNOW WHERE TO AIM.
SENDING YOU WHAT I GOT NOW, STORM.
...YES, I UNDERSTAND, THE TIMELINE. BUT LET'S ASSUME YOU DIDN'T ALTER IT BY KILLING THAT MAN, KYMERA...
WHAT HAPPENS NEXT?
PSYLOCKE
THERE IS NO "B" TEAM HERE. THE STUDENT BODY WAS HIT, THE STUDENT BODY WILL BE PART OF THE RESPONSE.
WHILE STORM'S TEAM TAKES THE FIGHT TO FUTURE, YOU WILL BE THE SCHOOL'S LAST LINE OF DEFENSE.
BEAST
YOUR MOM WILL BE BACK SOON, LITTLE ONE, I PROMISE.
BUH.
SHOGO
THE X-MEN DON'T GIVE UP ON ONE OF THEIR OWN.
PRIMAL
SPRITE

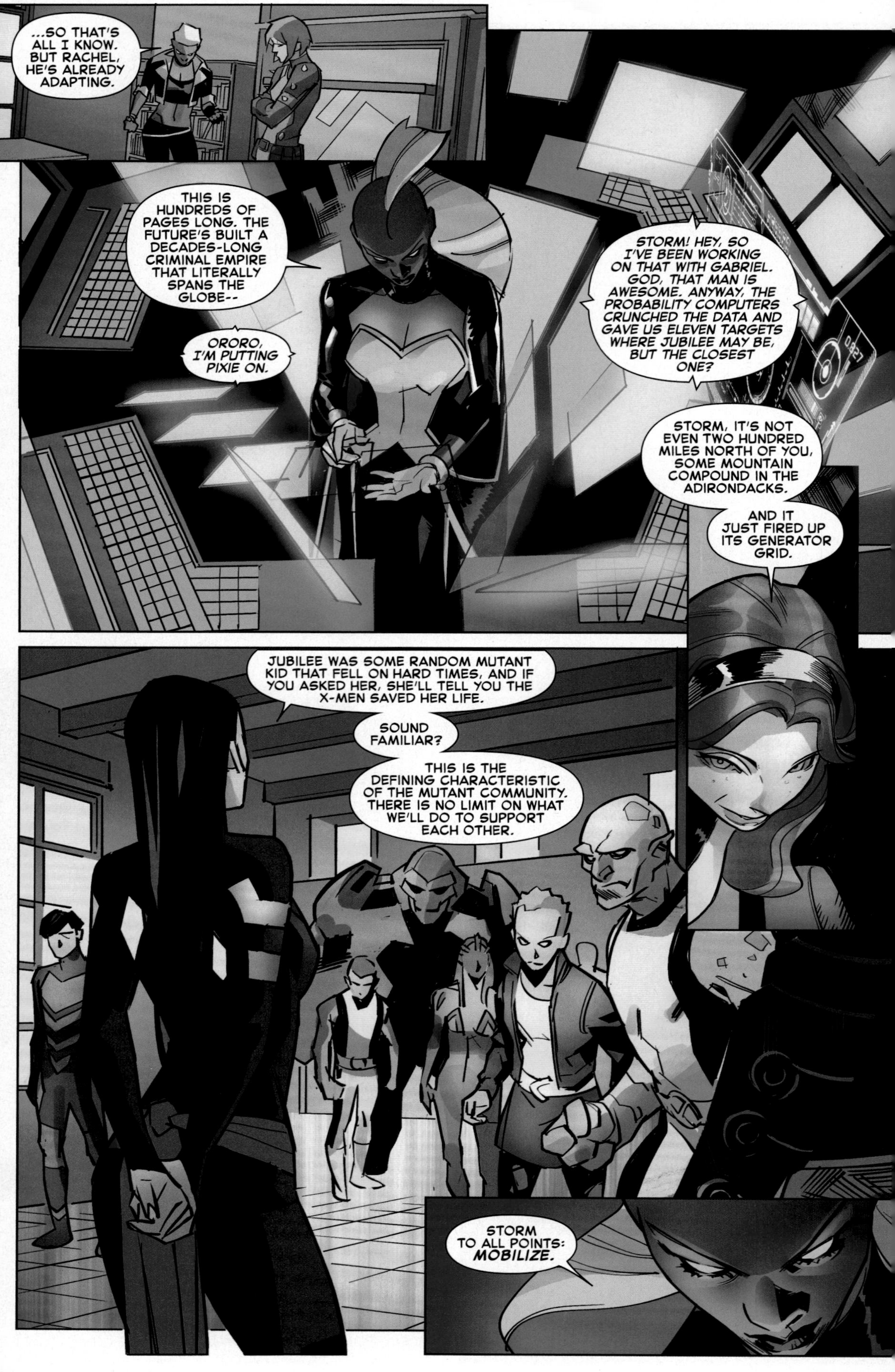
...SO THAT'S ALL I KNOW. BUT RACHEL, HE'S ALREADY ADAPTING.
THIS IS HUNDREDS OF PAGES LONG. THE FUTURE'S BUILT A DECADES-LONG CRIMINAL EMPIRE THAT LITERALLY SPANS THE GLOBE--
ORORO, I'M PUTTING PIXIE ON.
STORM! HEY, SO I'VE BEEN WORKING ON THAT WITH GABRIEL. GOD, THAT MAN IS AWESOME. ANYWAY, THE PROBABILITY COMPUTERS CRUNCHED THE DATA AND GAVE US ELEVEN TARGETS WHERE JUBILEE MAY BE, BUT THE CLOSEST ONE?
STORM, IT'S NOT EVEN TWO HUNDRED MILES NORTH OF YOU, SOME MOUNTAIN COMPOUND IN THE ADIRONDACKS.
AND IT JUST FIRED UP ITS GENERATOR GRID.
JUBILEE WAS SOME RANDOM MUTANT KID THAT FELL ON HARD TIMES, AND IF YOU ASKED HER, SHE'LL TELL YOU THE X-MEN SAVED HER LIFE.
SOUND FAMILIAR?
THIS IS THE DEFINING CHARACTERISTIC OF THE MUTANT COMMUNITY. THERE IS NO LIMIT ON WHAT WE'LL DO TO SUPPORT EACH OTHER.
STORM TO ALL POINTS: *MOBILIZE.*

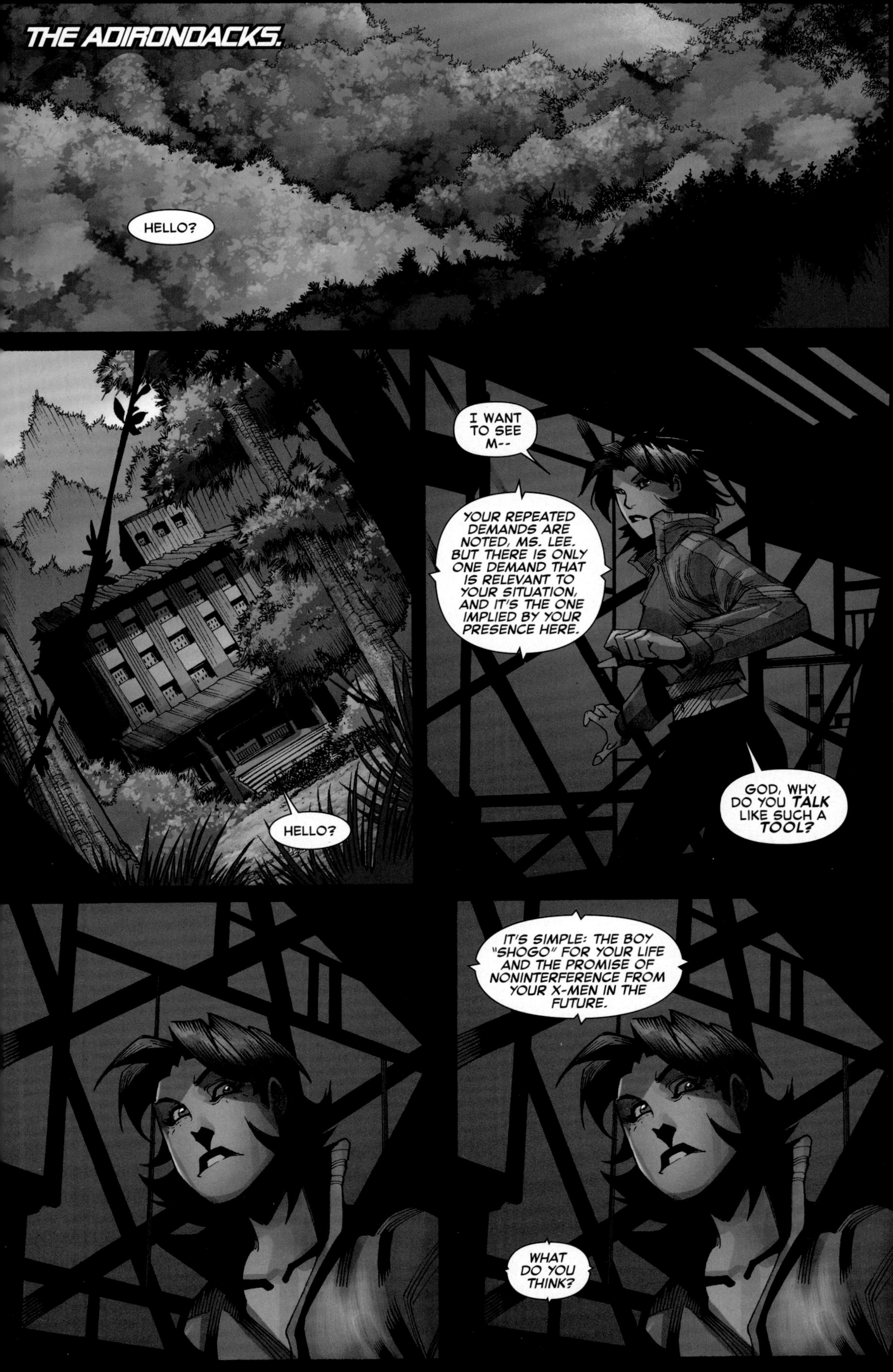
THE ADIRONDACKS.
HELLO?
HELLO?
I WANT TO SEE M--
YOUR REPEATED DEMANDS ARE NOTED, MS. LEE. BUT THERE IS ONLY ONE DEMAND THAT IS RELEVANT TO YOUR SITUATION, AND IT'S THE ONE IMPLIED BY YOUR PRESENCE HERE.
GOD, WHY DO YOU TALK LIKE SUCH A TOOL?
IT'S SIMPLE: THE BOY "SHOGO" FOR YOUR LIFE AND THE PROMISE OF NONINTERFERENCE FROM YOUR X-MEN IN THE FUTURE.
WHAT DO YOU THINK?

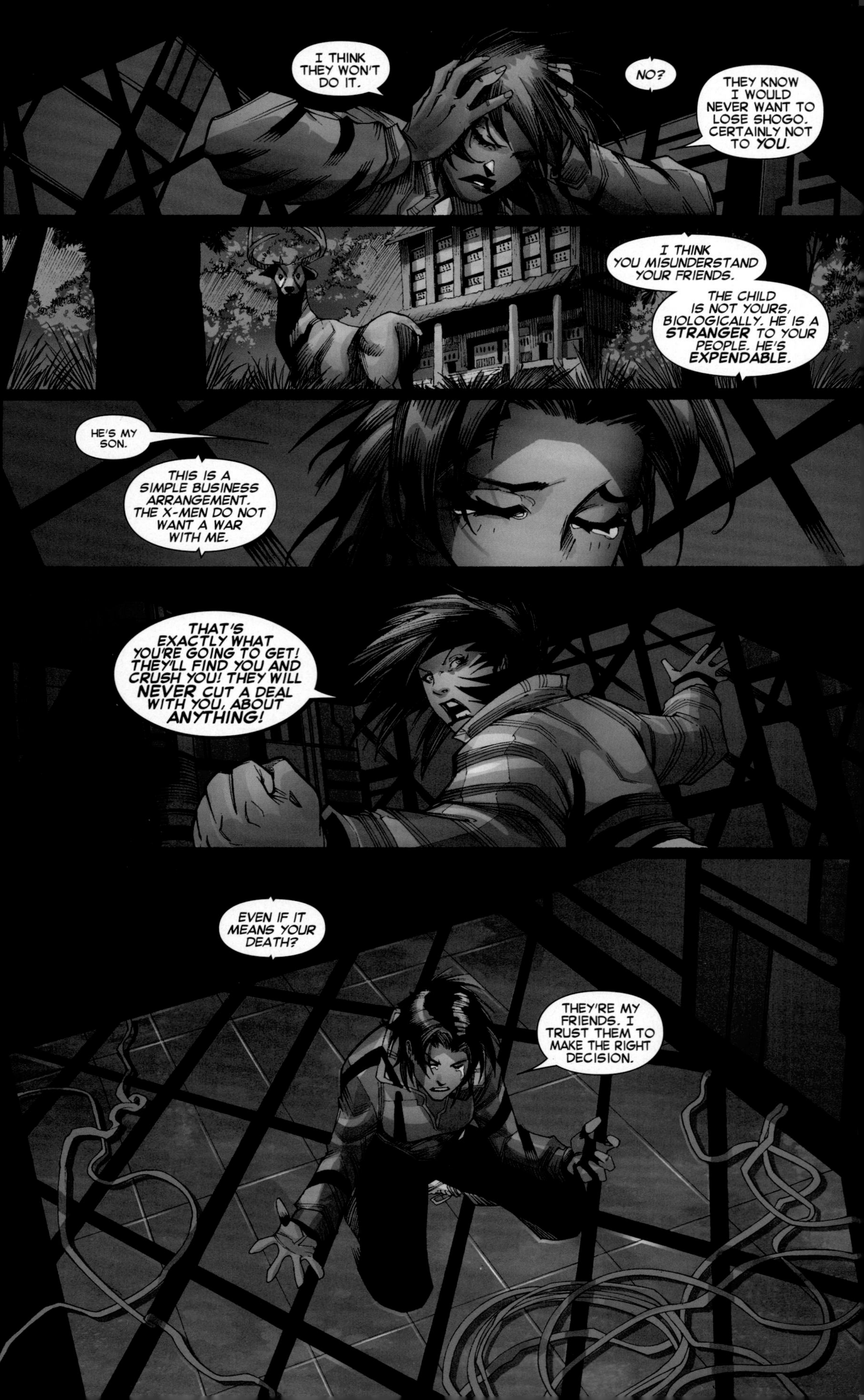
I THINK THEY WON'T DO IT.
NO?
THEY KNOW I WOULD NEVER WANT TO LOSE SHOGO. CERTAINLY NOT TO YOU.
I THINK YOU MISUNDERSTAND YOUR FRIENDS.
THE CHILD IS NOT YOURS, BIOLOGICALLY. HE IS A STRANGER TO YOUR PEOPLE. HE'S EXPENDABLE.
HE'S MY SON.
THIS IS A SIMPLE BUSINESS ARRANGEMENT. THE X-MEN DO NOT WANT A WAR WITH ME.
THAT'S EXACTLY WHAT YOU'RE GOING TO GET! THEY'LL FIND YOU AND CRUSH YOU! THEY WILL NEVER CUT A DEAL WITH YOU, ABOUT ANYTHING!
EVEN IF IT MEANS YOUR DEATH?
THEY'RE MY FRIENDS. I TRUST THEM TO MAKE THE RIGHT DECISION.

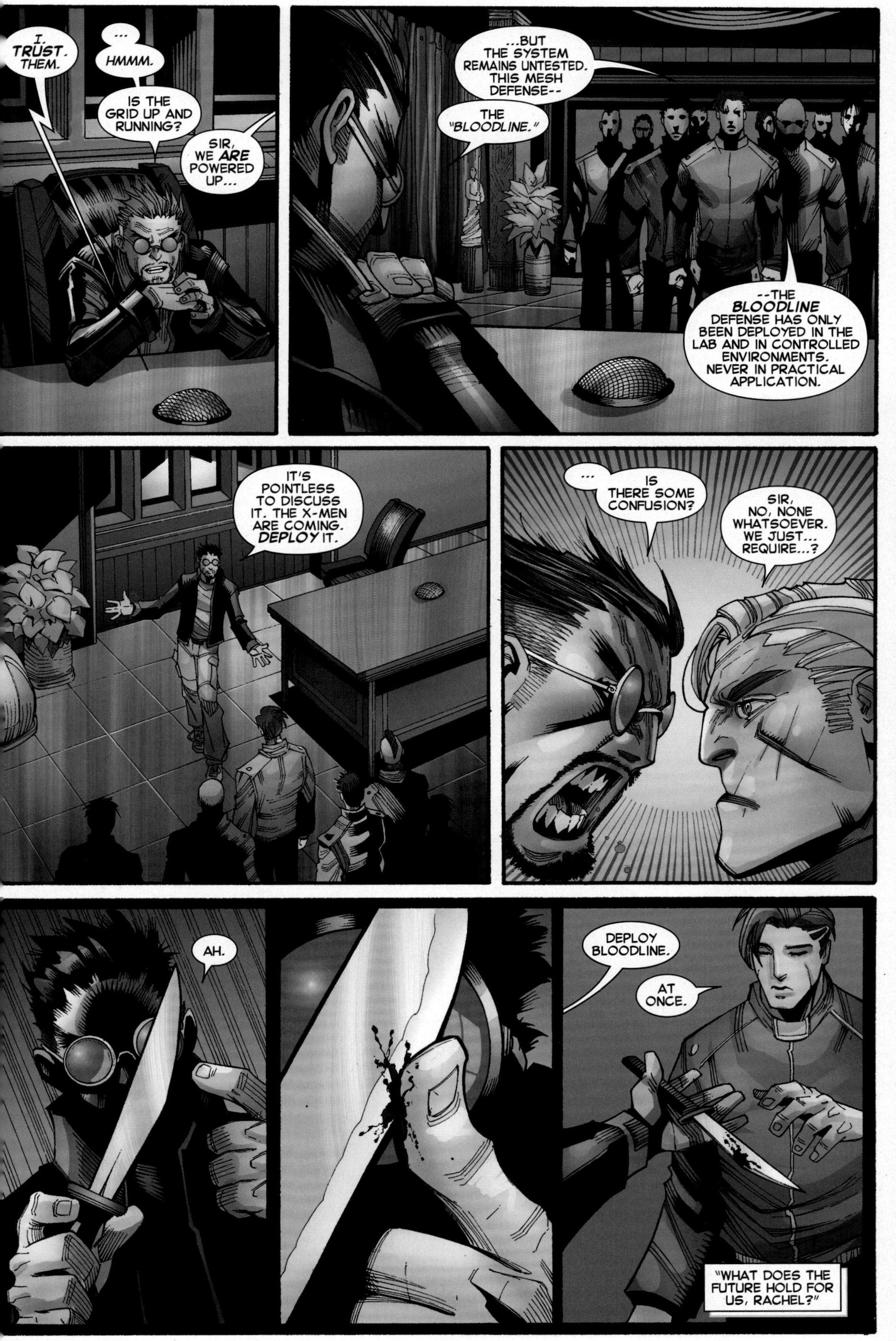

I. TRUST. THEM.
...
HMMM.
IS THE GRID UP AND RUNNING?
SIR, WE ARE POWERED UP...
...BUT THE SYSTEM REMAINS UNTESTED. THIS MESH DEFENSE--
THE "BLOODLINE."
--THE BLOODLINE DEFENSE HAS ONLY BEEN DEPLOYED IN THE LAB AND IN CONTROLLED ENVIRONMENTS. NEVER IN PRACTICAL APPLICATION.
IT'S POINTLESS TO DISCUSS IT. THE X-MEN ARE COMING. DEPLOY IT.
...
IS THERE SOME CONFUSION?
SIR, NO, NONE WHATSOEVER. WE JUST... REQUIRE...?
AH.
DEPLOY BLOODLINE.
AT ONCE.
"WHAT DOES THE FUTURE HOLD FOR US, RACHEL?"

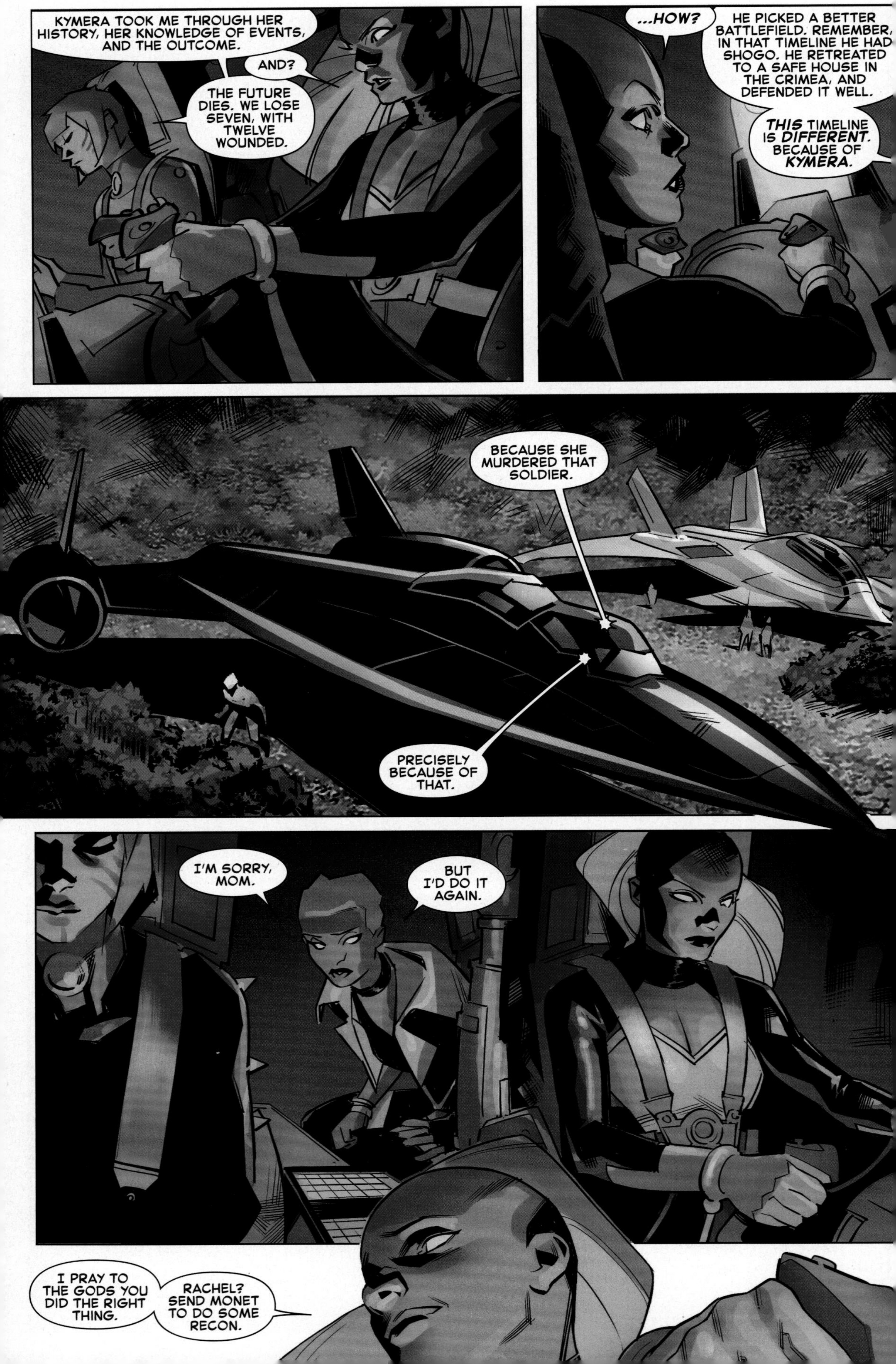
KYMERA TOOK ME THROUGH HER HISTORY, HER KNOWLEDGE OF EVENTS, AND THE OUTCOME.
AND?
THE FUTURE DIES. WE LOSE SEVEN, WITH TWELVE WOUNDED.
...HOW?
HE PICKED A BETTER BATTLEFIELD. REMEMBER, IN THAT TIMELINE HE HAD SHOGO. HE RETREATED TO A SAFE HOUSE IN THE CRIMEA, AND DEFENDED IT WELL.
THIS TIMELINE IS DIFFERENT. BECAUSE OF KYMERA.
BECAUSE SHE MURDERED THAT SOLDIER.
PRECISELY BECAUSE OF THAT.
I'M SORRY, MOM.
BUT I'D DO IT AGAIN.
I PRAY TO THE GODS YOU DID THE RIGHT THING.
RACHEL? SEND MONET TO DO SOME RECON.

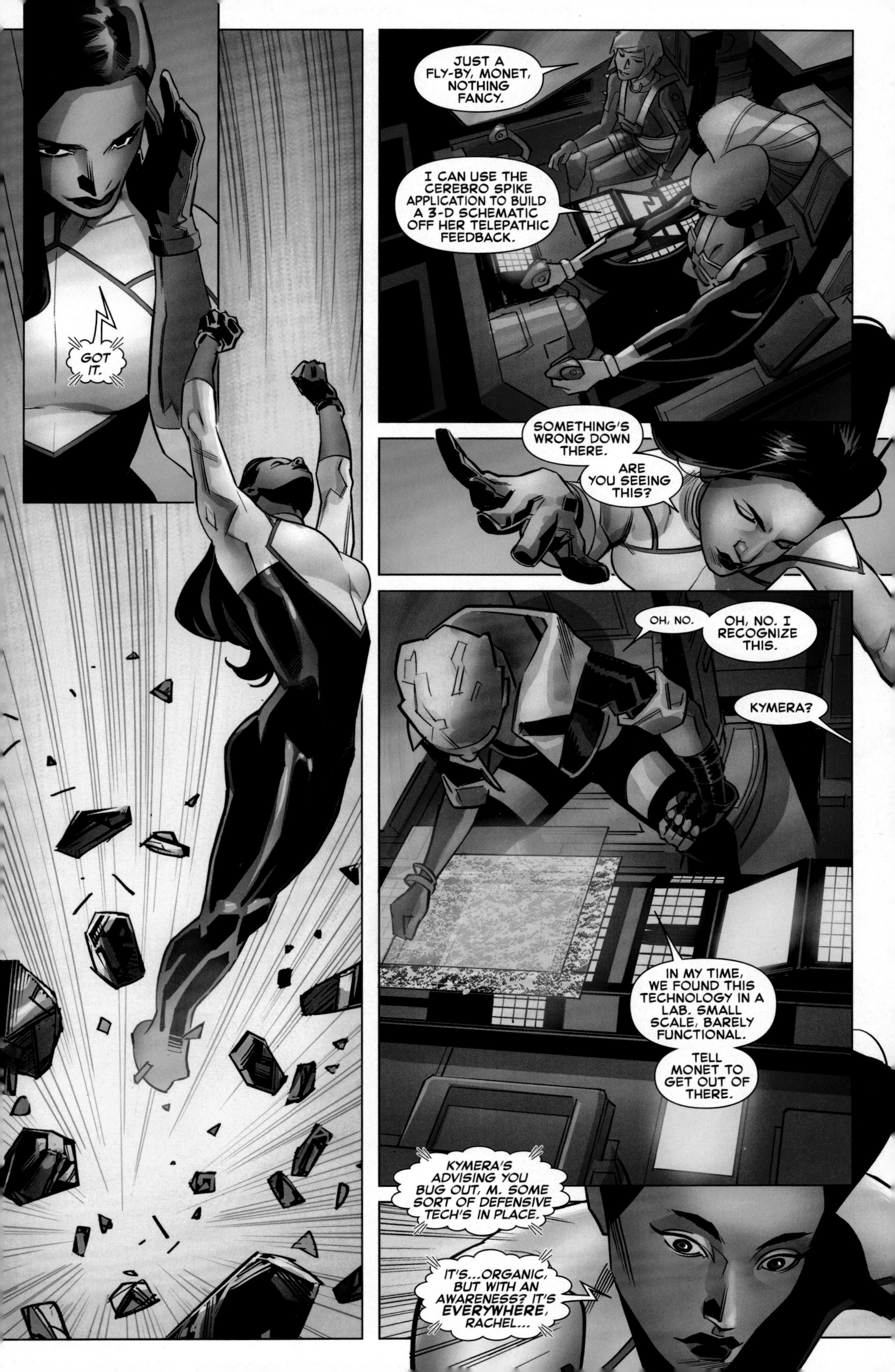
GOT IT.
JUST A FLY-BY, MONET, NOTHING FANCY.
I CAN USE THE CEREBRO SPIKE APPLICATION TO BUILD A 3-D SCHEMATIC OFF HER TELEPATHIC FEEDBACK.
SOMETHING'S WRONG DOWN THERE.
ARE YOU SEEING THIS?
OH, NO.
OH, NO. I RECOGNIZE THIS.
KYMERA?
IN MY TIME, WE FOUND THIS TECHNOLOGY IN A LAB. SMALL SCALE, BARELY FUNCTIONAL.
TELL MONET TO GET OUT OF THERE.
KYMERA'S ADVISING YOU BUG OUT, M. SOME SORT OF DEFENSIVE TECH'S IN PLACE.
IT'S...ORGANIC, BUT WITH AN AWARENESS? IT'S EVERYWHERE, RACHEL...

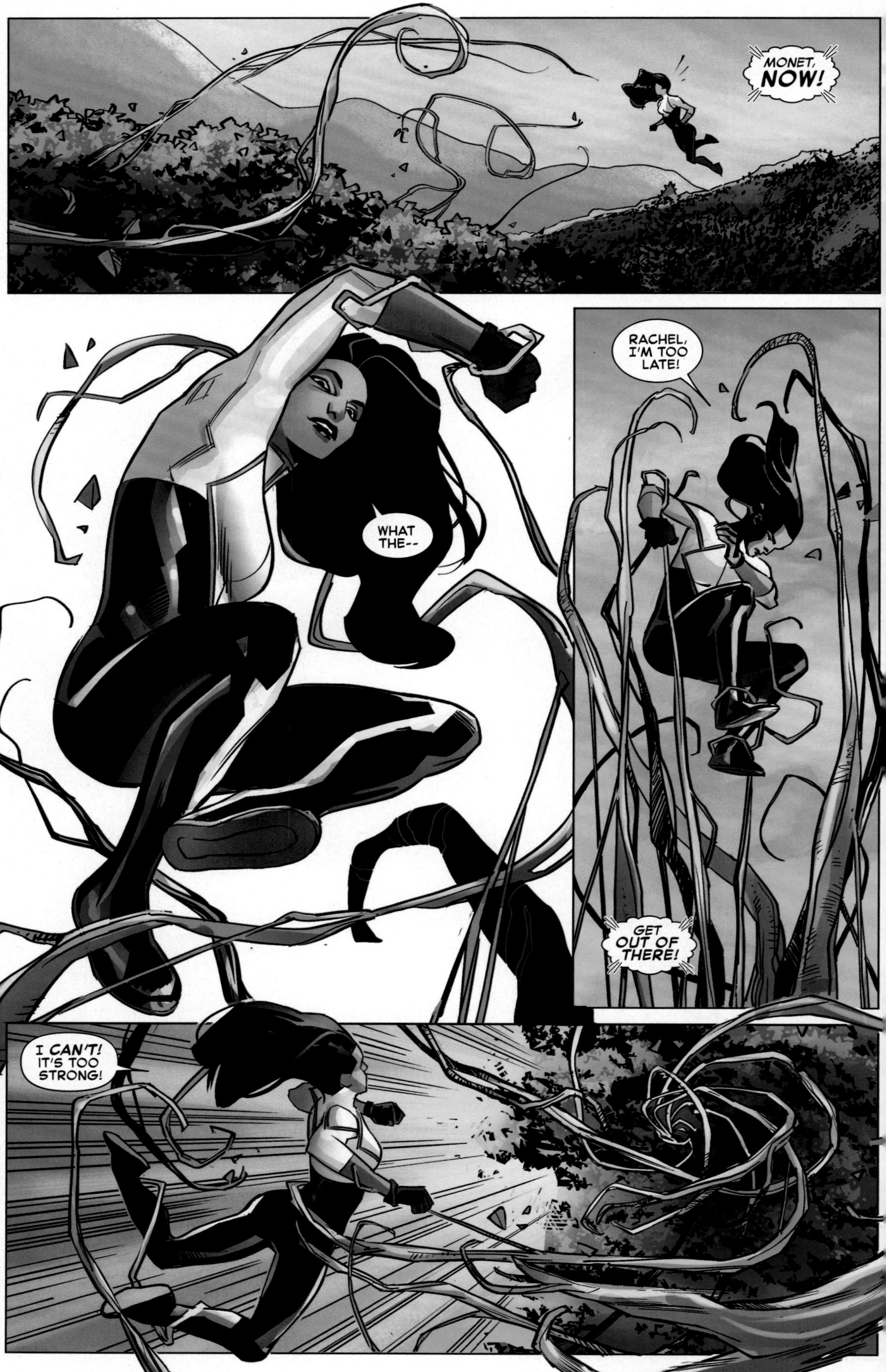
MONET, NOW!
WHAT THE--
RACHEL, I'M TOO LATE!
GET OUT OF THERE!
I CAN'T! IT'S TOO STRONG!

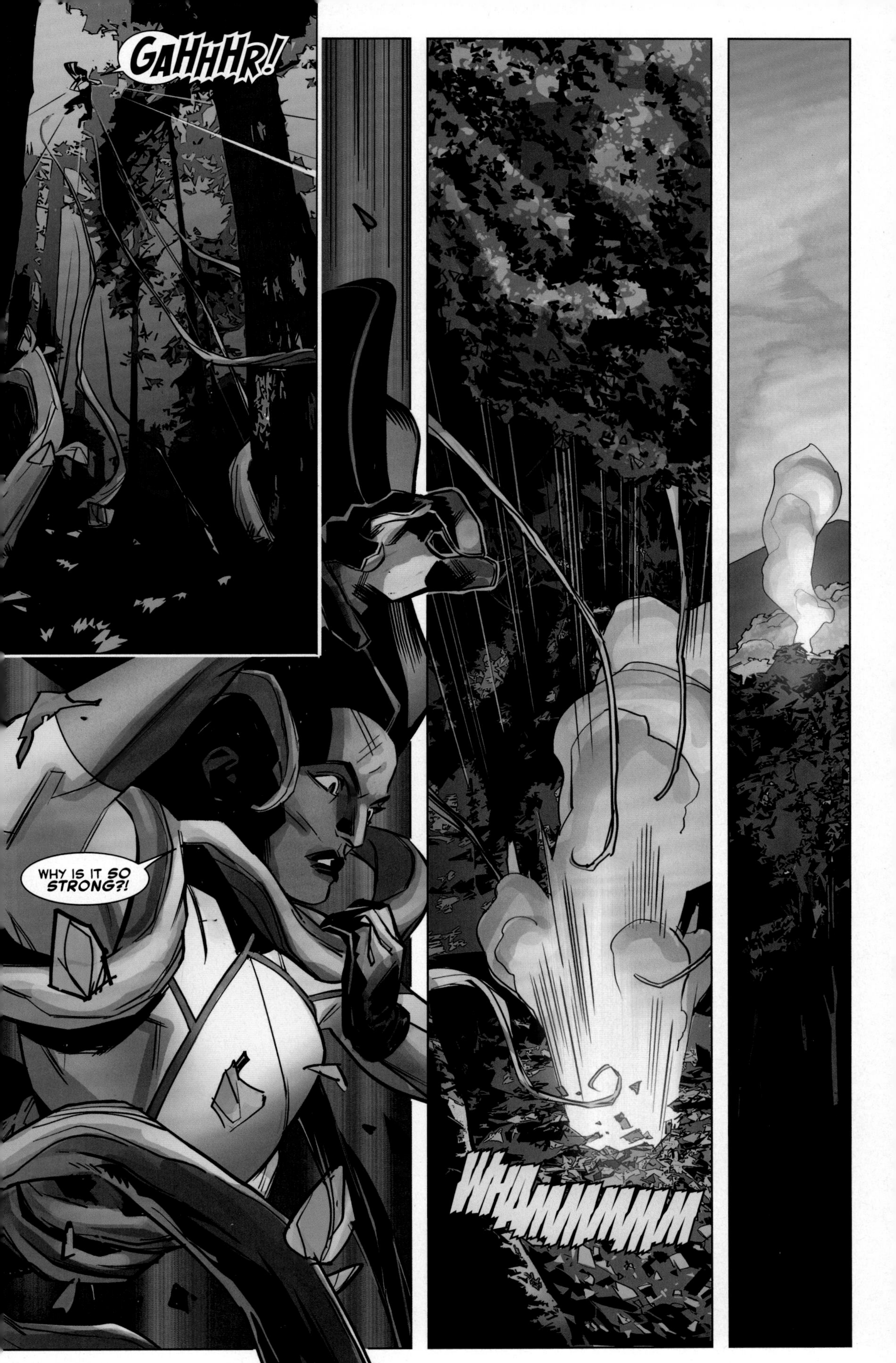
GAHHHR!
WHY IS IT SO STRONG?!
WHAMMMMMM

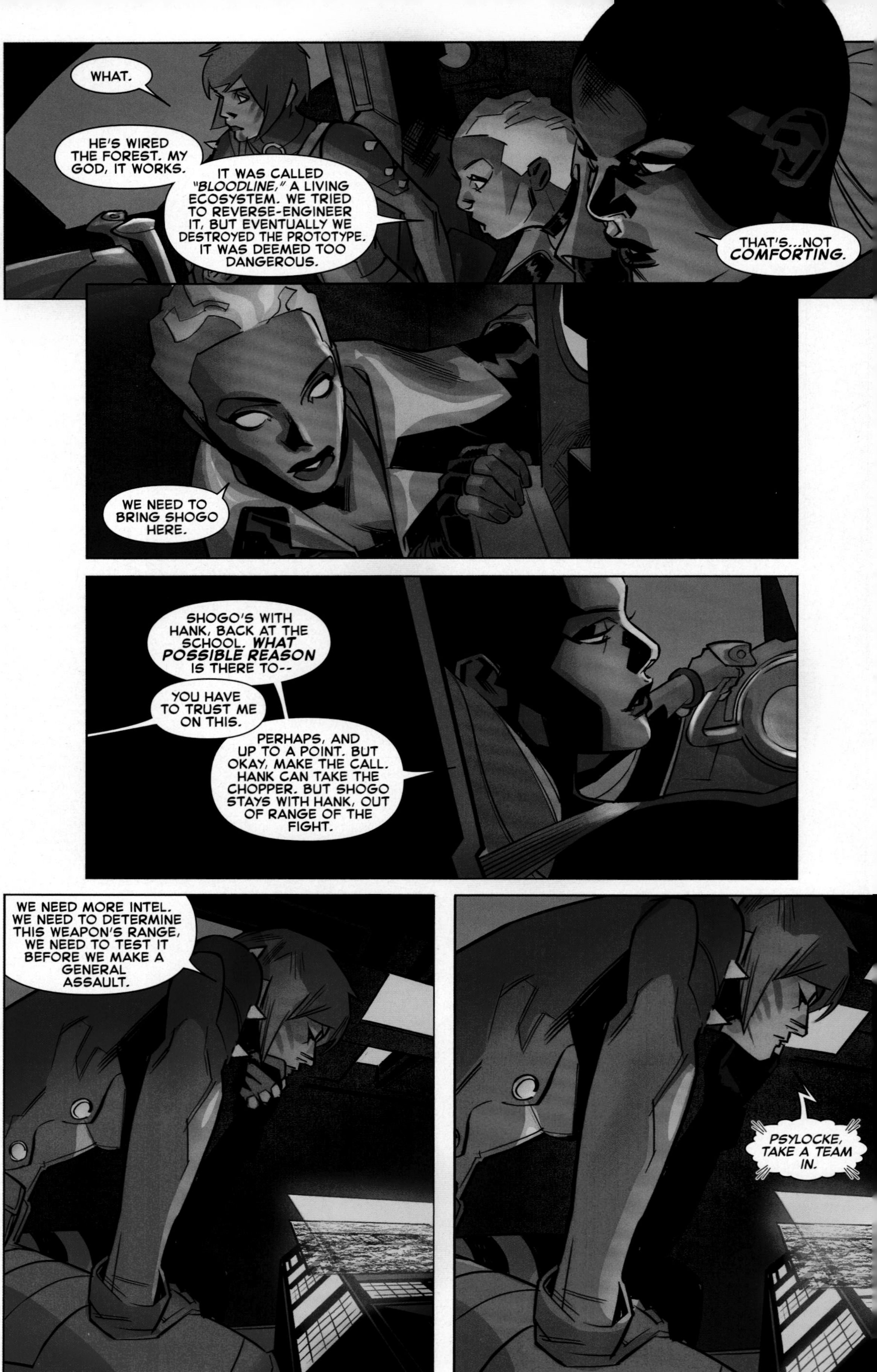
WHAT.
HE'S WIRED THE FOREST. MY GOD, IT WORKS.
IT WAS CALLED "BLOODLINE," A LIVING ECOSYSTEM. WE TRIED TO REVERSE-ENGINEER IT, BUT EVENTUALLY WE DESTROYED THE PROTOTYPE. IT WAS DEEMED TOO DANGEROUS.
THAT'S...NOT COMFORTING.
WE NEED TO BRING SHOGO HERE.
SHOGO'S WITH HANK, BACK AT THE SCHOOL. WHAT POSSIBLE REASON IS THERE TO--
YOU HAVE TO TRUST ME ON THIS.
PERHAPS, AND UP TO A POINT. BUT OKAY, MAKE THE CALL. HANK CAN TAKE THE CHOPPER. BUT SHOGO STAYS WITH HANK, OUT OF RANGE OF THE FIGHT.
WE NEED MORE INTEL. WE NEED TO DETERMINE THIS WEAPON'S RANGE, WE NEED TO TEST IT BEFORE WE MAKE A GENERAL ASSAULT.
PSYLOCKE, TAKE A TEAM IN.

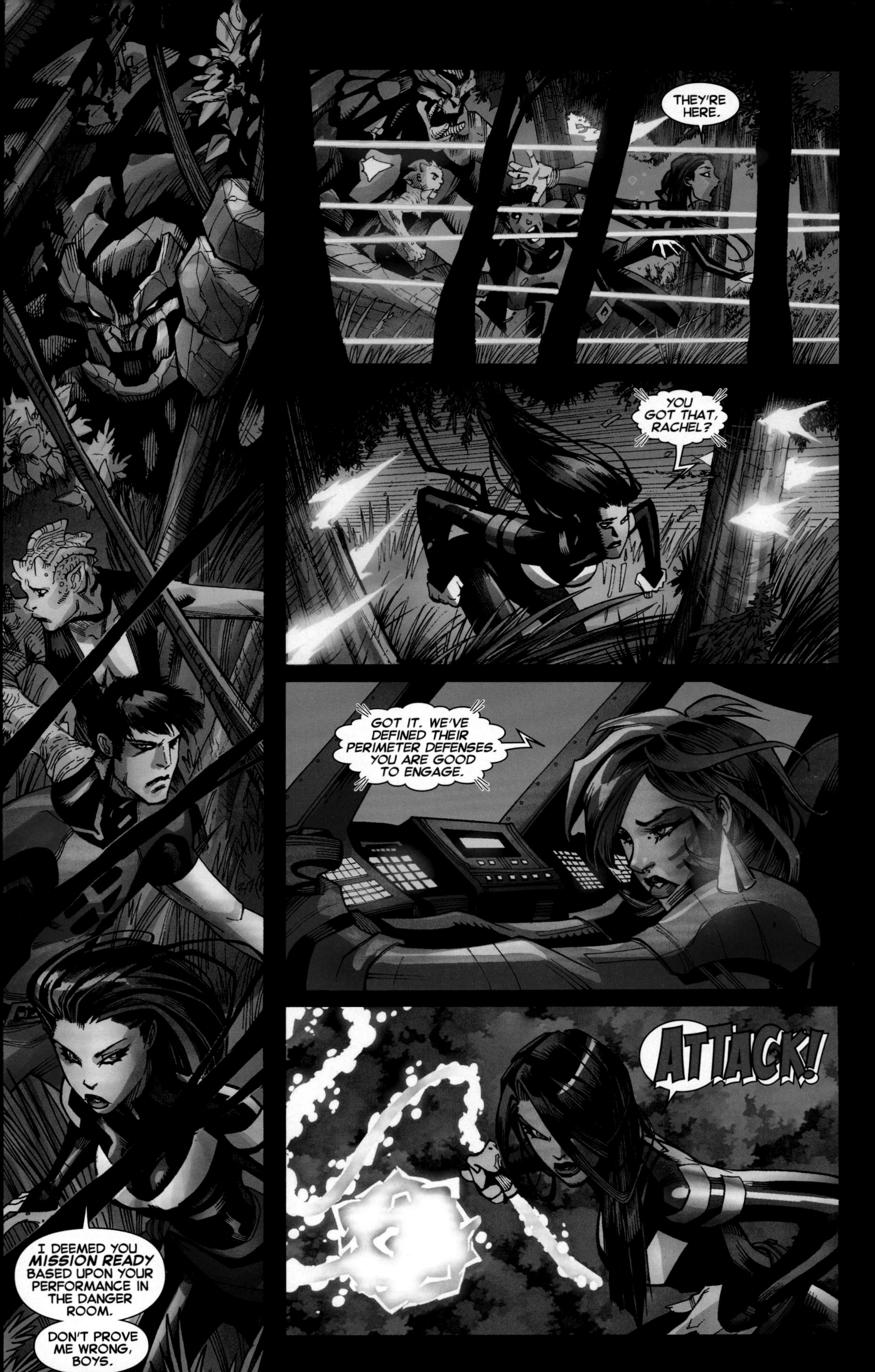
THEY'RE HERE.
YOU GOT THAT, RACHEL?
GOT IT. WE'VE DEFINED THEIR PERIMETER DEFENSES. YOU ARE GOOD TO ENGAGE.
ATTACK!
I DEEMED YOU MISSION READY BASED UPON YOUR PERFORMANCE IN THE DANGER ROOM.
DON'T PROVE ME WRONG, BOYS.

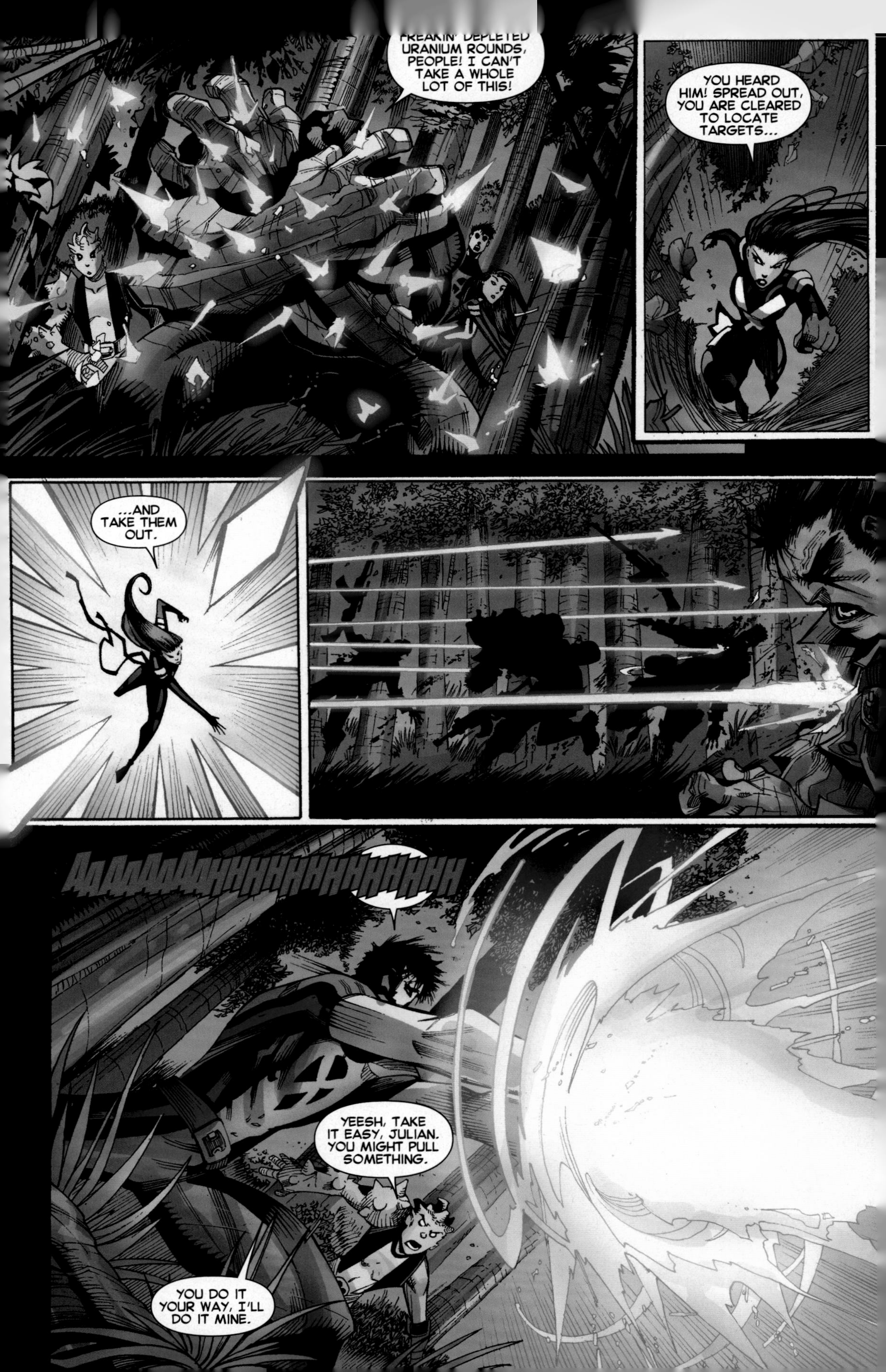
FREAKIN' DEPLETED URANIUM ROUNDS, PEOPLE! I CAN'T TAKE A WHOLE LOT OF THIS!
YOU HEARD HIM! SPREAD OUT, YOU ARE CLEARED TO LOCATE TARGETS...
...AND TAKE THEM OUT.
AAAAAAAHHHHHHHHHHHHHH
YEESH, TAKE IT EASY, JULIAN. YOU MIGHT PULL SOMETHING.
YOU DO IT YOUR WAY, I'LL DO IT MINE.

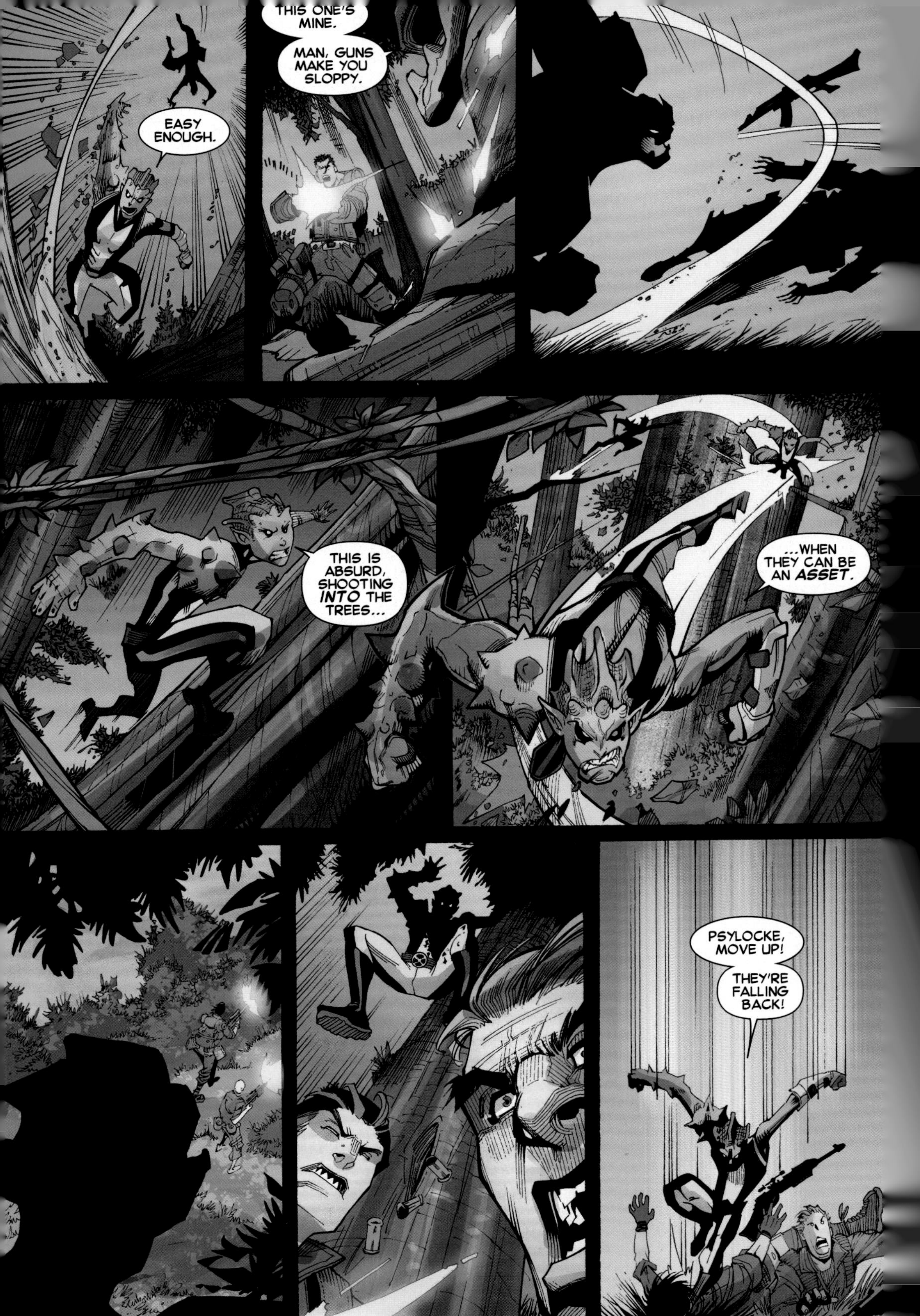
EASY ENOUGH.
THIS ONE'S MINE.
MAN, GUNS MAKE YOU SLOPPY.
THIS IS ABSURD, SHOOTING *INTO* THE TREES...
...WHEN THEY CAN BE AN *ASSET*.
PSYLOCKE, MOVE UP!
THEY'RE FALLING BACK!

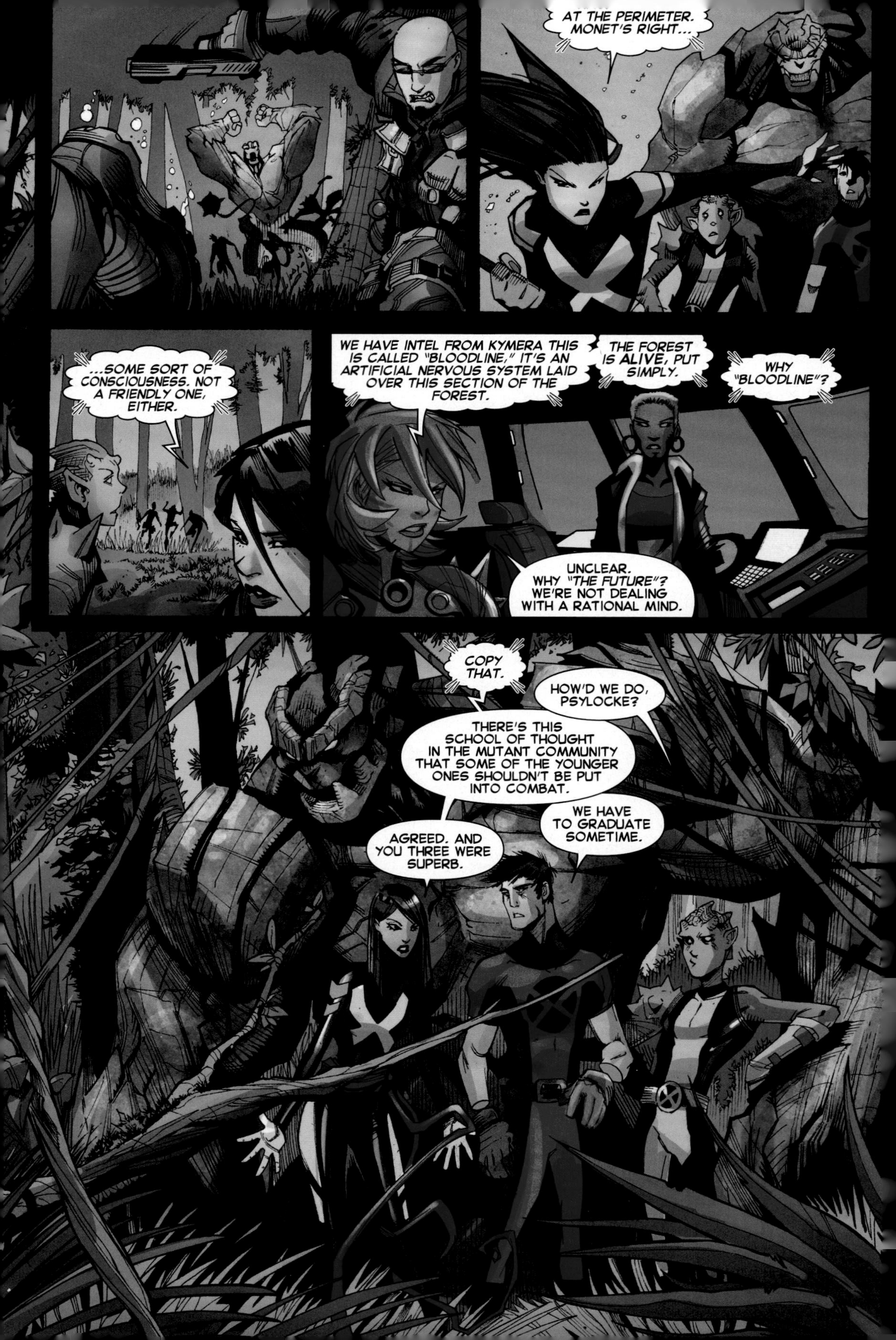
AT THE PERIMETER. MONET'S RIGHT...
...SOME SORT OF CONSCIOUSNESS. NOT A FRIENDLY ONE, EITHER.
WE HAVE INTEL FROM KYMERA THIS IS CALLED "BLOODLINE," IT'S AN ARTIFICIAL NERVOUS SYSTEM LAID OVER THIS SECTION OF THE FOREST.
THE FOREST IS ALIVE, PUT SIMPLY.
WHY "BLOODLINE"?
UNCLEAR. WHY "THE FUTURE"? WE'RE NOT DEALING WITH A RATIONAL MIND.
COPY THAT.
HOW'D WE DO, PSYLOCKE?
THERE'S THIS SCHOOL OF THOUGHT IN THE MUTANT COMMUNITY THAT SOME OF THE YOUNGER ONES SHOULDN'T BE PUT INTO COMBAT.
AGREED. AND YOU THREE WERE SUPERB.
WE HAVE TO GRADUATE SOMETIME.

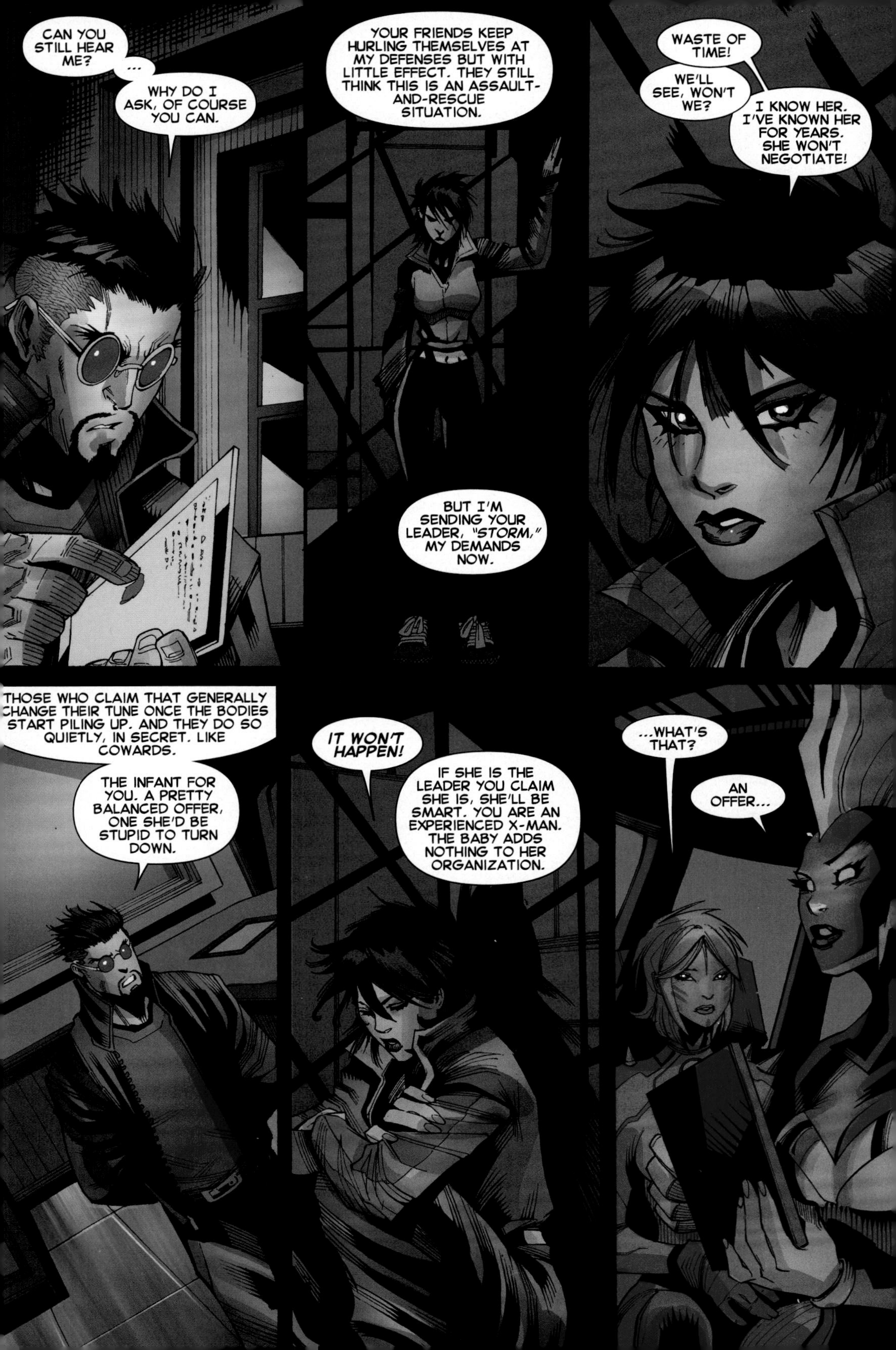
CAN YOU STILL HEAR ME?
...
WHY DO I ASK, OF COURSE YOU CAN.
YOUR FRIENDS KEEP HURLING THEMSELVES AT MY DEFENSES BUT WITH LITTLE EFFECT. THEY STILL THINK THIS IS AN ASSAULT-AND-RESCUE SITUATION.
BUT I'M SENDING YOUR LEADER, "STORM," MY DEMANDS NOW.
WASTE OF TIME!
WE'LL SEE, WON'T WE?
I KNOW HER. I'VE KNOWN HER FOR YEARS. SHE WON'T NEGOTIATE!
THOSE WHO CLAIM THAT GENERALLY CHANGE THEIR TUNE ONCE THE BODIES START PILING UP. AND THEY DO SO QUIETLY, IN SECRET. LIKE COWARDS.
THE INFANT FOR YOU. A PRETTY BALANCED OFFER, ONE SHE'D BE STUPID TO TURN DOWN.
IT WON'T HAPPEN!
IF SHE IS THE LEADER YOU CLAIM SHE IS, SHE'LL BE SMART. YOU ARE AN EXPERIENCED X-MAN. THE BABY ADDS NOTHING TO HER ORGANIZATION.
...WHAT'S THAT?
AN OFFER...

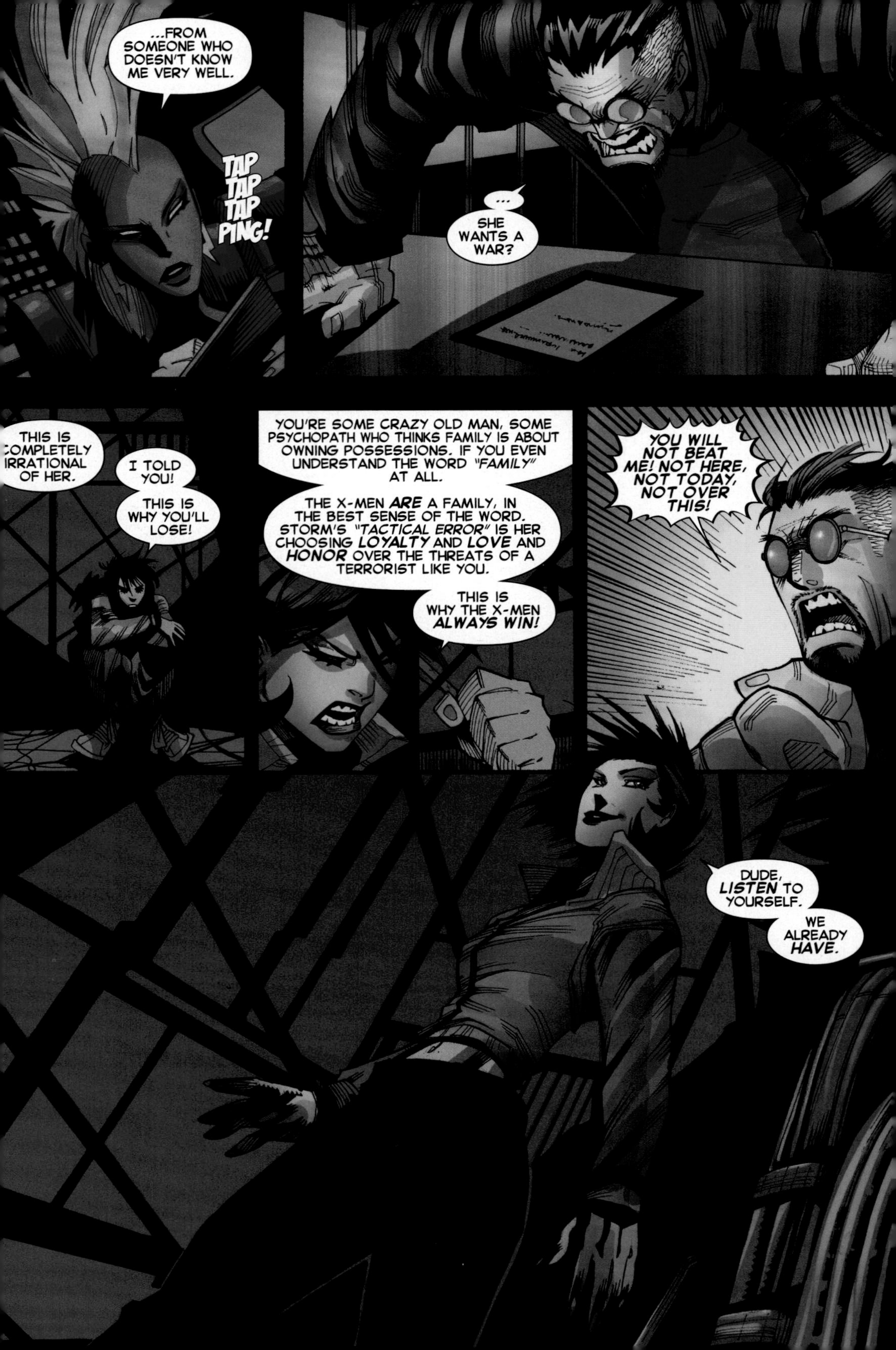
...FROM SOMEONE WHO DOESN'T KNOW ME VERY WELL.
TAP TAP TAP PING!
...
SHE WANTS A WAR?
THIS IS COMPLETELY IRRATIONAL OF HER.
I TOLD YOU!
THIS IS WHY YOU'LL LOSE!
YOU'RE SOME CRAZY OLD MAN, SOME PSYCHOPATH WHO THINKS FAMILY IS ABOUT OWNING POSSESSIONS. IF YOU EVEN UNDERSTAND THE WORD "FAMILY" AT ALL.
THE X-MEN ARE A FAMILY, IN THE BEST SENSE OF THE WORD. STORM'S "TACTICAL ERROR" IS HER CHOOSING LOYALTY AND LOVE AND HONOR OVER THE THREATS OF A TERRORIST LIKE YOU.
THIS IS WHY THE X-MEN ALWAYS WIN!
YOU WILL NOT BEAT ME! NOT HERE, NOT TODAY, NOT OVER THIS!
DUDE, LISTEN TO YOURSELF.
WE ALREADY HAVE.

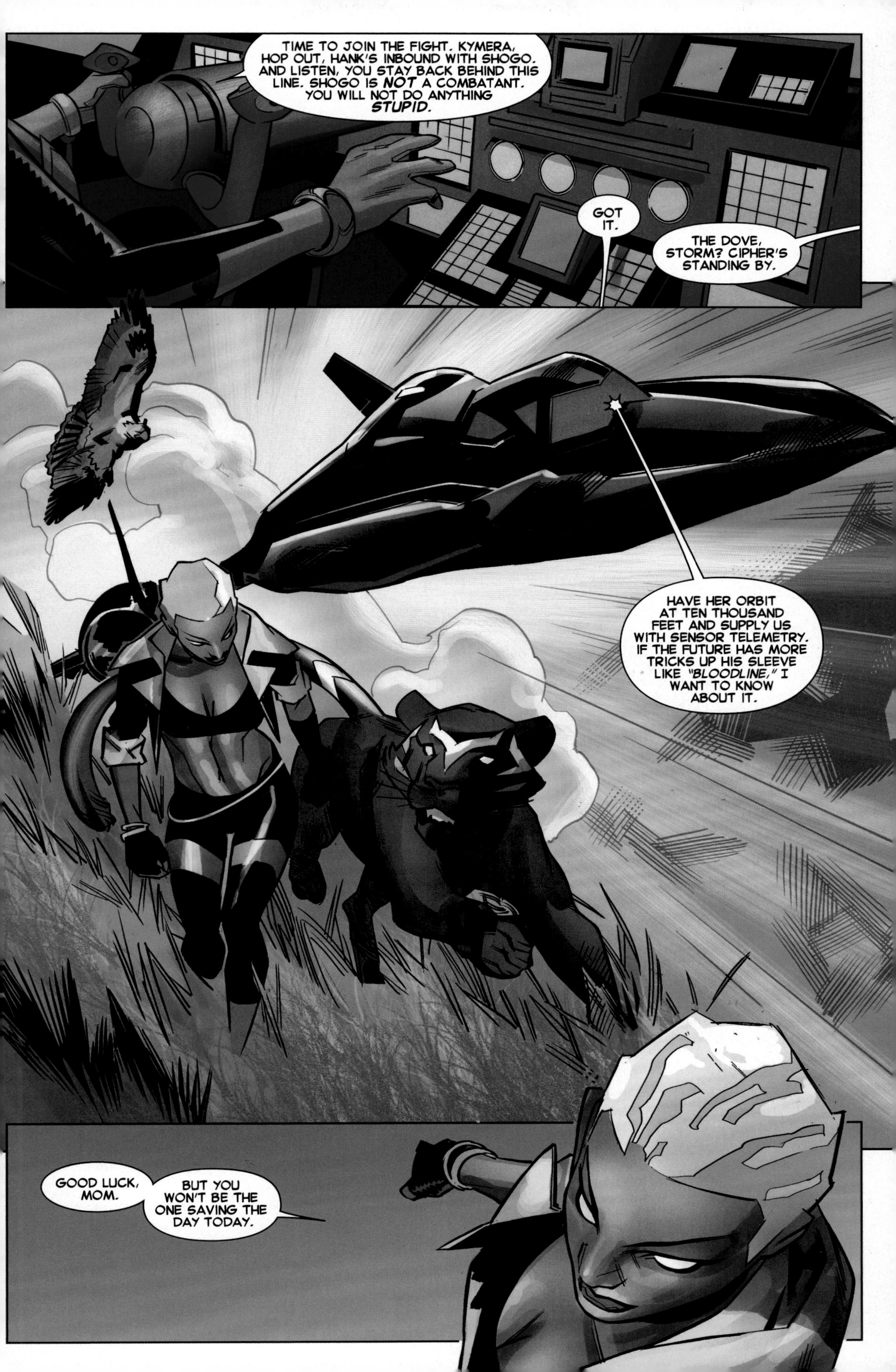
TIME TO JOIN THE FIGHT. KYMERA, HOP OUT, HANK'S INBOUND WITH SHOGO. AND LISTEN, YOU STAY BACK BEHIND THIS LINE. SHOGO IS NOT A COMBATANT. YOU WILL NOT DO ANYTHING STUPID.
GOT IT.
THE DOVE, STORM? CIPHER'S STANDING BY.
HAVE HER ORBIT AT TEN THOUSAND FEET AND SUPPLY US WITH SENSOR TELEMETRY. IF THE FUTURE HAS MORE TRICKS UP HIS SLEEVE LIKE "BLOODLINE," I WANT TO KNOW ABOUT IT.
GOOD LUCK, MOM.
BUT YOU WON'T BE THE ONE SAVING THE DAY TODAY.

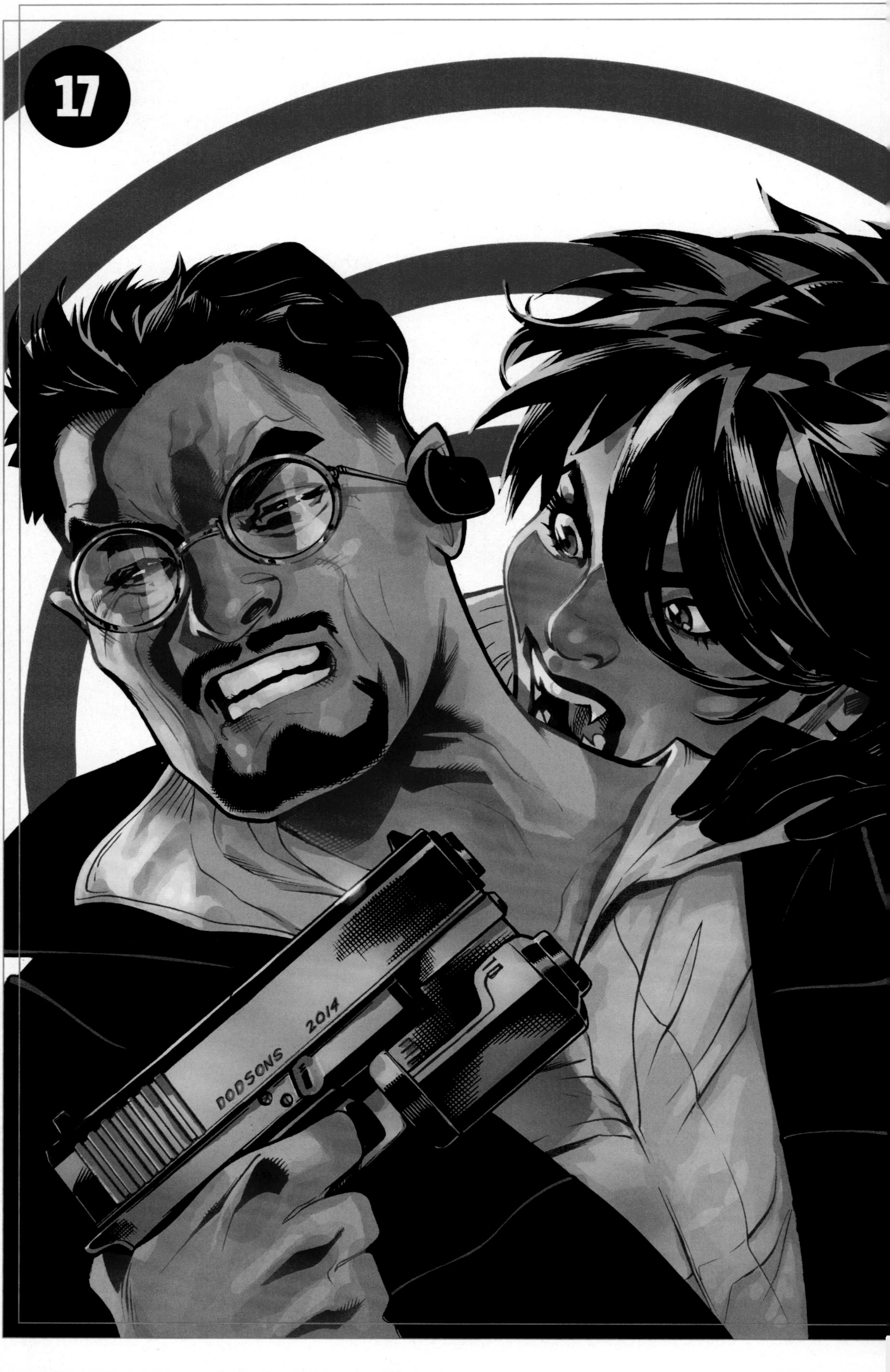
17
DODSONS 2014

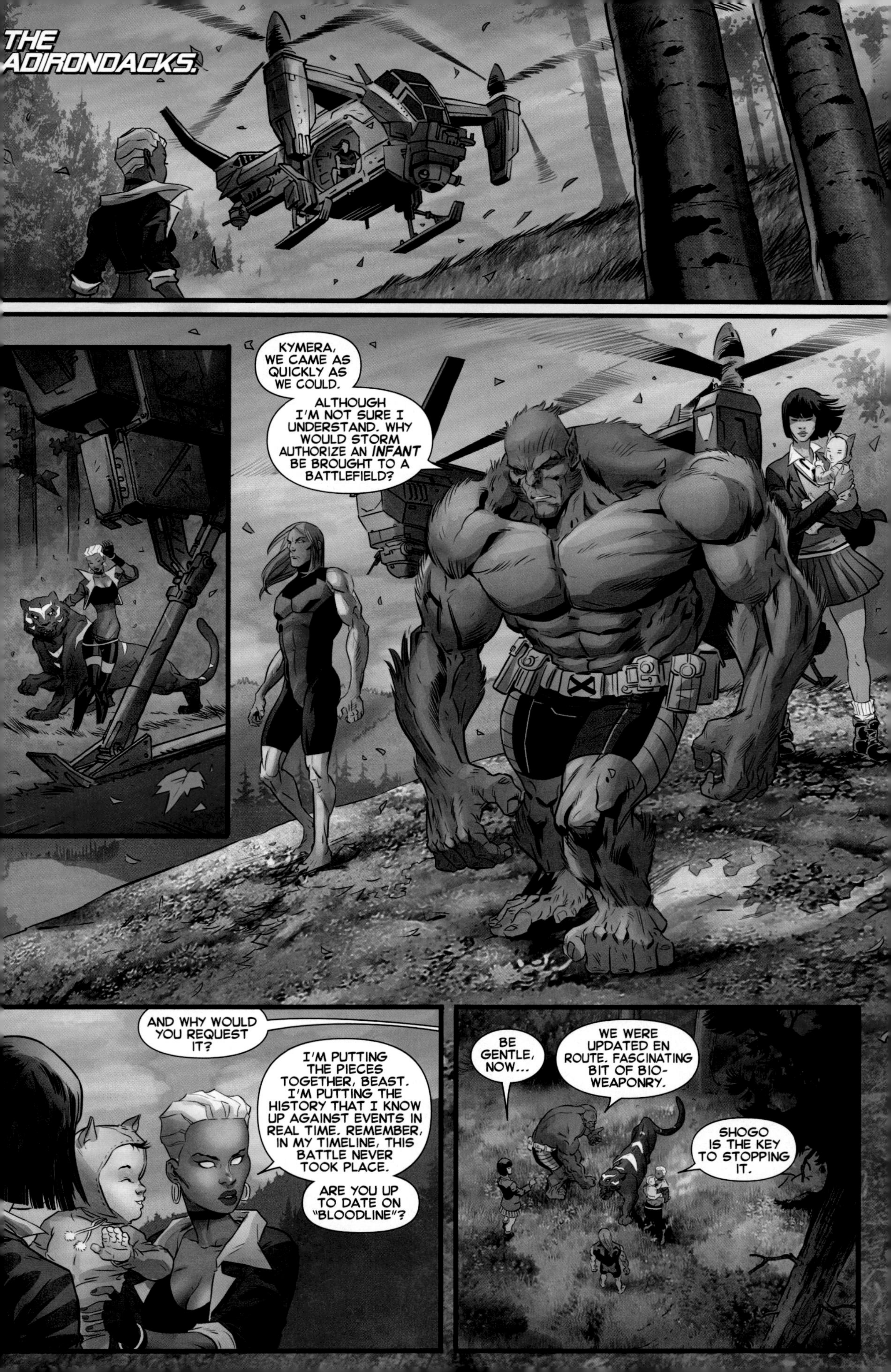
THE ADIRONDACKS.
KYMERA, WE CAME AS QUICKLY AS WE COULD.
ALTHOUGH I'M NOT SURE I UNDERSTAND. WHY WOULD STORM AUTHORIZE AN INFANT BE BROUGHT TO A BATTLEFIELD?
AND WHY WOULD YOU REQUEST IT?
I'M PUTTING THE PIECES TOGETHER, BEAST. I'M PUTTING THE HISTORY THAT I KNOW UP AGAINST EVENTS IN REAL TIME. REMEMBER, IN MY TIMELINE, THIS BATTLE NEVER TOOK PLACE.
ARE YOU UP TO DATE ON "BLOODLINE"?
BE GENTLE, NOW...
WE WERE UPDATED EN ROUTE. FASCINATING BIT OF BIO-WEAPONRY.
SHOGO IS THE KEY TO STOPPING IT.

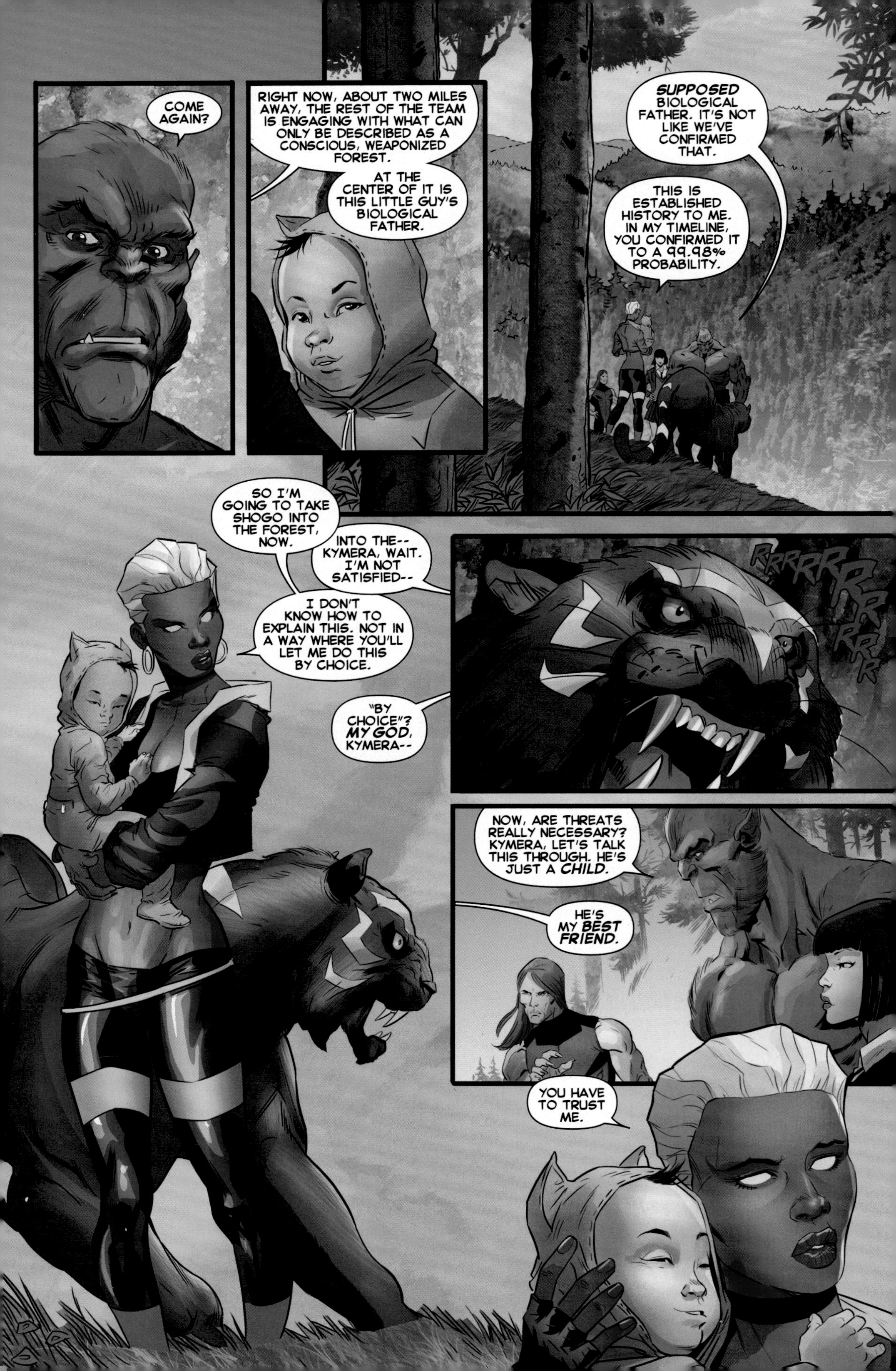
COME AGAIN?
RIGHT NOW, ABOUT TWO MILES AWAY, THE REST OF THE TEAM IS ENGAGING WITH WHAT CAN ONLY BE DESCRIBED AS A CONSCIOUS, WEAPONIZED FOREST.
AT THE CENTER OF IT IS THIS LITTLE GUY'S BIOLOGICAL FATHER.
SUPPOSED BIOLOGICAL FATHER. IT'S NOT LIKE WE'VE CONFIRMED THAT.
THIS IS ESTABLISHED HISTORY TO ME. IN MY TIMELINE, YOU CONFIRMED IT TO A 99.98% PROBABILITY.
SO I'M GOING TO TAKE SHOGO INTO THE FOREST, NOW.
INTO THE-- KYMERA, WAIT. I'M NOT SATISFIED--
I DON'T KNOW HOW TO EXPLAIN THIS. NOT IN A WAY WHERE YOU'LL LET ME DO THIS BY CHOICE.
"BY CHOICE"? MY GOD, KYMERA--
RRRRRRRRRRRR
NOW, ARE THREATS REALLY NECESSARY? KYMERA, LET'S TALK THIS THROUGH. HE'S JUST A CHILD.
HE'S MY BEST FRIEND.
YOU HAVE TO TRUST ME.

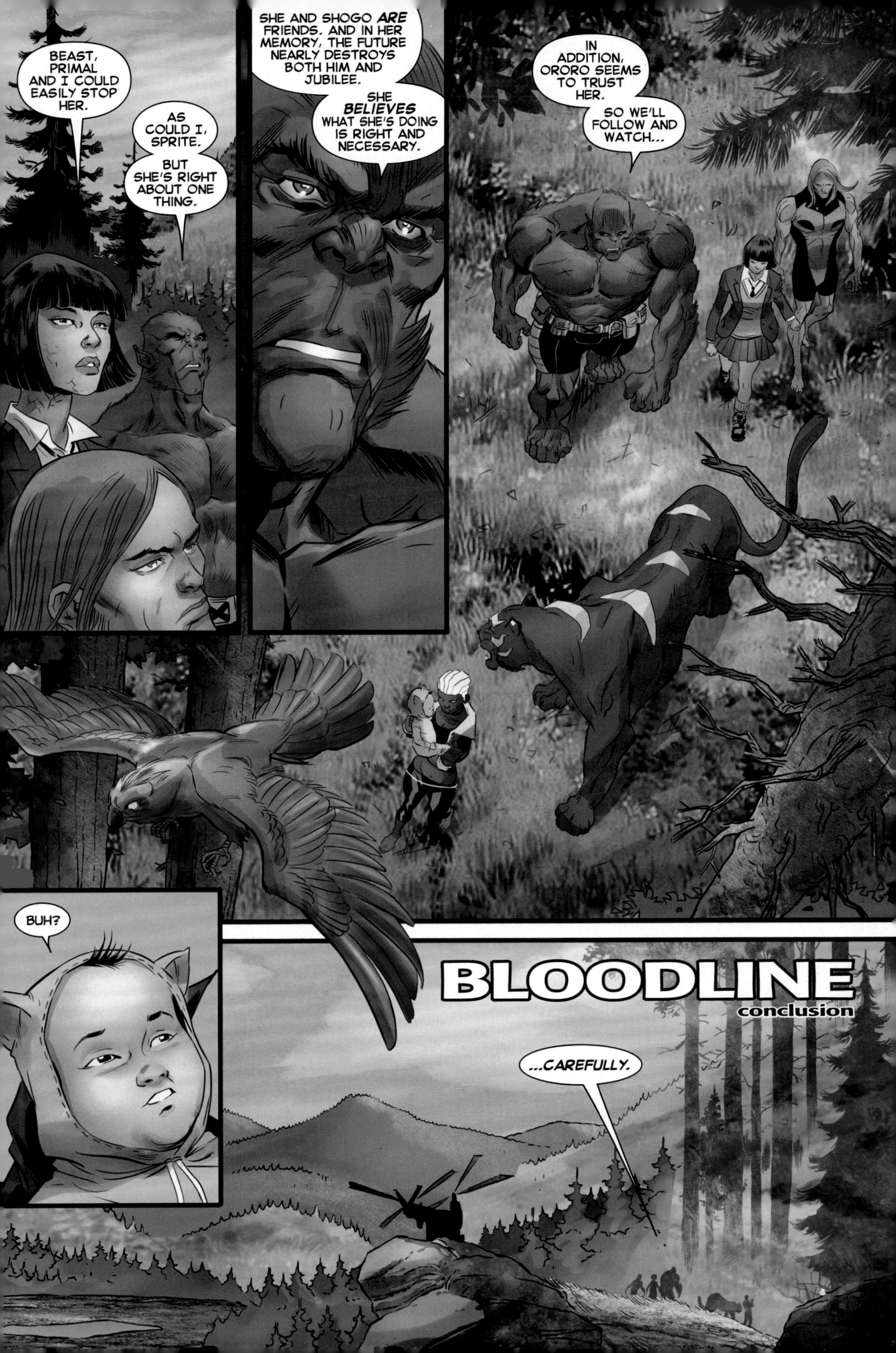

BEAST, PRIMAL AND I COULD EASILY STOP HER.
AS COULD I, SPRITE.
BUT SHE'S RIGHT ABOUT ONE THING.
SHE AND SHOGO ARE FRIENDS. AND IN HER MEMORY, THE FUTURE NEARLY DESTROYS BOTH HIM AND JUBILEE.
SHE BELIEVES WHAT SHE'S DOING IS RIGHT AND NECESSARY.
IN ADDITION, ORORO SEEMS TO TRUST HER.
SO WE'LL FOLLOW AND WATCH...
BUH?
BLOODLINE
conclusion
...CAREFULLY.

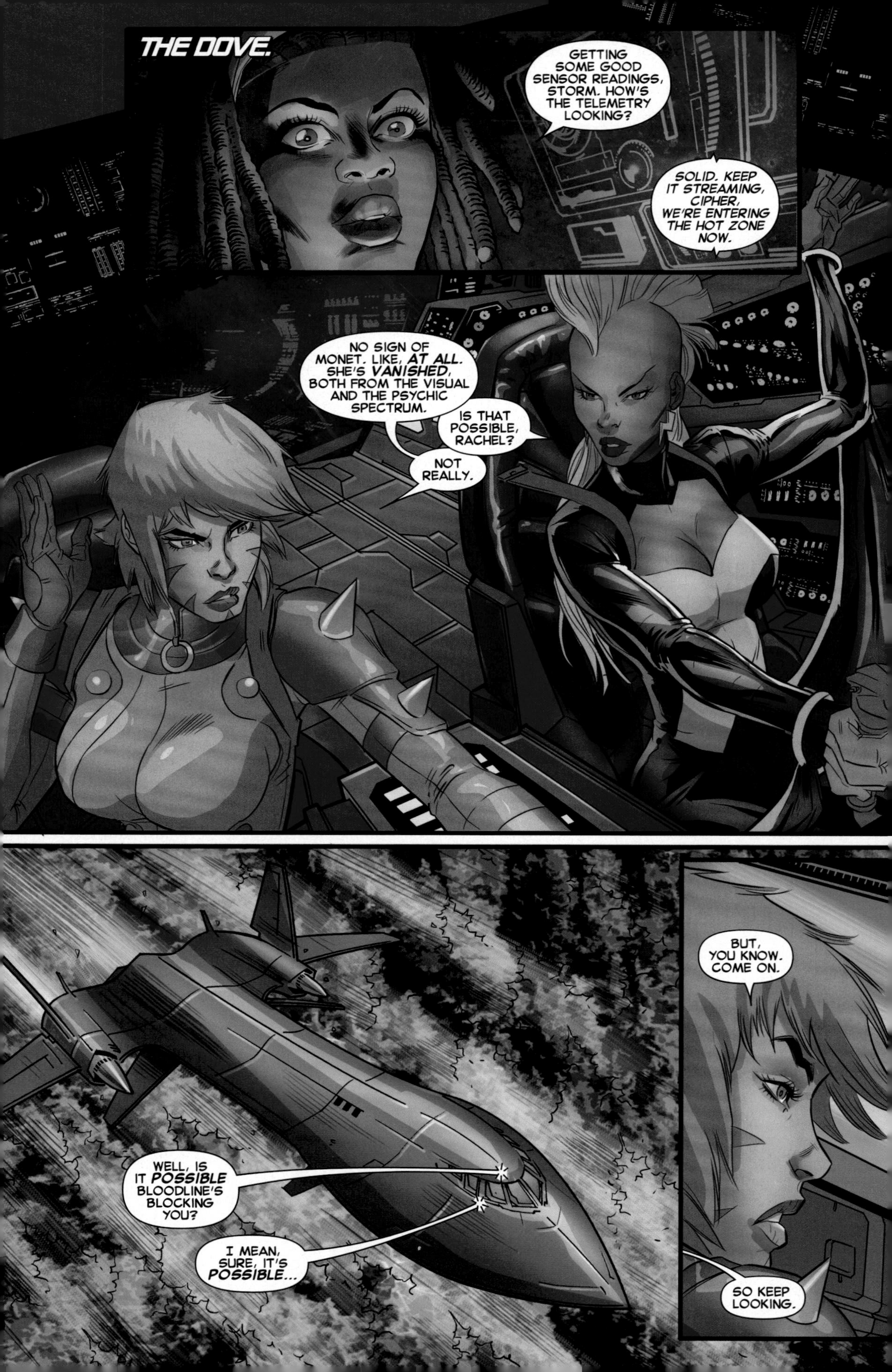
THE DOVE.
GETTING SOME GOOD SENSOR READINGS, STORM. HOW'S THE TELEMETRY LOOKING?
SOLID. KEEP IT STREAMING, CIPHER, WE'RE ENTERING THE HOT ZONE NOW.
NO SIGN OF MONET. LIKE, AT ALL. SHE'S VANISHED, BOTH FROM THE VISUAL AND THE PSYCHIC SPECTRUM.
IS THAT POSSIBLE, RACHEL?
NOT REALLY.
WELL, IS IT POSSIBLE BLOODLINE'S BLOCKING YOU?
I MEAN, SURE, IT'S POSSIBLE...
BUT, YOU KNOW. COME ON.
SO KEEP LOOKING.

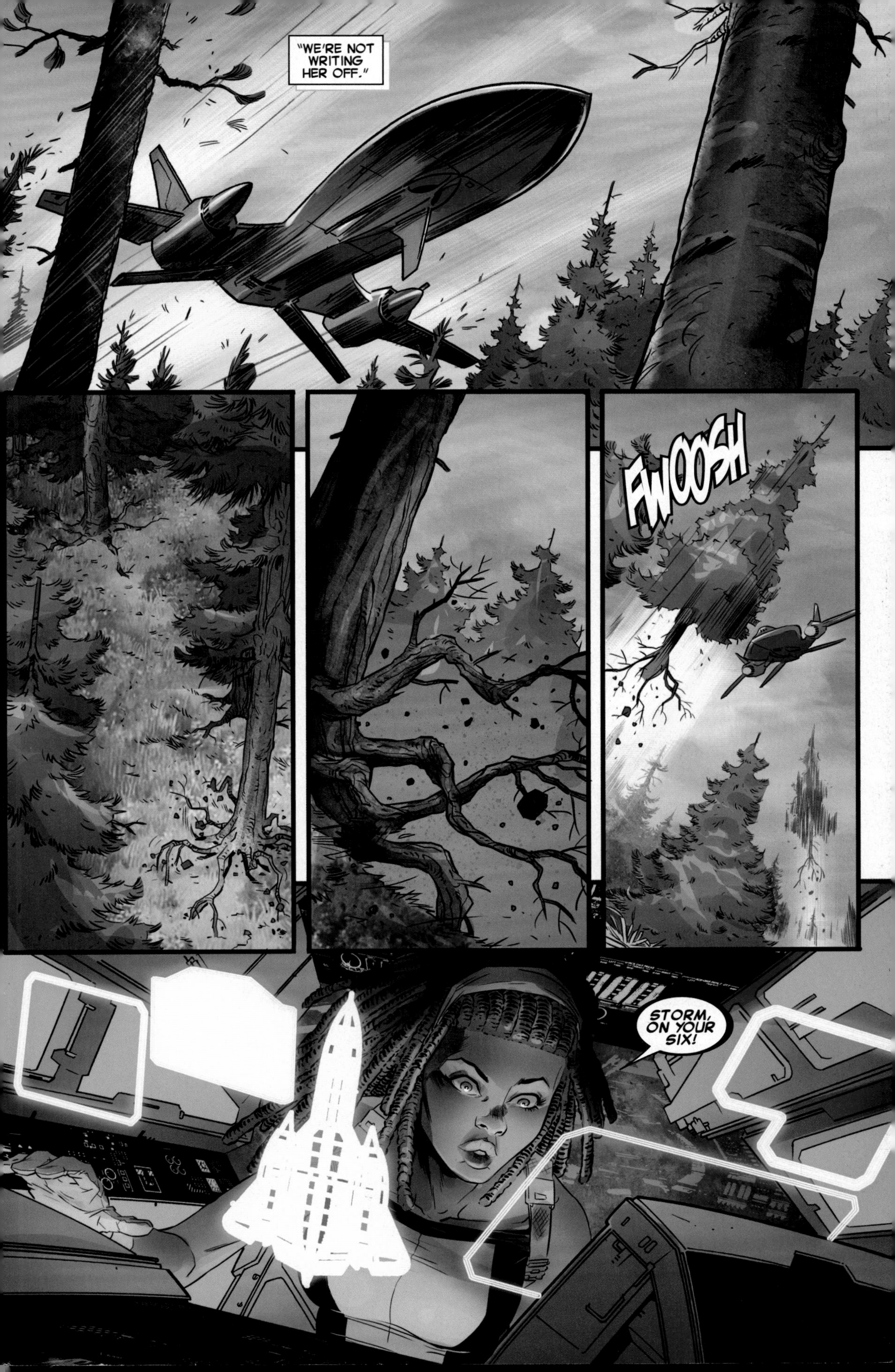
"WE'RE NOT WRITING HER OFF."
FWOOSH
STORM, ON YOUR SIX!

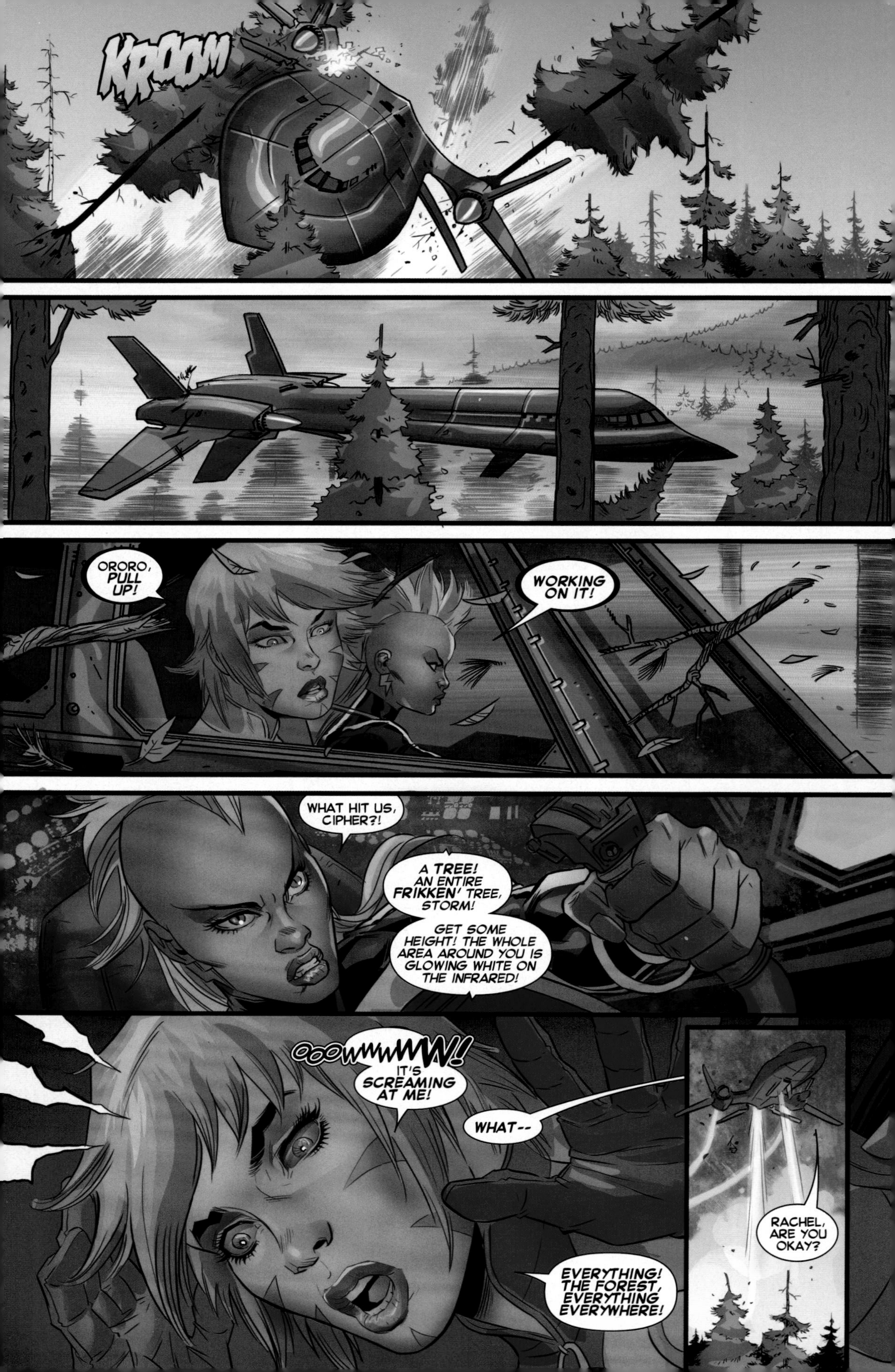
KROOM
ORORO, PULL UP!
WORKING ON IT!
WHAT HIT US, CIPHER?!
A TREE! AN ENTIRE FRIKKEN' TREE, STORM!
GET SOME HEIGHT! THE WHOLE AREA AROUND YOU IS GLOWING WHITE ON THE INFRARED!
OOOWWWWWW!
IT'S SCREAMING AT ME!
WHAT--
EVERYTHING! THE FOREST, EVERYTHING EVERYWHERE!
RACHEL, ARE YOU OKAY?

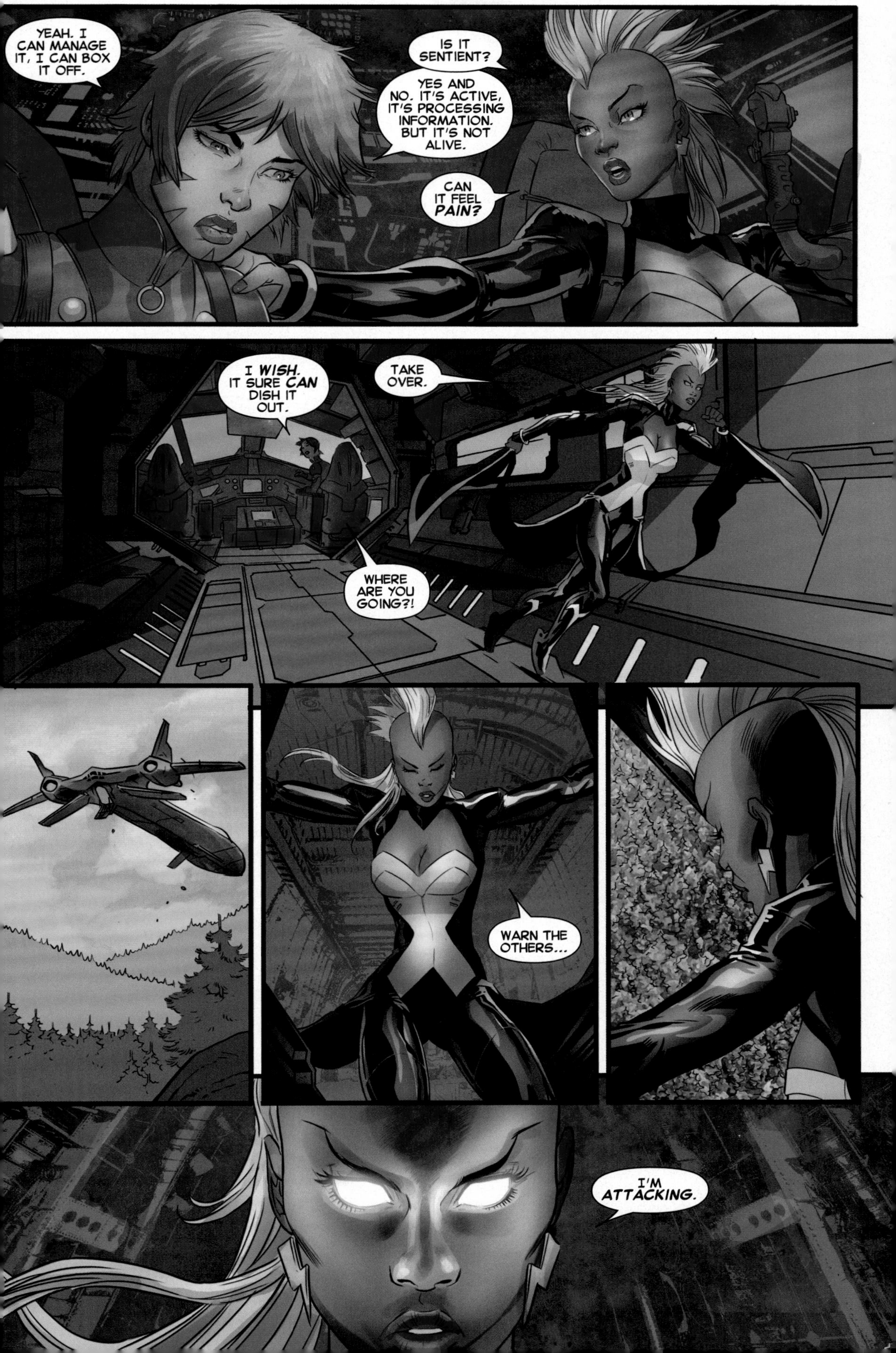
YEAH. I CAN MANAGE IT, I CAN BOX IT OFF.
IS IT SENTIENT?
YES AND NO. IT'S ACTIVE, IT'S PROCESSING INFORMATION. BUT IT'S NOT ALIVE.
CAN IT FEEL **PAIN?**
I ***WISH.*** IT SURE ***CAN*** DISH IT OUT.
TAKE OVER.
WHERE ARE YOU GOING?!
WARN THE OTHERS...
I'M **ATTACKING.**

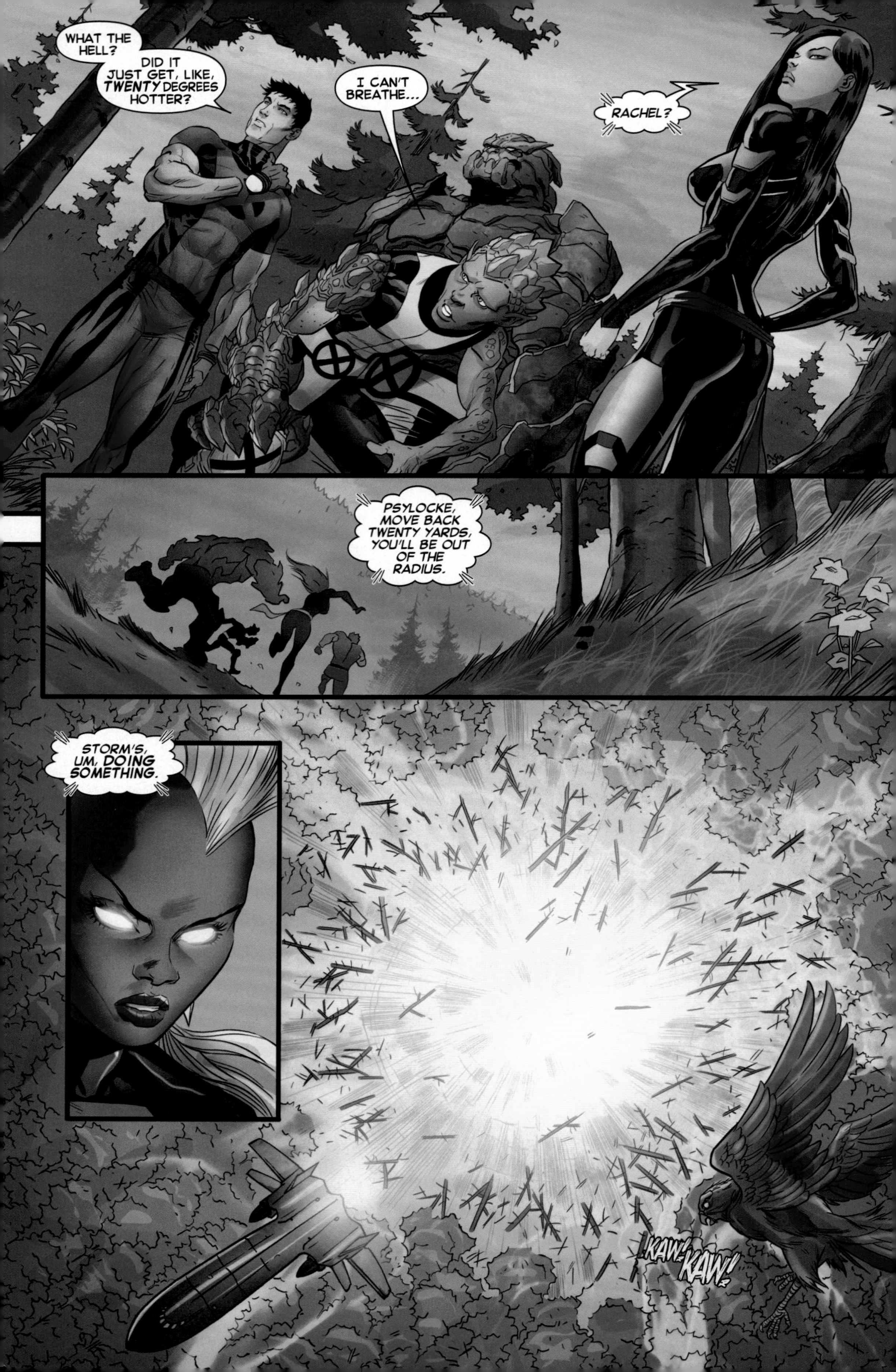
WHAT THE HELL?
DID IT JUST GET, LIKE, TWENTY DEGREES HOTTER?
I CAN'T BREATHE...
RACHEL?
PSYLOCKE, MOVE BACK TWENTY YARDS, YOU'LL BE OUT OF THE RADIUS.
STORM'S, UM, DOING SOMETHING.
KAW-KAW!

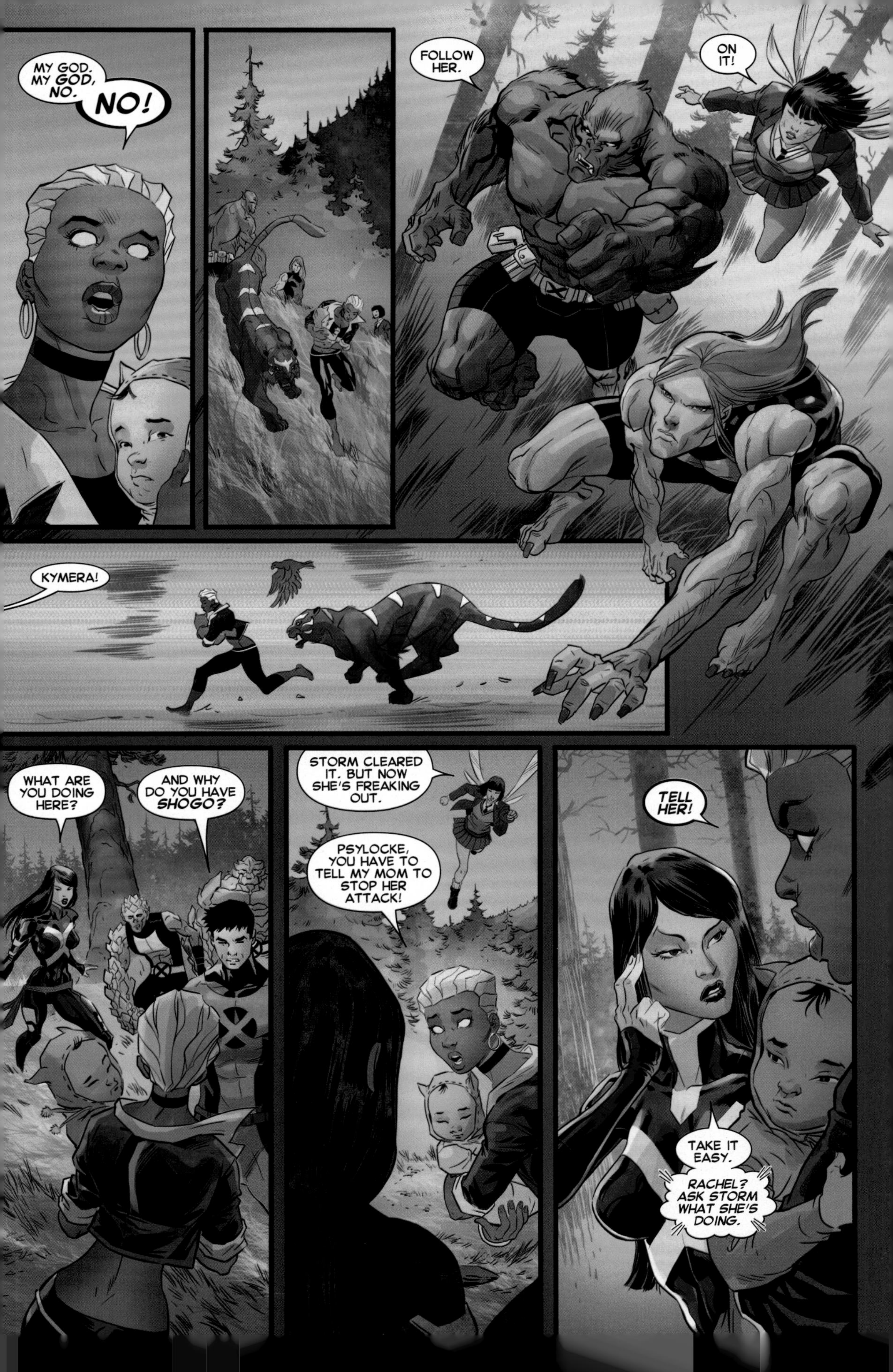

MY GOD. MY GOD, NO. NO!
FOLLOW HER.
ON IT!
KYMERA!
WHAT ARE YOU DOING HERE?
AND WHY DO YOU HAVE SHOGO?
STORM CLEARED IT. BUT NOW SHE'S FREAKING OUT.
PSYLOCKE, YOU HAVE TO TELL MY MOM TO STOP HER ATTACK!
TELL HER!
TAKE IT EASY.
RACHEL? ASK STORM WHAT SHE'S DOING.

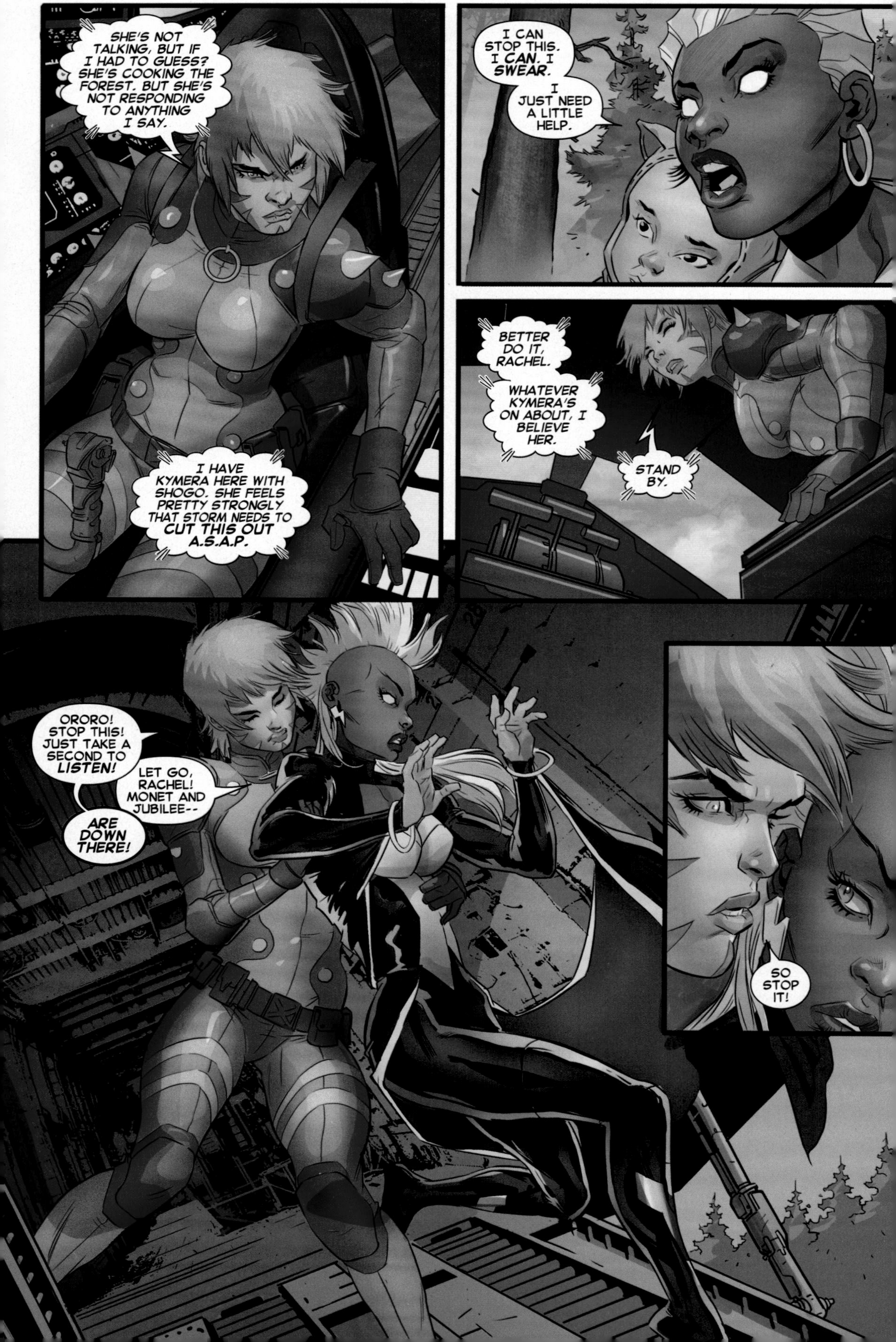
SHE'S NOT TALKING, BUT IF I HAD TO GUESS? SHE'S COOKING THE FOREST. BUT SHE'S NOT RESPONDING TO ANYTHING I SAY.
I HAVE KYMERA HERE WITH SHOGO. SHE FEELS PRETTY STRONGLY THAT STORM NEEDS TO CUT THIS OUT A.S.A.P.
I CAN STOP THIS. I CAN. I SWEAR.
I JUST NEED A LITTLE HELP.
BETTER DO IT, RACHEL.
WHATEVER KYMERA'S ON ABOUT, I BELIEVE HER.
STAND BY.
ORORO! STOP THIS! JUST TAKE A SECOND TO LISTEN!
LET GO, RACHEL! MONET AND JUBILEE--
ARE DOWN THERE!
SO STOP IT!

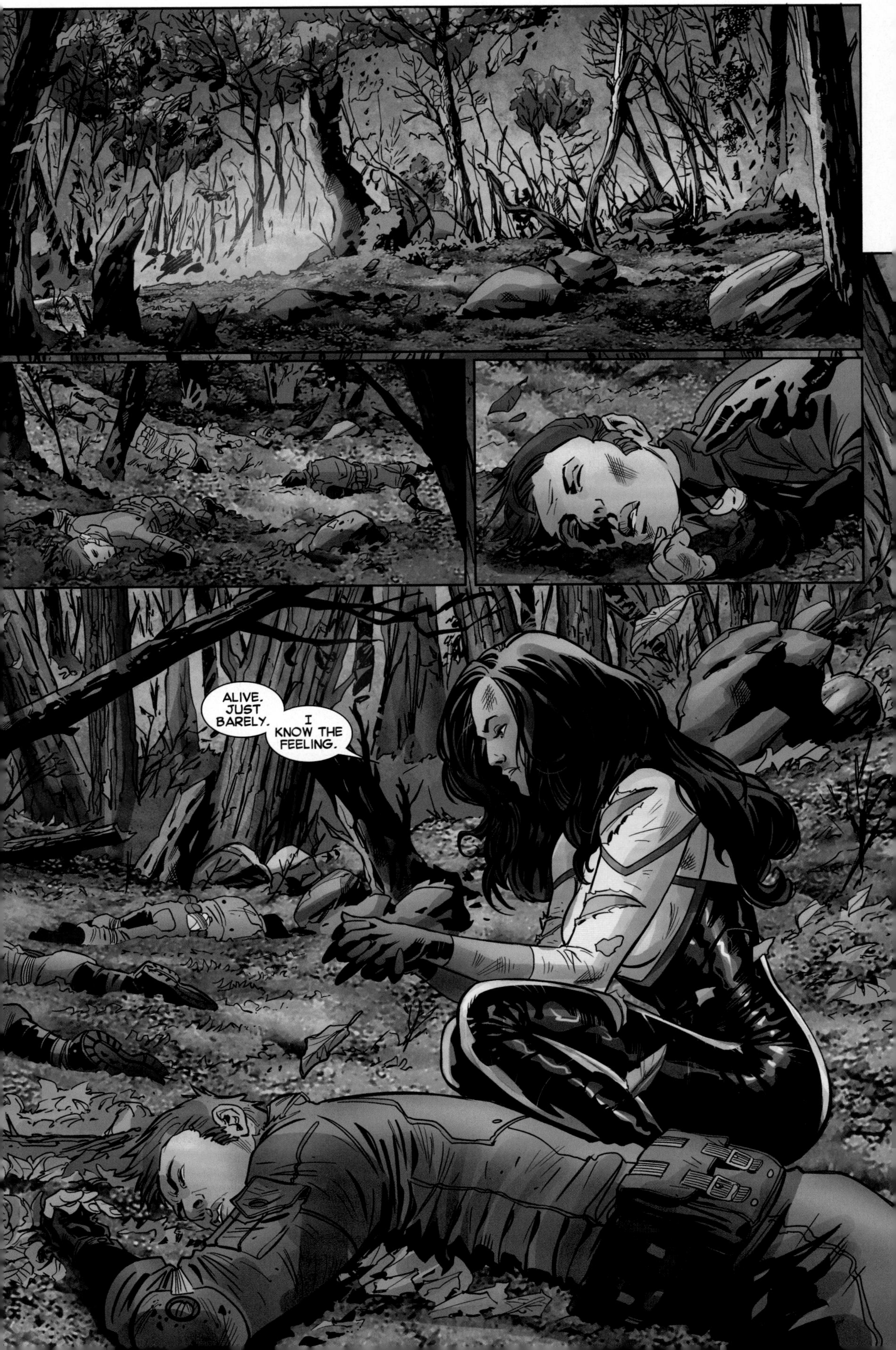
ALIVE. JUST BARELY.
I KNOW THE FEELING.

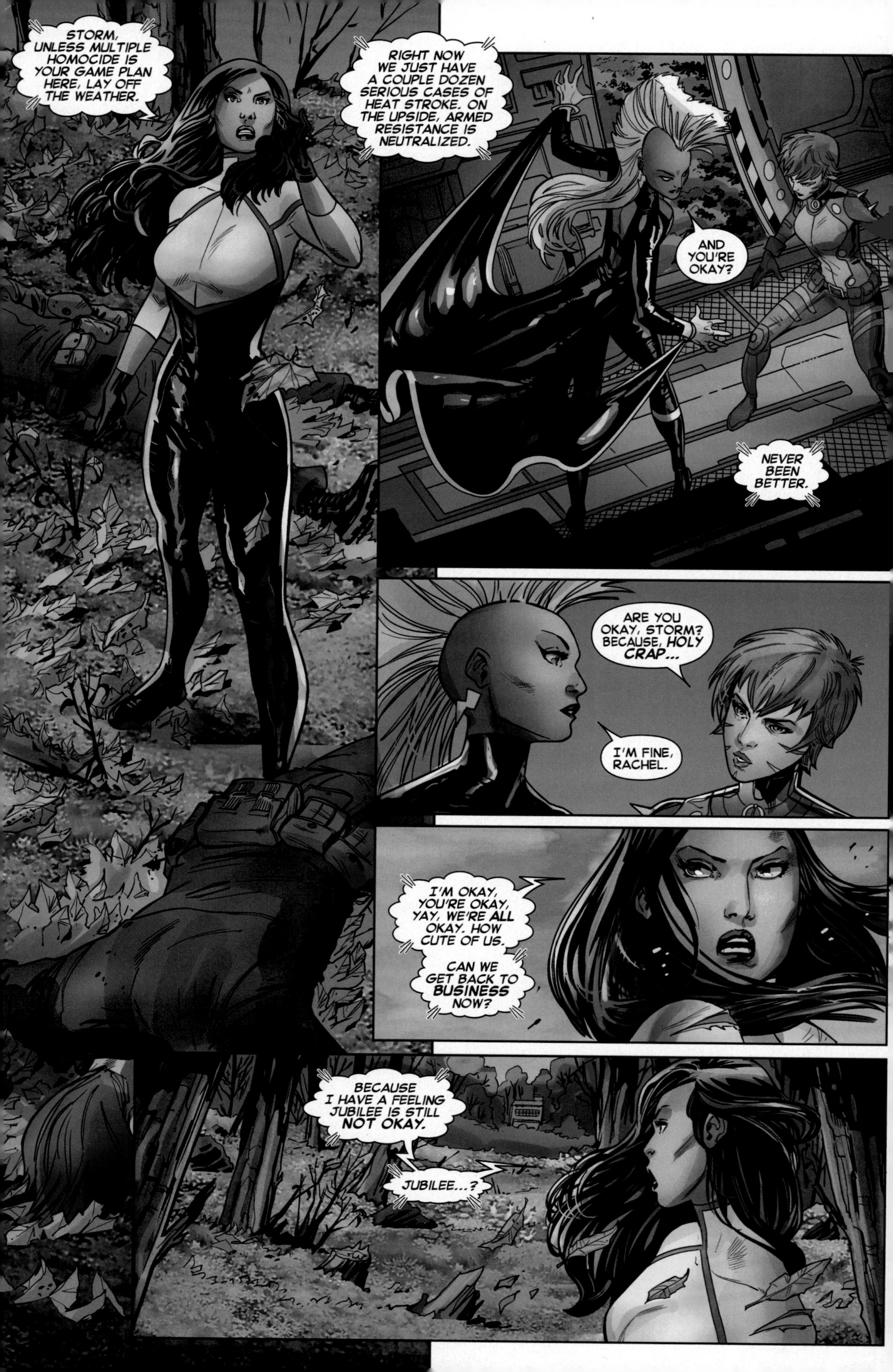
STORM, UNLESS MULTIPLE HOMOCIDE IS YOUR GAME PLAN HERE, LAY OFF THE WEATHER.
RIGHT NOW WE JUST HAVE A COUPLE DOZEN SERIOUS CASES OF HEAT STROKE. ON THE UPSIDE, ARMED RESISTANCE IS NEUTRALIZED.
AND YOU'RE OKAY?
NEVER BEEN BETTER.
ARE YOU OKAY, STORM? BECAUSE, HOLY CRAP...
I'M FINE, RACHEL.
I'M OKAY, YOU'RE OKAY, YAY, WE'RE ALL OKAY. HOW CUTE OF US.
CAN WE GET BACK TO BUSINESS NOW?
BECAUSE I HAVE A FEELING JUBILEE IS STILL NOT OKAY.
JUBILEE...?

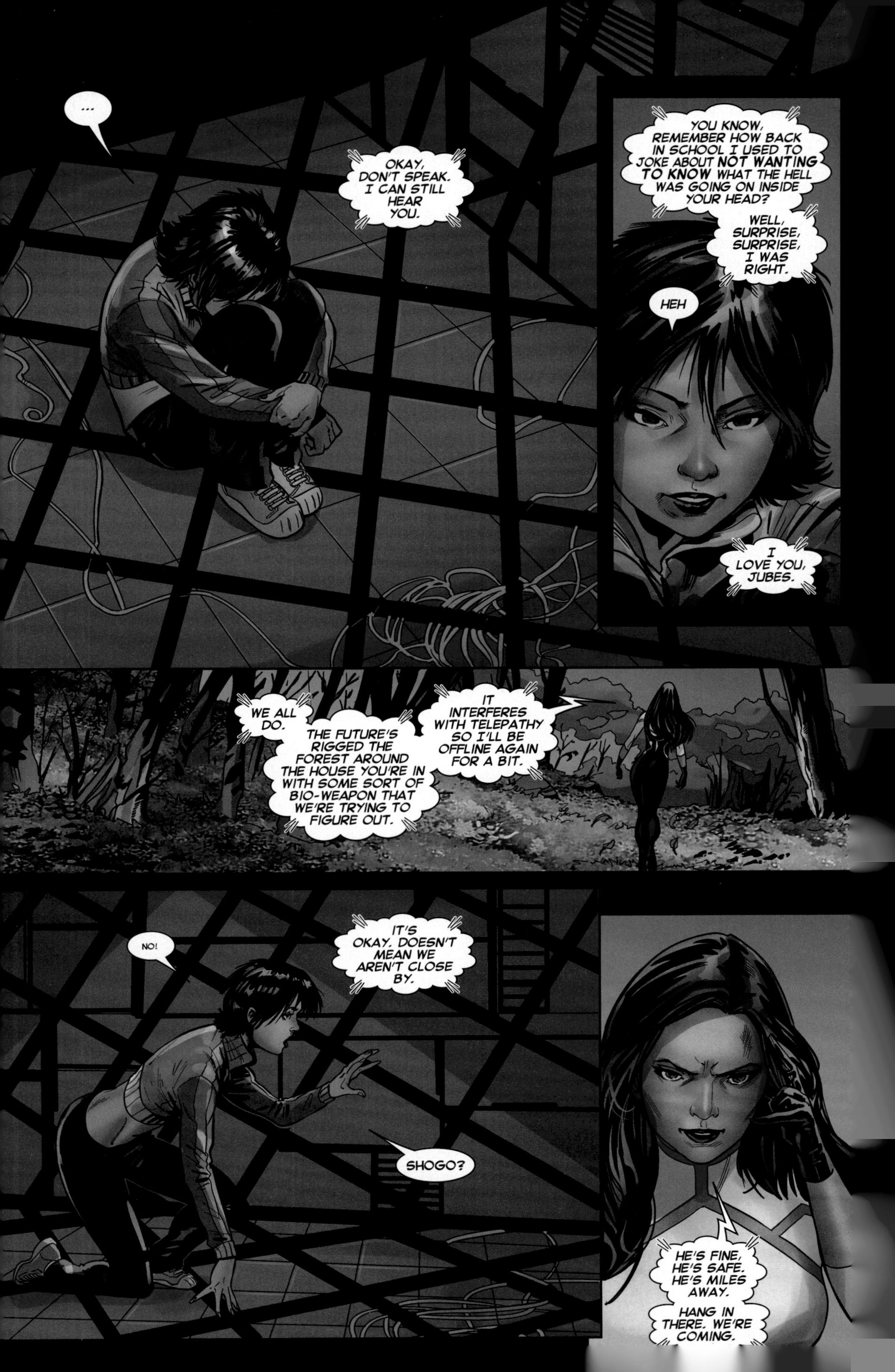
...
OKAY, DON'T SPEAK. I CAN STILL HEAR YOU.
YOU KNOW, REMEMBER HOW BACK IN SCHOOL I USED TO JOKE ABOUT NOT WANTING TO KNOW WHAT THE HELL WAS GOING ON INSIDE YOUR HEAD?
WELL, SURPRISE, SURPRISE, I WAS RIGHT.
HEH
I LOVE YOU, JUBES.
WE ALL DO.
THE FUTURE'S RIGGED THE FOREST AROUND THE HOUSE YOU'RE IN WITH SOME SORT OF BIO-WEAPON THAT WE'RE TRYING TO FIGURE OUT.
IT INTERFERES WITH TELEPATHY SO I'LL BE OFFLINE AGAIN FOR A BIT.
NO!
IT'S OKAY. DOESN'T MEAN WE AREN'T CLOSE BY.
SHOGO?
HE'S FINE, HE'S SAFE. HE'S MILES AWAY.
HANG IN THERE. WE'RE COMING.

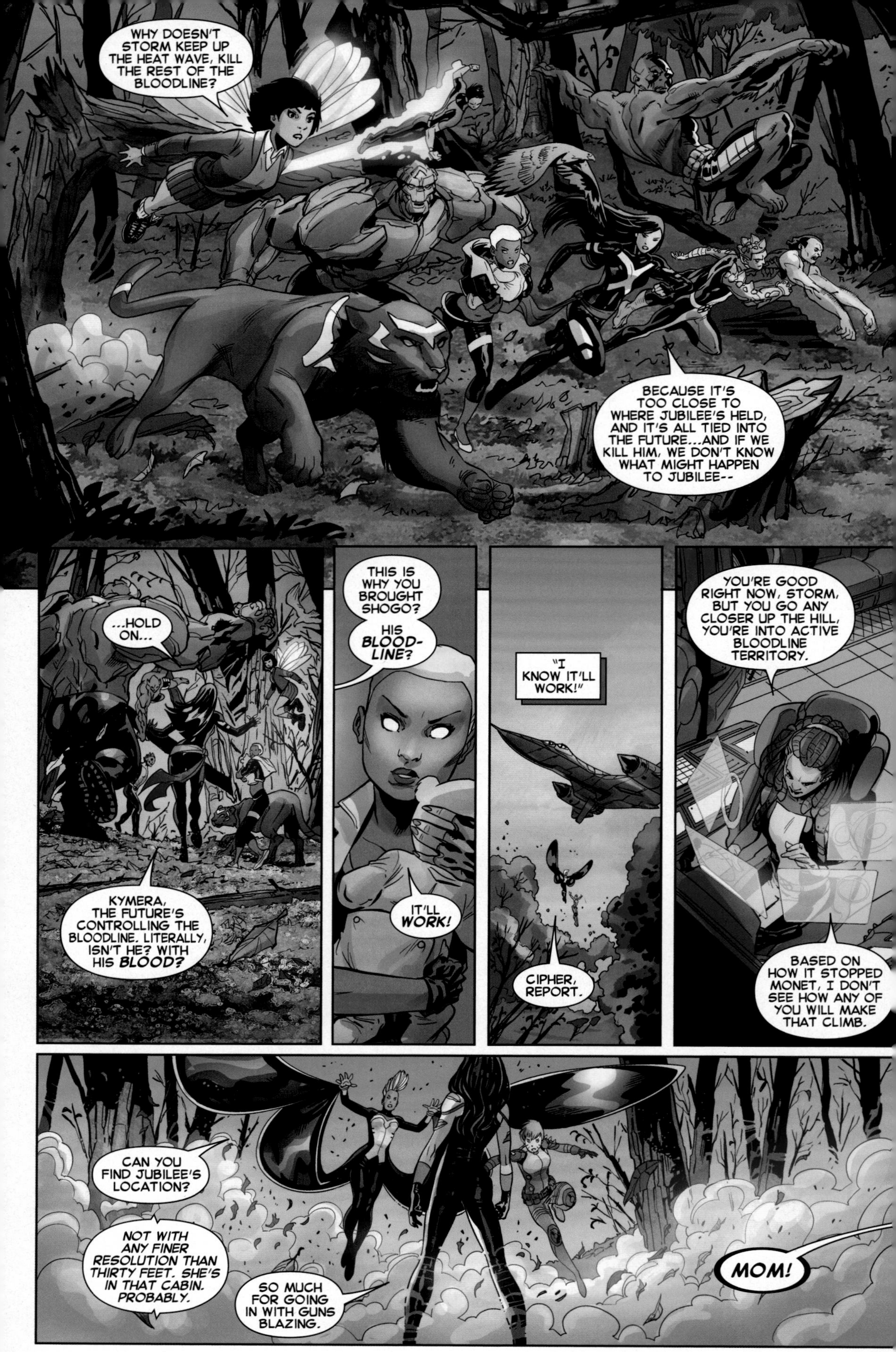
WHY DOESN'T STORM KEEP UP THE HEAT WAVE, KILL THE REST OF THE BLOODLINE?
BECAUSE IT'S TOO CLOSE TO WHERE JUBILEE'S HELD, AND IT'S ALL TIED INTO THE FUTURE...AND IF WE KILL HIM, WE DON'T KNOW WHAT MIGHT HAPPEN TO JUBILEE--
...HOLD ON...
KYMERA, THE FUTURE'S CONTROLLING THE BLOODLINE. LITERALLY, ISN'T HE? WITH HIS BLOOD?
THIS IS WHY YOU BROUGHT SHOGO? HIS BLOODLINE?
IT'LL WORK!
"I KNOW IT'LL WORK!"
CIPHER, REPORT.
YOU'RE GOOD RIGHT NOW, STORM, BUT YOU GO ANY CLOSER UP THE HILL, YOU'RE INTO ACTIVE BLOODLINE TERRITORY.
BASED ON HOW IT STOPPED MONET, I DON'T SEE HOW ANY OF YOU WILL MAKE THAT CLIMB.
CAN YOU FIND JUBILEE'S LOCATION?
NOT WITH ANY FINER RESOLUTION THAN THIRTY FEET. SHE'S IN THAT CABIN. PROBABLY.
SO MUCH FOR GOING IN WITH GUNS BLAZING.
MOM!

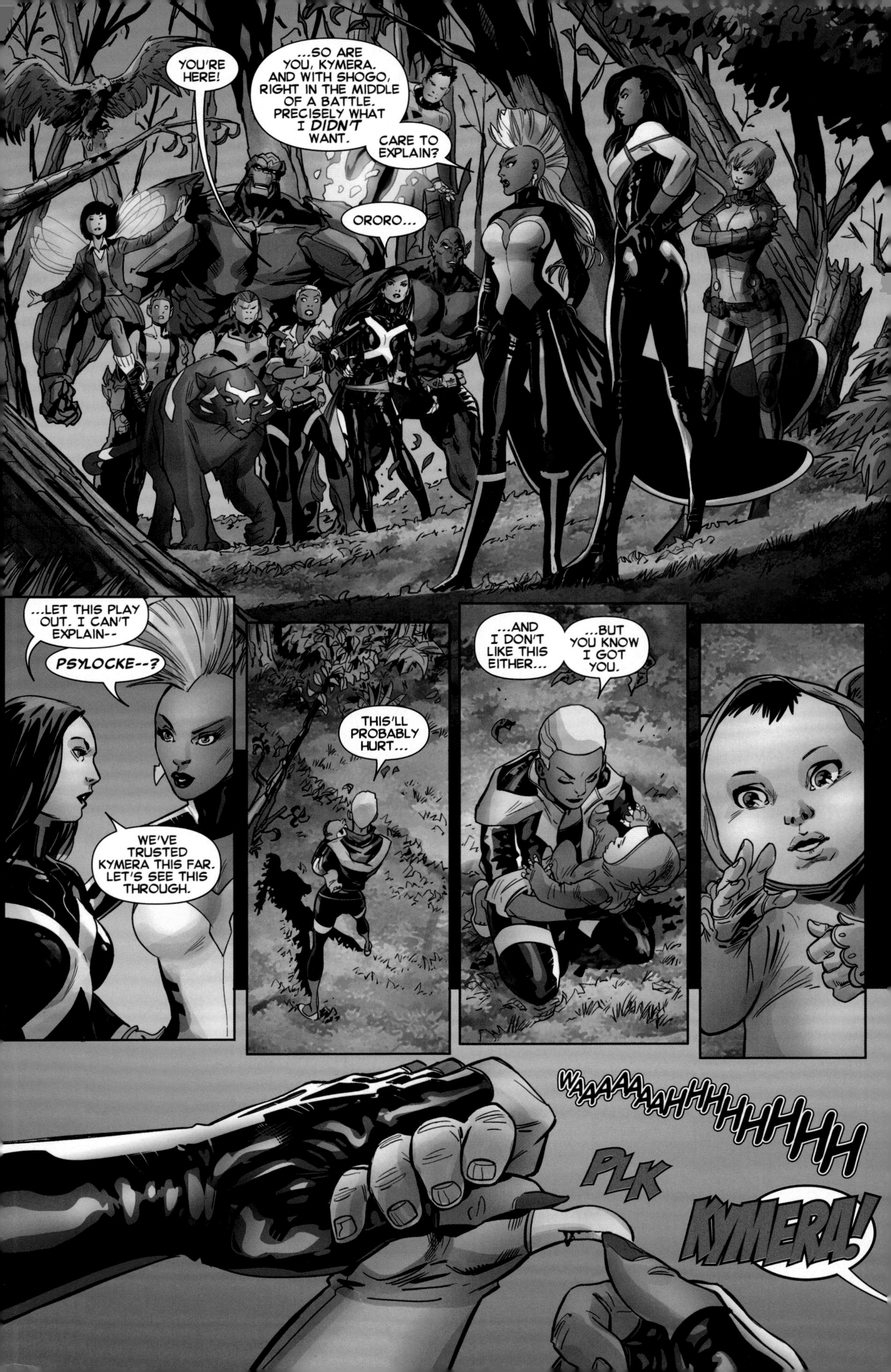
YOU'RE HERE!
...SO ARE YOU, KYMERA. AND WITH SHOGO, RIGHT IN THE MIDDLE OF A BATTLE. PRECISELY WHAT I *DIDN'T* WANT.
CARE TO EXPLAIN?
ORORO...
...LET THIS PLAY OUT. I CAN'T EXPLAIN--
PSYLOCKE--?
WE'VE TRUSTED KYMERA THIS FAR. LET'S SEE THIS THROUGH.
THIS'LL PROBABLY HURT...
...AND I DON'T LIKE THIS EITHER...
...BUT YOU KNOW I GOT YOU.
WAAAAAAAHHHHHHHHH
PLK
KYMERA!

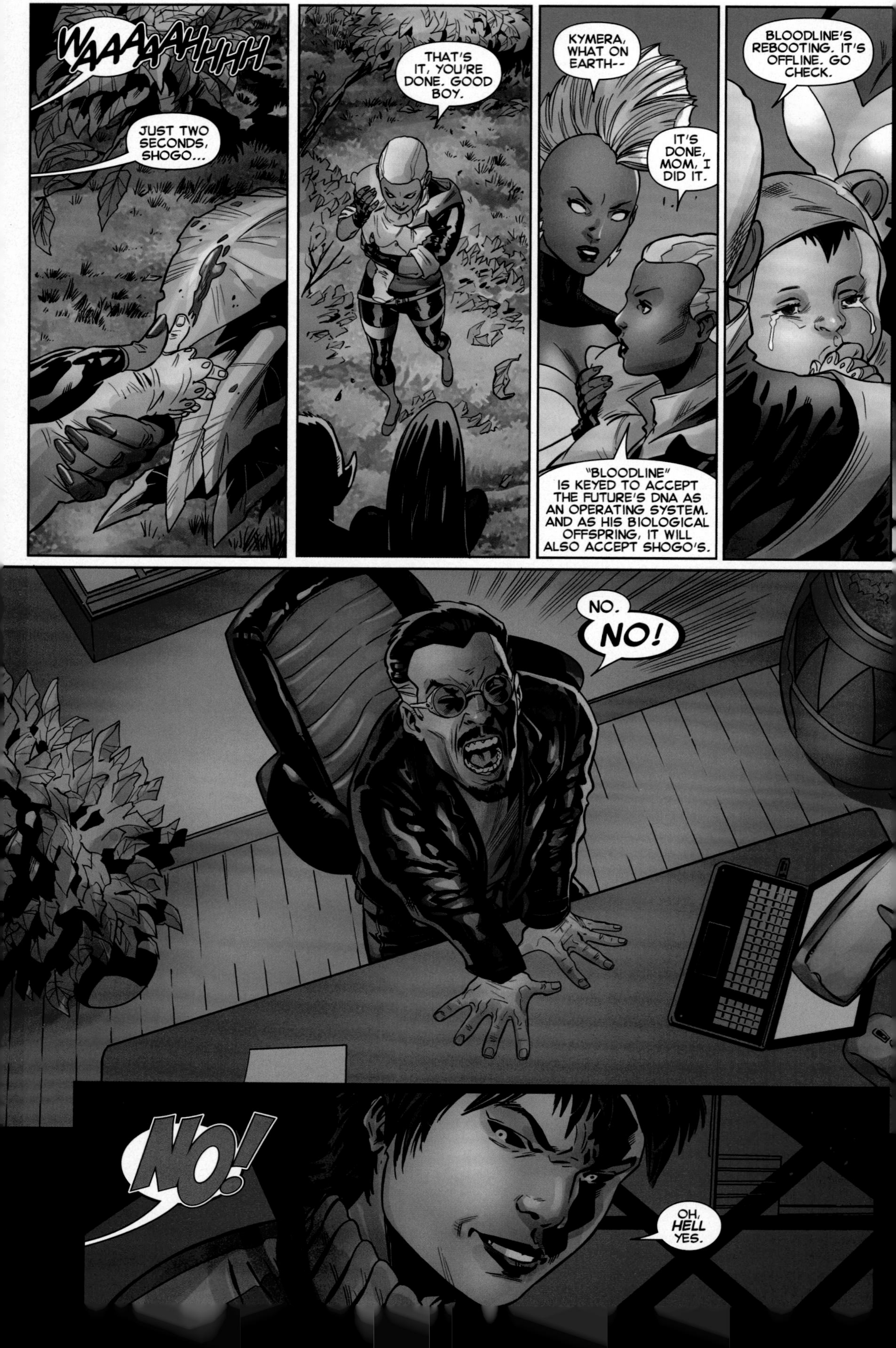
WAAAAAHHHH
JUST TWO SECONDS, SHOGO...
THAT'S IT, YOU'RE DONE. GOOD BOY.
KYMERA, WHAT ON EARTH--
IT'S DONE, MOM, I DID IT.
"BLOODLINE" IS KEYED TO ACCEPT THE FUTURE'S DNA AS AN OPERATING SYSTEM. AND AS HIS BIOLOGICAL OFFSPRING, IT WILL ALSO ACCEPT SHOGO'S.
BLOODLINE'S REBOOTING. IT'S OFFLINE. GO CHECK.
NO. NO!
NO!
OH, HELL YES.

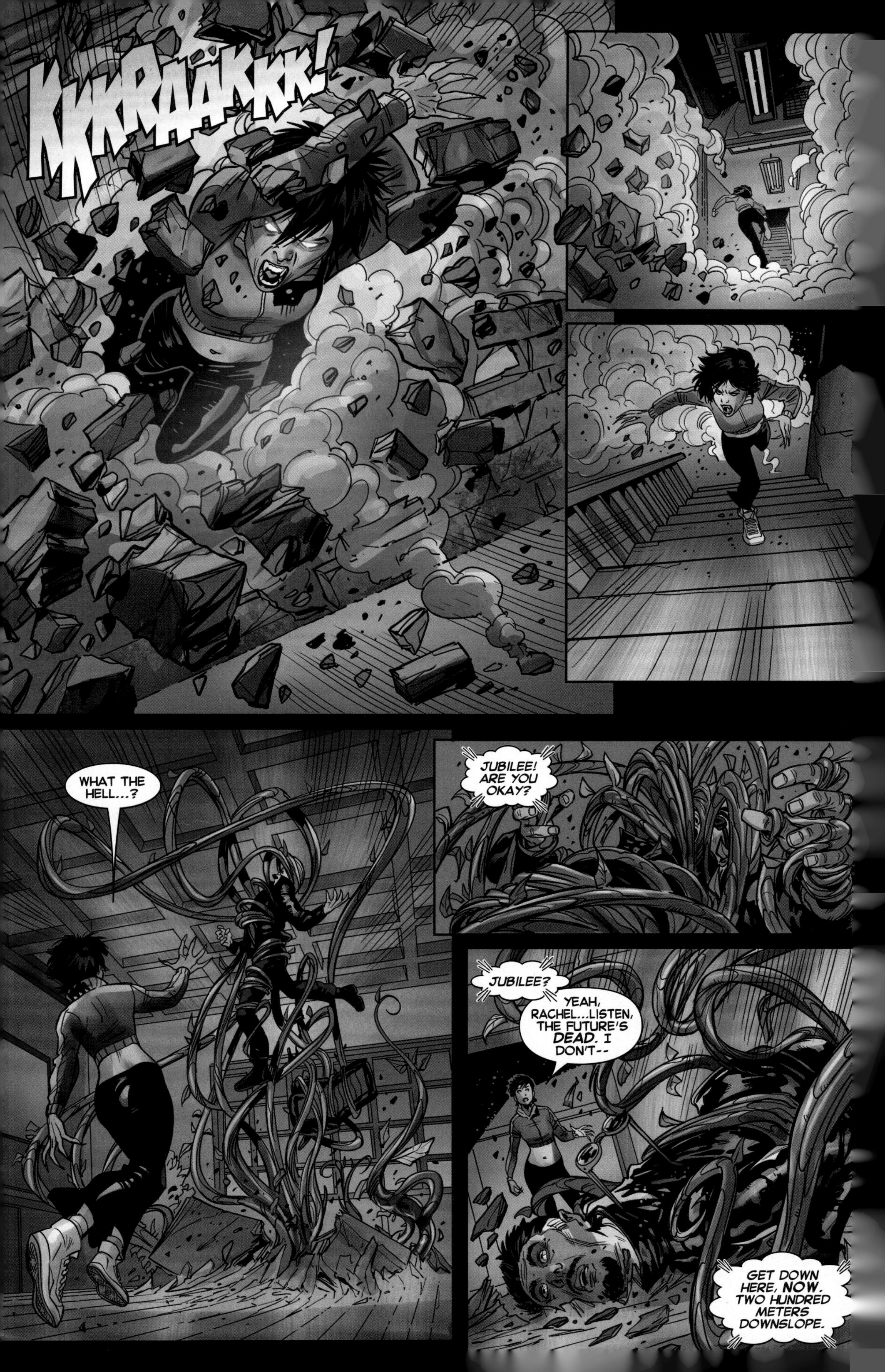
KKKRAAKKK!
WHAT THE HELL...?
JUBILEE! ARE YOU OKAY?
JUBILEE?
YEAH, RACHEL...LISTEN, THE FUTURE'S DEAD. I DON'T--
GET DOWN HERE, NOW. TWO HUNDRED METERS DOWNSLOPE.

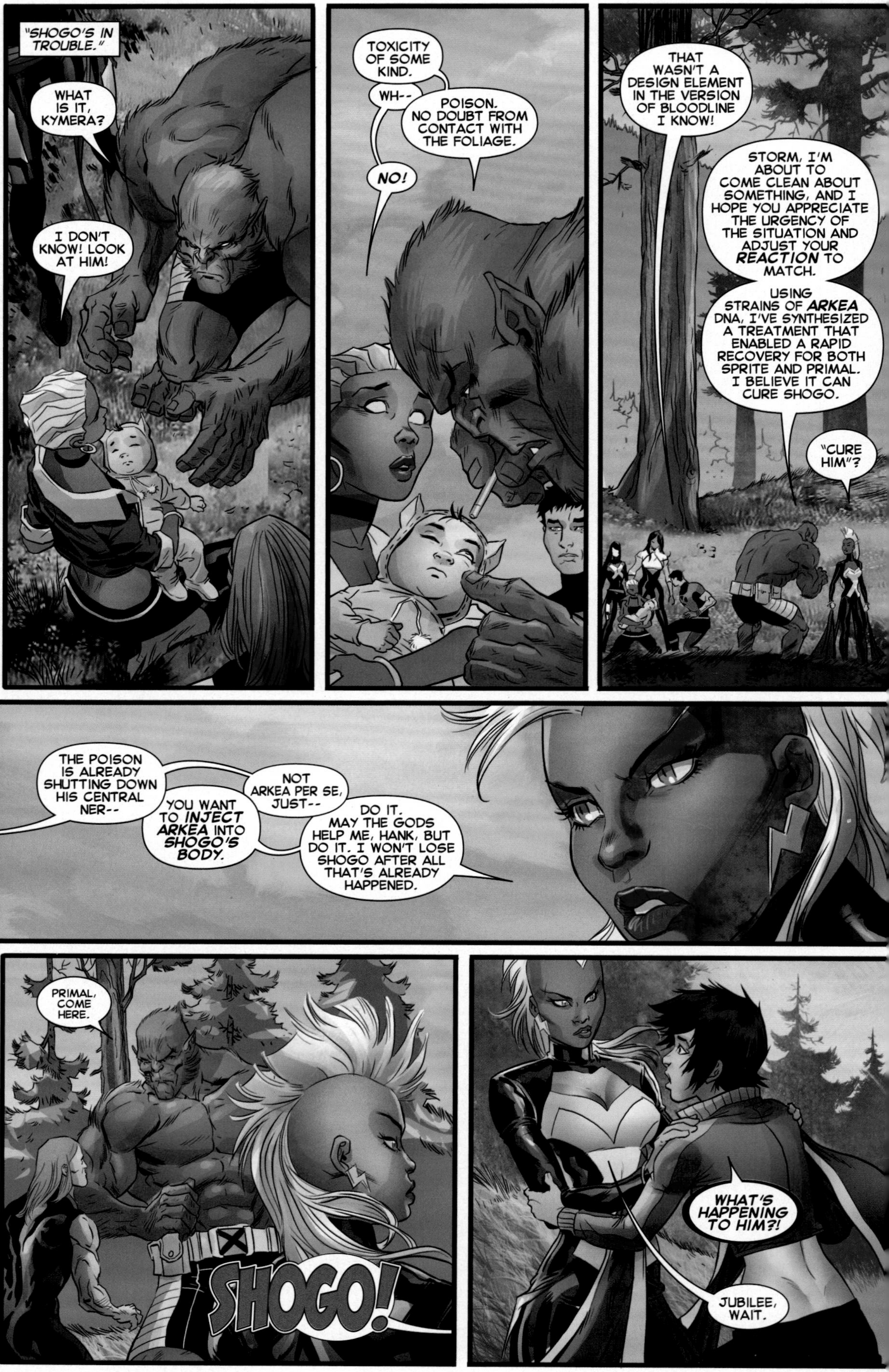
"SHOGO'S IN TROUBLE."
WHAT IS IT, KYMERA?
I DON'T KNOW! LOOK AT HIM!
TOXICITY OF SOME KIND.
WH--
POISON. NO DOUBT FROM CONTACT WITH THE FOLIAGE.
NO!
THAT WASN'T A DESIGN ELEMENT IN THE VERSION OF BLOODLINE I KNOW!
STORM, I'M ABOUT TO COME CLEAN ABOUT SOMETHING, AND I HOPE YOU APPRECIATE THE URGENCY OF THE SITUATION AND ADJUST YOUR REACTION TO MATCH.
USING STRAINS OF ARKEA DNA, I'VE SYNTHESIZED A TREATMENT THAT ENABLED A RAPID RECOVERY FOR BOTH SPRITE AND PRIMAL. I BELIEVE IT CAN CURE SHOGO.
"CURE HIM"?
THE POISON IS ALREADY SHUTTING DOWN HIS CENTRAL NER--
YOU WANT TO INJECT ARKEA INTO SHOGO'S BODY.
NOT ARKEA PER SE, JUST--
DO IT. MAY THE GODS HELP ME, HANK, BUT DO IT. I WON'T LOSE SHOGO AFTER ALL THAT'S ALREADY HAPPENED.
PRIMAL, COME HERE.
SHOGO!
WHAT'S HAPPENING TO HIM?!
JUBILEE, WAIT.

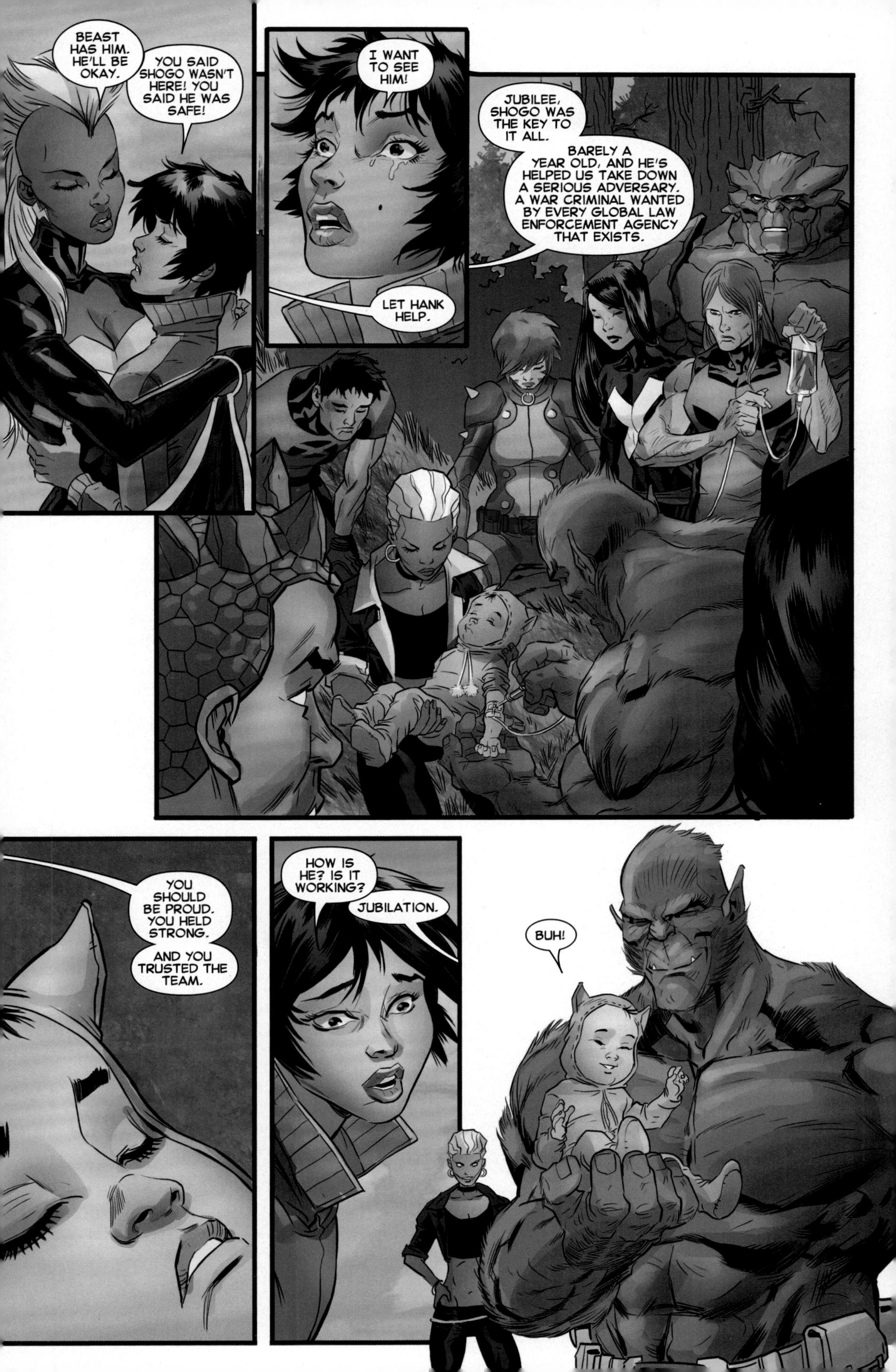
BEAST HAS HIM. HE'LL BE OKAY.
YOU SAID SHOGO WASN'T HERE! YOU SAID HE WAS SAFE!
I WANT TO SEE HIM!
JUBILEE, SHOGO WAS THE KEY TO IT ALL.
BARELY A YEAR OLD, AND HE'S HELPED US TAKE DOWN A SERIOUS ADVERSARY. A WAR CRIMINAL WANTED BY EVERY GLOBAL LAW ENFORCEMENT AGENCY THAT EXISTS.
LET HANK HELP.
YOU SHOULD BE PROUD. YOU HELD STRONG.
AND YOU TRUSTED THE TEAM.
HOW IS HE? IS IT WORKING?
JUBILATION.
BUH!

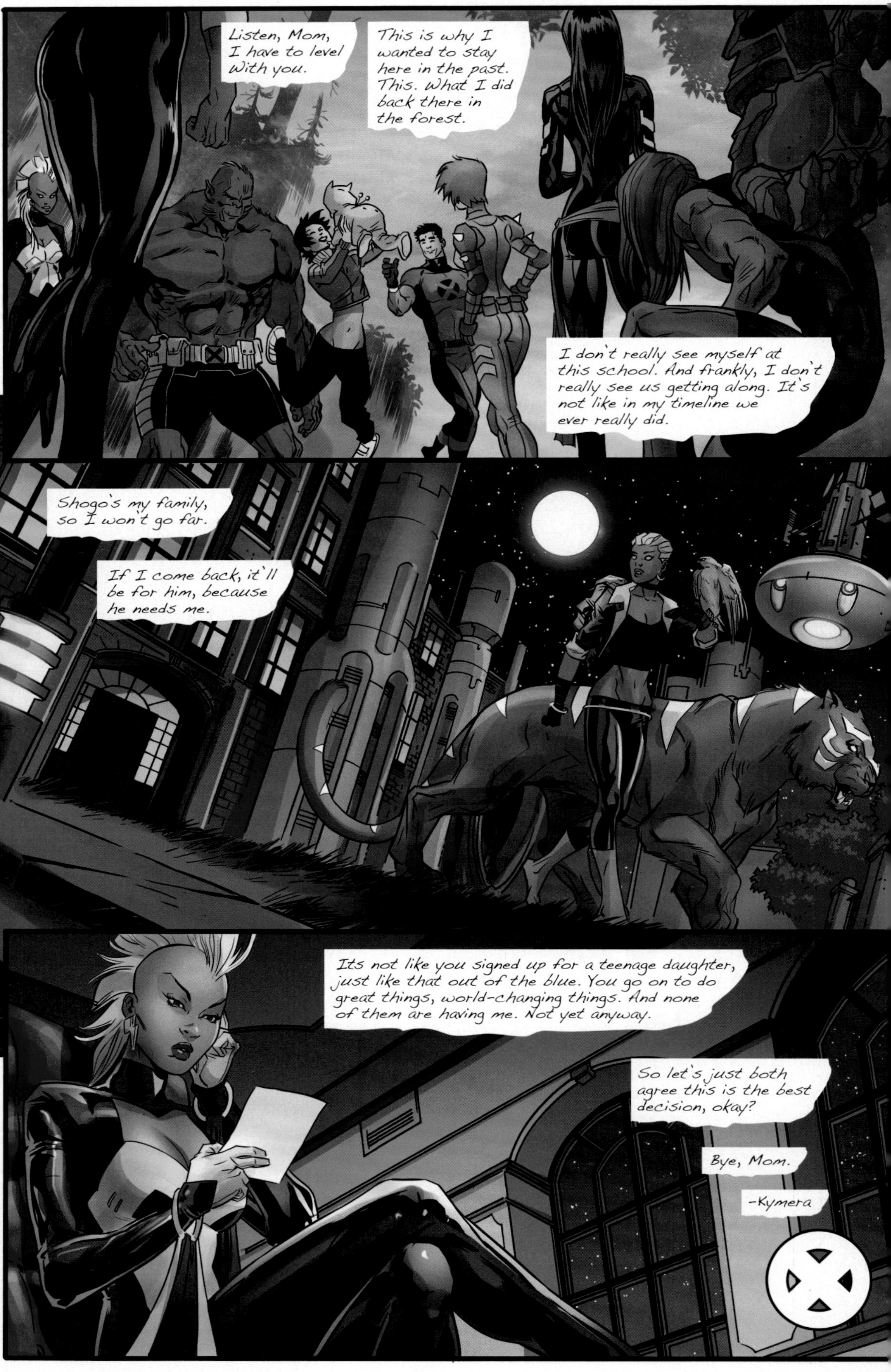
Listen, Mom, I have to level with you.
This is why I wanted to stay here in the past. This. What I did back there in the forest.
I don't really see myself at this school. And frankly, I don't really see us getting along. It's not like in my timeline we ever really did.
Shogo's my family, so I won't go far.
If I come back, it'll be for him, because he needs me.
Its not like you signed up for a teenage daughter, just like that out of the blue. You go on to do great things, world-changing things. And none of them are having me. Not yet anyway.
So let's just both agree this is the best decision, okay?
Bye, Mom.
-Kymera

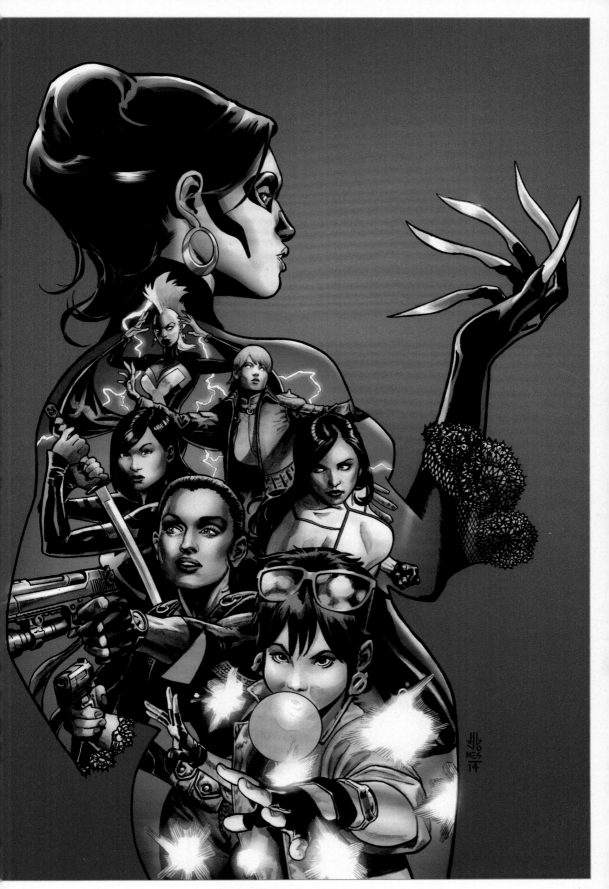

X-MEN #13 VARIANT
BY J.G. JONES